A New Model
of the
Authentic Church

ROBERT FUGGI

WESTBOW
PRESS®
A DIVISION OF THOMAS NELSON
& ZONDERVAN

WestBow Press books may be ordered through booksellers or by contacting:

WestBow Press
A Division of Thomas Nelson & Zondervan
1663 Liberty Drive
Bloomington, IN 47403
www.westbowpress.com
1 (866) 928-1240

ISBN: 978-1-9736-1094-6 (sc)
ISBN: 978-1-9736-1095-3 (e)

Library of Congress Control Number: 2017919182

Print information available on the last page.

WestBow Press rev. date: 2/7/2018

There is only one way to avoid criticism:
do nothing, say nothing and be nothing.

ARISTOTLE

If you want to change the world, pick up your pen and write.

MARTIN LUTHER

To change something, Build A New Model
that makes the existing model obsolete.

RICHARD BUCKMINSTER FULLER

ACKNOWLEDGMENTS

I am grateful to the Princeton Theological Seminary for allowing me to develop this new paradigm of the Authentic Church as part of my M.Div. and Th.M. studies.

I am also grateful for having a mentor in Professor George Hunsinger, who has taught me the deep truths of the person and work of Jesus Christ and to voice unpopular opinions.

To Professor Richard Osmer, who supported and encouraged much of this research as part of my independent studies and thesis.

To artist Peggy Drinkard, who captures in the cover painting the beauty and simplicity of the Authentic Church.

Last, to my beautiful wife, Lana, and my family for allowing me to pursue these studies.

In communion,
Robert Fuggi

... for Chief and Dino

INTRODUCTION

The last thing I want to burden readers with is another how-to book that repeats or replicates what has been said about how to successfully start a ministry or "do church." In the book of Haggai, the prophet says, "The glory of this present house will be greater than the glory of the former house."[1] If that is true, why is the church in the condition it is in, a shadow of its former glory?

With this book, I intend to bring forth a groundbreaking new paradigm for reintroducing authenticity into church, ministry, and practice. Though it may appear odd to some that I am stepping back in time to the beginning, when the church began to bring about a new paradigm, that is what I propose to do. We must unlearn how we have been taught to do church and get back to the basics and simplicity of the gospel centered on Christ to truly be the Authentic Church.

This book or model will redefine how church should and ought to function in Christendom today. It proffers a very different and sometimes problematic model that will certainly ruffle some feathers, offend some, and challenge existing models of church in America in this new millennium and help bring forth a revival of faith and change.

I hope this book will encourage many across this nation to build the kind of ministry depicted in the book of Acts.[i] If this is carried out, I believe it has the potential to be one of the greatest spiritual awakenings in American history; what starts out as a mustard seed grows into a large bush.[2] For this revival of faith and change to occur, there needs to be a foundation built in lay discovery and training of the Word. More qualified ministers are needed to teach, and more churches are needed to be biblically and Christ-centered as well as more missionally minded and relevant to society. For that to occur, there must be a successful model of church

---

[i] The Acts of the Apostles is often referred to as the book of Acts in the New Testament. The book documents the early beginnings of the Christian Church circa AD 80–90. When reference is made to the book of Acts, the principle I am attempting to draw attention to is the simplicity and effectiveness of the early church as it began after the death of Jesus Christ. The apostles were ordinary people who were compelled to leave the security of everyday life to pursue building the kingdom of God.

for this time and culture. A working model must be developed that has proven itself successful and is simple, cost-effective, and spiritually and biblically based. The purpose of this book is to formulate a working model of what *A New Model of the Authentic Church* should be and how it should function. This book will challenge the way we think about how church has been done and more important, point to what changes need to be made to revive the church and make it more effective.

Readers, whether ordained ministers or lay, will be inspired and encouraged to build a ministry based on community, self-sacrifice, love, and commitment. These new and authentic ministries would enhance and benefit the Christian church and society. I have faith that those who read this book will begin this journey prayerfully and immediately.

Jesus said, "The harvest is plentiful but the workers are few. Ask the Lord of the harvest therefore to send out workers into the harvest field."[3] Why can't that be you? This book will be a trumpet call for many people who have been called by God but have not yet responded. I've heard, "You find more pastors in the cemetery than in the seminary"; many do not realize their call to God until it is too late or never. Don't be one of them. Many Americans, both white- and blue-collar professionals who have established comfortable existences, need to ask themselves, What have I done for God? Can I do more?

The great theologian Pastor Dietrich Bonhoeffer said, "We must be ready to allow ourselves to be interrupted by God."[4] Americans need to contemplate their eternal call to build the kingdom of God on earth. Many need to leave their status-quo existences and be transformed by God and His power to build His house, the Authentic Church. We can do this in everyday life. God has given us His revelation in His Word. If we search diligently through scripture, we will find the mind of God. We do not need to find complex mathematical equations or formulae hidden under layers of theological terms; God's Word is plainly visible to all who incline their eyes to see, their ears to hear, and their minds to understand.[5] I am confident that this book will challenge Christendom in our time and will encourage you to think about your ministry or the beginning of your ministry as it relates to the universal Christian church.

This book is a step-by-step analysis of what the American church—in its institutional and independent branches—can and should do to radically change the landscape of the church and align it with the missional purpose of the Authentic Church. The faith that has inspired me to write this book will, I hope, challenge many ministers, laypeople, and nonministers to begin training, educating, and studying how to build a local work. I believe that if others catch on to this model and vision, it will bring renewal, revival, and transformation to a stagnating church.

In communion,
Robert Fuggi

PREFACE

The title of this book, *A New Model of the Authentic Church*, should stir up a person's interest in the status and effectiveness of the contemporary American church. Many of the concepts in this book may seem radical to some, but the purpose for raising these issues is to challenge the reader to ask basic questions about the role of the Christian church in society today. Not many would argue with the overall thesis of the book—that we need a new model for the American church, a new reformation because the church is in decline and continues to lose influence and relevance in American culture. The data and research provided in this book on the anemic condition of the church ought to cause us to examine the current state of the church and look for solutions.

The American church will be challenged by this book; it will provide a new paradigm of effectiveness and how to develop it. These provocative questions must be asked and answered thoughtfully: Can a church function if it does not have a paid, full-time staff? Should church leaders get nonministerial jobs to sustain a startup or ongoing ministry? *A New Model of the Authentic Church* allows for full-time pastors and staff to become salaried by their ministry in time, but it suggests the church would be better off—enriched and strengthened—if the leaders were committed to studying and ministering without salaried positions. This would eliminate any motivation for financial gain by starting a ministry. This would allow small churches to multiply in number, which would enrich the church's overall impact in society and neutralize the overwhelming need to create finances through the ministry.

Robert Fuggi's marshalling of the data is thorough and provokes readers to examine the overall status of the American church—not just where they are at in their own churches but where the church is collectively. Too often, many small churches try to duplicate the models of larger TV churches that are financially successful. His thesis clearly shows the flaws in this thinking. According to him, what are needed now are more new, vibrant, and developing churches led by unpaid devoted ministers and laypeople. He uses the model of St. Paul, the tentmaker,[ii] and other apostles who gave up their status-quo way of life in exchange for a life of service to God and humanity who were motivated directly by the Lord to interact with society out of love for the unchurched along with a desire to see the church bring people into a personal relationship with God.

Another bonus in this book is the author's treatment of one of the major issues facing Christian society today—the treatment and understanding of Israel and the Jews by the Christian church. He deals with this thorny issue very well by invoking the historical and theological relationship between the Jewish people and the Christian church. He deals deftly with the touchy and often controversial subject of supersessionism—the issue of whether the Christian church has replaced Israel and the Jews.

The erudition and careful scholarly research is revealed by his thoroughness in treating each chapter's subject. I very much appreciated the intelligent and sober manner in which he handled the need for significant change or reformation in how we do church. The model he develops for how church should and ought to be done today is easy to follow. It may very well change the landscape of the American church.

Having spent more than forty-five years in ministry in the Middle East as one of America's early missionaries to Jordan, I noticed early on that some of the most effective ministry was done by people who were gainfully employed outside the church as "tentmakers"; their attitude and commitment to their ministry consumed them. That doesn't mean they were less qualified or less trained than full-time, professional ministers. One church leader worked in a printing press but was always ready to be called on to preach effectively. Another was a tailor who possessed an eloquent speaking style when teaching biblical studies. The list goes on, but the point is that some of the most effective leaders of churches have been those who are set on serving God because the love of Christ and neighbor compels them to.

Those who seek a salaried position have weakened their call and their ministry by relying on deriving income from their ministry. We have seen how numerous problems have occurred as the result of some pastors trying to align themselves to be successful financially but not spiritually. This question needs to be asked, was the early church affluent, or did it simply meet the needs of the people—spiritually and physically—where they were?

In many countries in the Middle East, volunteer and unpaid leadership has produced vibrant and powerful church ministries. Lay leaders are seen as those who love the Lord and are doing ministry from their hearts, not from the prospects of lucrative salaries. This is lacking in the American church today.

[ii] Paul was called a tentmaker because he worked full-time at that occupation while maintaining and supporting his ministry.

While some may not appreciate or agree with the thesis of this book, it offers a new paradigm or model more akin to the early church depicted in the book of Acts. In this thought-provoking book, Robert Fuggi puts forth a challenging new concept while courageously and convincingly dealing thoroughly with the subject.

At first, I thought the thesis of this book would be too controversial for the American church; then I came to realize that because of the challenging nature of this work, it is greatly needed. I therefore endorse it without hesitation, and I encourage God's workers to wrestle with these concepts.

Rev. Dr. George E. Kelsey
American Missionary (Jordan, 1955–2000)

INTEGRATED LESSONS

The objective of the lessons at the end of each chapter is to allow you to encounter and work through the theological concepts, practical applications, and challenges of Christian ministry presented in *A New Model of the Authentic Church*.

Each lesson will follow the format and chapter of the book. The lessons are an interactive tool designed to enhance discussion of the materials presented in *A New Model of the Authentic Church*. By using the lessons, you will more easily integrate the book's concepts into your personal ministry. My expectation is that as you interact with the lesson materials and the subject matter in the book, the process will inspire your own thoughts and ideas, which will in turn allow you to apply the concepts in your own life and ministry. The lessons have numerous sections at the end of each chapter that are designed to make a place for personal reflection, analysis, and discussion.

As you work through each lesson, you will be asked to think not only about specific scriptures and themes but also about how they relate to the accompanying section of the book and to the church at large. Then you will be asked to write your own thoughts and reflections on the material and its application. As you do this, the lessons will begin to fill up with your thoughts, ideas, and philosophy about ministry. My expectation is that engaging with the lessons will help you to develop your own application of *A New Model of the Authentic Church*—one that you can use in existing ministries or use to birth new ministries. We believe this model, when applied, could birth 1000 new churches.

These lessons are a blueprint for your own ministry. Its text will present not only the challenges you will face but also the accomplishments your ministry will achieve in accordance with the concepts developed and implemented by Jesus Christ and the disciples in the early church. The lessons will help pastors, ministers, or students of ministry to develop a mission and vision of the church that integrates their own principles of ministry with a biblical and Christological balance that will build the kingdom of God rather than erode it. That is the objective of *A New Model of the Authentic Church* and the practical application of the lessons. May God bless you in your journey to build an Authentic Church.

Contents

CHAPTER 1
The Decline of the American Church

To the angel of the church in Sardis write: These are the words of him who holds the seven spirits of God and the seven stars. I know your deeds; you have a reputation of being alive, but you are dead. Wake up! Strengthen what remains and is about to die, for I have not found your deeds complete in the sight of my God. Remember, therefore, what you have received and heard; obey it, and repent. But if you do not wake up, I will come like a thief, and you will not know at what time I will come to you.

REVELATION 3:1–3 (NIV)

I have a disclaimer here: in this book, I am attempting to formulate a new paradigm for how church should and ought to be done in the new millennium. For us to be successful in developing this new paradigm of the Authentic Church, we must first take a cold, hard look at the status and condition of the contemporary American church.

This chapter compiles data from well-conducted surveys about where the church is now, and it includes data about its trends. It may read laboriously, but it is important to have a working knowledge about the raw data of church attendance, associations, and beliefs, and it is just as important to have a breakdown in the demographics of the church including information about geographical areas, race, age, denominations, and the group called the "nones." With this data, we are in a better position to look at the American church and formulate a model for bringing lasting change and relevancy to the Authentic Church.

This directive may be even more relevant now than it was to the early church at Sardis.[iii] One foundational issue that needs to be addressed is to understand where the American church is now. We need to answer this question to evaluate the effectiveness of churches in

---

[iii] The reference to the early church at Sardis was the church referred to by the Apostle John, the author of the book of Revelation. He warned the church at Sardis that it must reform.

society today. In light of that, you might not be surprised to learn that Brazil is the number-one nation for receiving foreign missionaries in the world. And it may surprise you to find out who is second in the world when it comes to receiving missionaries—the United States.[6]

- Of the 250,000 Protestant churches in America, 200,000 are either stagnant (with no growth) or declining. That is 80% of the Protestant churches in America.
- 3,000 American churches close their doors every year.
- 6,000 Americans leave the church each day.
- Since 1950, there are one-third fewer churches in the United States.[7]

Perhaps now you can see why the United States is the number-two nation for receiving foreign missionaries. Churches in America are declining, following the trend that has been occurring throughout Europe in recent years.

The church in America is desperately in need of a revival, but where does that revival start? A revival should not be an appeal to those outside the church. Nowadays, we cannot pitch a tent and put up a sign reading "Revival Tonight." A revival is not for the lost but for the church from which the beneficial effects of the revival can then spread to the lost. The church is the only place where a revival can begin. If you are standing in the sand, draw a circle around yourself. Inside that circle is where the revival must begin.[8] Once we understand the conditions of the church—and ourselves—we can then begin to formulate a solution.

Christianity started out strong in America, but we must ask ourselves, has the church lost its effectiveness and relevancy in our society and culture today? In a 2012 *New York Times* article entitled "One Nation Under God?" the author writes,

> The colonies were relatively unchurched, but European visitors to the early republic marveled at Americans' fervent piety. Alexis de Tocqueville[iv] wrote in 1840 that the absence of an established state church nurtured a society in which "Christian sects are infinitely diversified and perpetually modified; but Christianity itself is a fact so irresistibly established that no one undertakes either to attack or defend it."[9]

Tocqueville visited America during a wave of religious revival, so he underestimated the degree to which some Americans held Christianity at arm's length.

[iv] Alexis-Charles-Henri Clérel de Tocqueville was a French political thinker and historian best known for his works *Democracy in America* and *The Old Regime and the Revolution.*

Nevertheless, America's rates of church affiliation have long been higher than those of Europe—perhaps because of the First Amendment, which permitted a religious "free market" that encouraged innovation and competition between spiritual entrepreneurs. Yet membership, as every exasperated pastor knows, is not the same as showing up on Sunday morning.[10]

Rates of church attendance have fluctuated and recently have shown a steady decline.

Before the Civil War, regular attendance probably never exceeded 30%, rising to a high of 40% around 1965 and declining to under 30% in recent years—even as 77% still identify (themselves) as Christians and 69% say they are "very" or "moderately" religious, according to a 2012 Gallup survey.[11]

The *Times* article goes on to say,

Christianity, as a label, is the largest religion in the world. Over 2 billion people can be counted as "Christians." Their actual practices, beliefs, and lifestyles are another matter entirely. The west is responsible for Christianity's expansion around the world since the late medieval period. Ironically, it was the scientific and industrial advancements of the west that enabled the label of Christianity to spread, while nevertheless causing the substantive religion to shrink in significance … Christianity is defined as the major world religion that includes beliefs such as the virgin birth and resurrection of Jesus Christ, a personal God, the second coming of Christ, and the need to accept Jesus as one's personal savior for salvation. This will also be referred to as "traditional Christianity" to distinguish it from newer sects and denominations.

The United States is among the most religious societies in the western, developed world. Yet the hold of traditional Christianity on people's lives has been significantly eroded, even among people who call themselves "Christian." General belief in God has remained high and stable in the US since World War II, ranging from 92 to 98%. However, depending on the poll's question wording, belief in God declines notably. In 2010, 80% of people said they believe in God, while 12% believed in a "universal spirit." In 2006, 73% of Americans said they were "convinced God exists," and 19% said God probably exists, but they have some doubt. From 1948 to 2008, the self-reported Christian population of America fell from 92% to 78% and the nonreligious population rose from 2% to between 13–15%. Nonbelievers have mostly come from the ranks of Christian defectors.[12]

As this data indicates, over the last forty years, Americans have attended church less and less frequently.

In 1972, the majority attended religious services once a month or more frequently. In 2008, a majority attended several times a year or less often. When asked, 40–45% of Americans claim they attend church weekly. However, actual weekly church attendance is estimated at somewhere between 10 and 30%. The majority of Americans do not attend church regularly.[13]

Why is this? These are the questions we are trying to answer.

The question of whether Christianity is in decline is a complex question with layers of answers. Based on data accumulated over the last several decades, it appears that though the numbers in some small pockets of Christian denominations may be growing, overall, traditional Christianity is on the decline in America. The number of Christians in America has been in steady decline while the population continues to grow rapidly. Though some studies suggest there are more Christians today than before, when factoring in the dramatic rise in population growth and immigration, things may be even worse for the church than it appears. Many studies have suggested that for the first time in American history, America is becoming a non-Christian nation. This could have significant implications for the country spiritually, politically, socially, and culturally.

Jesus preached the kingdom of God and was active in a social gospel of meeting the needs of the masses. America appears to be rejecting a biblical worldview in favor of a more politically correct and culturally acceptable one. It appears from some recent surveys that Americans are becoming more biblically illiterate and so is the American church. Look at some recent information obtained about biblical knowledge.

- Only 25% of Americans can name the four Gospels.
- Only 60% of Americans can list five of the Ten Commandments.
- At least 12% of Americans think Joan of Arc was Noah's wife[14]

These are just basic primary questions that in the past any third-grade Sunday-school class or child would know, yet the vast majority of the American public and Christian churches today do not. We, the American church, must admit we failed to stay relevant in the world today and have failed to inculcate our congregations at large with a biblical understanding and worldview.

When it relates to the core values of the Christian faith, fewer people are identifying themselves as Christians and fewer associate themselves with many of the tenets of the Christian faith. Though on the surface there appears to be a high percentage of self-proclaimed Christians in America, results of numerous polls support a decline of Christianity in America.

While many Americans identify with being Christian, less than 10% affirm Christian principles such as the infallibility of the Bible as well as other tenets of faith—receiving Christ as Savior, confessing their sins if they want to go to heaven when they die, or believing that Jesus lived a sinless life here on earth and that salvation is possible only by grace and not by works (though works would follow). They also do not affirm that God is all-powerful and relevant in the world today, nor do they believe Satan exists.[15] When the (so-called) Christians are asked whether they believe these statements of faith, the percentage of Christians is significantly less.

The foundational beliefs of the Christian faith are in danger, and there have been significant drops in other areas.

- Sunday school attendance declined 14%.
- Volunteerism in church was down almost 30%.
- Church attendance decreased 7%.
- Only 62% of Christians read the Bible weekly.[16]

Saving the worst for last is the millennials, those thirty and under who "are increasingly rejecting church attendance."[17] Some church scholars suggest they have fallen into a black hole.

It is estimated that a staggering six of ten millennials who grew up in the church have now left it. They do not believe the church is relevant in their daily lives. They believe they can find God in other places or not at all. They feel church is boring and outdated. Most would rather spend their time on social media.

The news appears bleak for the American church unless a solution is found.

The Pew Forum on Religious Public Life conducted one of the most comprehensive surveys in American religious history, the ARIS (American Religious Identification Survey). Its results are startling and illuminating. It concluded that 41% of Americans have switched their religion in their life. Many have left the religion they were raised in in favor of another religion or none.[18]

The U.S. Census does not ask about religion, so the ARIS survey was the first comprehensive study of how people identified their spiritual beliefs. A new category called the "nones" developed from that initial ARIS report. The 1990 survey interviewed 113,000 people, an update in 2001 interviewed 50,000, and in 2008, 54,000 were interviewed. This study led to quantifying the category of nones based on the survey question "What is your religious identity?" The answer was "None."[19] The nones appear to be one of the most significant reasons the American church is losing members and is in decline.

When you examine the numbers, it is simply not possible to come to any other conclusion. Millions of Christians in the United States simply do not believe many of the fundamental principles of the Christian faith any longer.[20] This is the most significant reason why there needs to be a reestablishment of Christocentric theology in which the Bible is taught at community churches. A strong Christology is the antidote that must be affirmed and taught to combat this theological lethargy and decline of the church.

> When we look historically at American religious history for the early settlers, "the Christian faith was the very center of their lives, and it deeply affected the laws that they made and the governmental structures that they established."[21] So what will America's future look like without a Christological understanding of the world and humanity? Christianity is not in danger of disappearing any time soon, but it is certainly not growing or expanding as it has in the past especially in America. Has the message lost its appeal, or are the messengers ill-equipped to proclaim it? Probably, it is a combination. Why then in some areas of the globe outside the United States is Christianity experiencing explosive growth? A recent study by the Barna Group discovered that nearly 60% of all Christians between the ages of 15 and 29 are no longer actively involved in any church. Just check out the results of one survey of young adults that was conducted by the LifeWay Christian Resources …
>
> - 65% rarely or never pray with others
> - 38% almost never pray by themselves
> - 65% rarely or never attend worship services of any kind
> - 67% don't read the Bible or any other religious texts regularly.[22]

If this does not change, churches (will be) closing as quickly as GM dealerships. The reality is that they are also rejecting the fundamental principles of the Christian faith. One survey conducted by the Barna Group found that less than 1% of all Americans between the ages of 18 and 23 hold a Biblical worldview.[23]

The Barna Group asked participants in the survey if they agreed with the following statements.

1. Absolute moral truth exists.
2. The Bible is completely accurate in all of the principles it teaches.
3. Satan is considered a real being or force, not merely symbolic.
4. A person cannot earn their way into Heaven by trying to be good or by doing good works.
5. Jesus Christ lived a sinless life on earth.
6. God is the all-knowing, all-powerful creator of the world who still rules the universe today.

Less than 1% of the participants agreed with all of those statements. For example, one survey found that 52% of all American Christians believe that "at least some non-Christian faiths can lead to eternal life." Another survey found that 29% of all American Christians claim to have been in contact with the dead, 23% believe in astrology and 22% believe in reincarnation. Without a doubt, the religious landscape of America is changing.[24]

Let's look at church around America and see what it tells us. The percentage of people who call themselves Christian in some way has dropped more than 11% in a generation. The faithful have scattered out of their traditional bases: the Bible Belt[v] is less Baptist, and the Rust Belt[vi] is less Catholic. Everywhere, more people are exploring spiritual frontiers or falling off the faith map completely. These dramatic shifts in just eighteen years are detailed in the ARIS survey. It finds that despite an increase in immigration and population growth that has added nearly 50 million adults to the U.S. population, almost all religious denominations have lost ground since the first ARIS survey in 1990. "More than ever before, people are just making up their own stories of who they are." They say, "I'm everything. I'm nothing. I believe in myself," says Barry Kosmin, survey co-author.[25]

These are among the key findings in the 2008 survey.

---

[v] The Bible Belt stretches from West Virginia and southern Virginia to southern Missouri in the north to Texas and northern Florida in the south.
[vi] The Rust Belt is in the Great Lakes region and covers much of the American Midwest that was utilized for transportation and natural resources.

- Many Americans claim no religion at all ("nones") (15%, up from 8% in 1990), that category now outranks every other major U.S. religious group except Catholics and Baptists. In a nation that has long been mostly Christian, 'the challenge to Christianity … does not come from other religions but from a rejection of all forms of organized religion,' the report concludes.

- Catholic strongholds in New England and the Midwest have faded as immigrants, retirees, and young job seekers have moved to the Sun Belt.[vii] While bishops from the Midwest to Massachusetts close down or consolidate historic parishes.

- Baptists, 15.8% of those surveyed, are down from 19.3% in 1990.

- Mainline Protestant denominations, once socially dominant, have seen sharp declines: The percentage of Methodists, for example, dropped from 8% to 5%.

- The percentage of those who choose a generic label, calling themselves simply Christian, Protestant, nondenominational, Evangelical, or "born again" was 14.2%, about the same as in 1990.

- Jewish numbers showed a steady decline, from 1.8% in 1990 to 1.2% today.

- The percentage of Muslims, while still slim, has doubled from 0.3% to 0.6%. Analysts within both groups (Jewish and Muslim) suggest those numbers understate the groups' populations."[26]

There seems to be two very significant trends in the religious landscape of America that have had a negative effect on the American church. First is the "development of the spectrum of organized unbelief presents a set of problems to any analysis of American religion."[27]

The actual number of the unaffiliated has remained about the same, between 40 and 50 million Americans. What has changed has been the number of nones; those with no religious affiliation have expanded from 14 million (1990) to 34 million (2008) and continue to grow, and the rise of Islam.[28]

The category of the nones and other sects of these diverse groupings have had an effect on the American church and may be causing much of the decline in traditional church participation. "This new level of religious pluralism even reaches out to the new Humanist-atheist community, whose observations are now welcomed into the discussion on basic religious concerns."[29] Though ecumenical dialogue is good, these groups clearly erode the American Christian church.

[vii] The Sun Belt stretches across the southern and southwestern portions of the country from Florida to California. The Sunbelt typically includes Florida, Georgia, South Carolina, Alabama, Mississippi, Louisiana, Texas, New Mexico, Arizona, Nevada, and California.

Those indicators of decline, taken from General Social Survey data, include,

- Oregon once led the nation in nones (18% in 1990), but in 2008 the leader, with 34%, was Vermont, where nones significantly outnumber every other group.[30]
- From 1990 to 2008, the percentage of people who never attend religious services rose from 13% to 22%.
- Just 45% of adult respondents born after 1970 reported growing up with religiously active fathers.
- In the 1960s, about 1% of college freshmen expected to become clergy. Now, about .03% has the same expectation.
- The percentage of people saying they have a great deal of confidence in leaders of religious institutions has declined from about 35% in the 1970s to about 25% today.[31]

America's so-called mainline Protestant churches aren't what they used to be. For generations on end, the Methodists, Presbyterians, Congregationalists, Episcopalians, and kindred denominations reported net annual membership gains. (In) the 1950s their growth rate equaled or exceeded that of the United States as a whole. But in the early 1960s their growth slowed down, and after the middle of the decade they had begun to lose members. With very few exceptions, the decline has continued to this date. Never before had any large religious body in this country lost members steadily for so many years. By 1990 these denominations had lost between 1/5 and 1/3 of the membership they claimed in 1965 and the proportion of Americans affiliated with them had reached a twentieth-century low. Many theories have been advanced to explain why these old denominations have fallen on hard times. The least credible theory attributes their decline to the secularizing effects of industrialization, urbanization, and the spread of mass education. If secularization were the sole explanation, all but the most culturally insulated sectors of American religion would be losing members. Biblically conservative nondenominational Christian fellowships, for example, (may be) growing and their typical location is not in rural Appalachia but in major metropolitan centers. To explain the decay of the mainline denominations, one must look instead for special factors at work within these churches themselves or in the lives of their constituents.[32]

Why is this happening? Why is the Christian church losing its mass appeal?

So the conclusion that we could draw is, "Only about 18% of Americans attend any church regularly—82% don't. From 2000 to 2005, overall church attendance declined in all fifty states. Even when broken down into subsets of "mainline," "Catholic" and "Evangelical," declines overwhelmed the infrequent small gains.[33]

All Christian churches in several states experienced a substantial decline in the percentage of their populations attending church on any given weekend from 2000 to 2005, the largest percentages as follows.

- Connecticut: -13.4%
- Maine: -11.9%
- Massachusetts: -13.7%
- New Hampshire: -17.5%
- New Jersey: -10.9% (-7.8% decline for mainline, -17.2% decline for Catholic, +2.3% growth for Evangelical)
- New Mexico: -11.4%
- New York: -10.7%
- Rhode Island: -14.1%
- Wisconsin: -13.3%[34]

Christine Wicker (a former evangelical) reports that evangelical Christianity in America—supposedly Christianity's cutting edge is dying. The facts are that about a thousand evangelicals walk away from their churches every day and most don't come back. As a whole, American Christians lose 6,000 members a day more than 2 million a year, while the U.S. population increases by 1.2%—currently 3.3 million people a year. The real figures are that fewer than 7% of the country are really evangelicals—only about 1 in 14, not 1 out of 4 as some have claimed. Southern Baptist growth isn't keeping up with population growth, and it hasn't for years.

Baptisms are going down in every age group except children under 5. And in the critical group of young adults ages 18 to 34, Southern Baptist baptisms fell 40%, from 100,000 in 1980 to 60,000 in 2005. During these 25 years, the U.S. population grew from about 226,545,805 to 296,000,000, a growth of about 30%. The Baptists would have had to baptize over 130,000 in 2005 just to stay even with population growth; they baptized fewer than half that number. The fastest growing groups in the country are atheists and nonbelievers (nones). In just the 11 years from 1990 to 2001, they more than doubled, from 14 million to 29 million, from 8% of the country to 14%. There are more than twice as many nonbelievers (nones) and atheists than there are evangelicals. Since it's hard to believe everyone would have the nerve to tell a pollster they were an atheist or a nonbeliever, the real figures are almost certainly higher."[35]

The halo effect may be responsible for the unreported figures.[viii]

The number of Americans who claim to have no religious affiliation is the highest it has even been since data on the subject started being collected in the 1930s.

Sociologists from the University of California, Berkeley, and Duke University analyzed results from the General Social Survey and found that the number of people who do not consider themselves part of an organized religion has jumped dramatically in recent years. Back in the 1930s and 1940s, the number of "nones,"—those who said they were religiously unaffiliated—hovered around 5%, Claude Fischer, one of the researchers with UC Berkeley, told The Huffington Post. That number had risen to only 8% by 1990.[36]

But since then, the number of people who don't consider themselves part of a religion has increased to 20%. Fischer told HuffPost, "One thing striking is the trend in terms of renouncing religious affiliation you might say continues to move up at a regular pace, while there is hardly any perceptible trend in the percentage of people who express atheist or agnostic beliefs." The research also found that men were more likely than women to claim they have no religion—24% compared to 16%—and that African Americans and Mexican Americans were more likely to associate themselves with a religion than whites.[37]

The results also echo some of the recent findings the Pew Research Center released in October [2012]. The center noted that a third of U.S. adults under the age of 30 don't identify with a religion. In addition to finding that many Americans don't associate with a specific faith, Pew discovered that many

---

[viii] The halo effect occurs when people are questioned about what society deems illicit or unpopular behavior and tend to downplay or underreport that conduct. When people are asked about good conduct or good behavior, i.e., such as attending church or belief in God, they tend to over report favorable conduct. The halo effect may alter respondents' answers as they relate to their actual lifestyle and religious choices compared to the responses.

aren't in the market for one. The report found that, "the unaffiliated say they are not looking for a religion that would be right for them. Overwhelmingly, they think that religious organizations are too concerned with money and power, too focused on rules and too involved in politics."[38]

One significant and telling fact of the condition of the American church is that in a survey conducted in 2002, of almost 1200 U.S. churches, only 6% were growing; conversely, 94% were not or were in decline. The significant point of this survey was finding that church growth was not increasing at a pace as fast as or faster than the communities' population growth rate.

Second, the concept of alternative fellowship—TV, Internet, social media, and home fellowship—has dramatically affected the attendance of the American church. With so many finding comfort, fellowship, and to a degree biblical teaching elsewhere, the church is further being eroded.

Though the directives in the Bible suggest that it is imperative to meet together (personally) for spiritual enrichment, many are finding that outside traditional church settings.

> Opinion polls indicate that over 40% of Americans attend worship services each week. However, attendance counts in several North American counties and Roman Catholic dioceses suggest that worship attendance may be much lower.[39]

So how many people attend traditional church services in America during an average week? Until recently, the most widely accepted answer was around 40%. This number can no longer be accepted based on the data collected on all Christian denominations in America. Churches are struggling to even stay in a nongrowth category; most are losing members, and few members if any show up consistently.

If the average church among the 300,000 American Christian churches has approximately 200 attending services each week, that comes to ca. 60 million people. The best estimate on the available data would be approximately 20% of Americans attend church services during an average week.

To support this proposition, Ed Stetzer, missiologist and director of the Center for Missional Research at the North American Mission Board of the Southern Baptist Convention, has found evidence of spiritual behavior occurring outside church walls. He recently finished a study on alternative faith communities and found that a growing number of people are finding Christian discipleship and community in places other than their local churches. The study found that 24.5% of Americans now say their primary form of spiritual nourishment is meeting with a small group of twenty or fewer every week. Stetzer says, "About 6 million people meet weekly with a small group and never or rarely go to church … There is a significant movement happening."[40] I suggest that this too is affecting consistent church attendance and the decline.

So with all this negative data and information, is there any hope to build and repair the American church? I believe there is, and I believe it could be found in the birth of small, Authentic churches all over America. Midsized churches are shrinking, but the smallest and largest churches are growing.

> While America's churches as a whole did not keep up with population growth from 1994 to 2004, the country's smallest (attendance 1-49) and largest churches (2,000-plus) did. During that period, the smallest churches grew 16.4%; the largest grew 21.5%, exceeding the national population growth of 12.2%. But mid-sized churches (100–299)—the average size of a Protestant church in America is 124—declined 1%.[41]
>
> As for why the smallest churches have kept up, Shawn McMullen, author of *Unleashing the Potential of the Smaller Church* notes that smaller churches cultivate an intimacy not easily found in larger churches. "In an age when human interaction is being supplanted by modern technology, many younger families are looking for a church that offers community, closeness and intergenerational relationships. For a church of 50 or less, the only place to go is up." They have a relatively small downside and a big upside. A church of 25 can't decline by 24 and still be on the radar. But it can grow by 200.[42]

This is an area where the Authentic Church can flourish.

Established churches 40 to 190 years old are on average declining. American churches started between 1810 and 1960 (excluding the 1920s) declined in attendance from 2003 to 2004.[43] This statistic is unfortunate. Some of the oldest and most-storied churches in America that have been part of American history are and have been in decline or are no longer in operation. How can this trend stop? Or will it?

In Europe, this trend is also continuing. A recent article in the *Wall Street Journal* was titled *Europe's Empty Churches Go on Sale*. Hundreds of churches have closed or are threatened by plunging membership; this poses the question, what to do with unused buildings? Look at what is happening to many historic churches in Europe.

> Two dozen scruffy skateboarders launched perilous jumps in a soaring old church building here on a recent night, watched over by a mosaic likeness of

Jesus and a solemn array of stone saints. This is the Arnhem Skate Hall, an uneasy reincarnation of the Church of St. Joseph, which once rang with the prayers of nearly 1,000 worshipers. It is one of hundreds of churches, closed or threatened by plunging membership, that pose a question for communities, and even governments, across Western Europe: What to do with once-holy, now-empty buildings that increasingly mark the countryside from Britain to Denmark? The Skate Hall's plight is replicated across a continent that long nurtured Christianity but is becoming relentlessly secular.[44]

The closing of Europe's churches reflects the rapid weakening of the faith in Europe, a phenomenon that is painful to both worshipers and others who see religion as a unifying factor in a disparate society. "In these little towns, you have a café, a church and a few houses and that is the village," says Lilian Grootswagers, an activist who fought to save the church in her Dutch town. "If the church is abandoned, we will have a huge change in our country." For Christians, a church's closure—often the centerpiece of the town square—is an emotional event."[45] Look at some statistics of Europe's closing churches:

- The Church of England closes about 20 churches a year.
- Roughly 200 Danish churches have been deemed non-viable or underused.
- The Roman Catholic Church in Germany has closed about 515 churches in the past decade.
- In the Netherlands, where the trend appears to be most advanced, the country's Roman Catholic leaders estimate that two-thirds of their 1,600 churches will be closed in a decade.
- 700 of Holland's Protestant churches are expected to close within 4 years.
- The U.S. has avoided a similar wave of church closings for now, because American Christians remain more religiously observant than Europeans. But religious researchers say the declining number of American churchgoers suggests the country could face the same problem in coming years.[46]

These once-prominent churches are often left vacant and deteriorate. The cost of maintaining these beautiful structures with their stained glass, chandeliers, and historic artifacts has become too high. Since attendance is down, it often means that tithes and financial support wane. There is also no funding for keeping up with daily operating costs much less additional finances to maintain, upkeep, and repair churches.

This is a consideration for building an Authentic Church. Finances ought not to be put into costly buildings that are some of the largest expenses in starting or continuing a work. Rather, spaces should be leased or rented to allow a ministry to start up without incurring significant costs. We have successfully developed and used this new concept I call the church share—more than one church sharing the same space. Different congregations worship at different times so there are no conflicts, but the space is being fully used saving and pooling valuable resources.

> In the U.S., church statisticians say roughly 5,000 new churches were added between 2000 and 2010 (but there needs to be significantly more). Some scholars think America's future will approach Europe's, since the number of actual churchgoers fell at the same time, according to Scott Thumma, professor of the sociology of religion at Connecticut's Hartford Seminary. Mr. Thumma says America's churchgoing population is graying. Unless these trends change, he says, "within another 30 years the situation in the U.S. will be at least as bad as what is currently evident in Europe."[47]
>
> The gap is a serious one for Christianity in America, as research and studies show that church plants are the most effective means of evangelism and church growth. "More evangelism happens through church planting than megachurches," Anderson says. He urges leaders to plant multicultural, missional churches.[48]

This supports *A New Model of the Authentic Church* and its objective to birth small new community churches.

Although America has seen a great dying-off of churches, missiologist Ed Stetzer says he is encouraged to see a renewed interest in missiology and Christology as well as churches that are striving to change themselves internally. "They're asking what a biblical church would look like."[49] "What's going to make an effective church plant in their community depends on what their community looks like," he explains. "Far too many pastors plant their church in their heads and not in their community."[50]

This is precisely what the Authentic Church is called to do—grow where it is planted. It is important to know and understand your community and grow a ministry organically. To be an effective church plant, the church and you must have established a clear biblical model and consistent doctrines. Any Authentic Church must be modeled after the early church in its simplicity as a model that will meet the spiritual and ministry demands of a community.

Jesus went through many towns and villages preaching the Good News of the kingdom of heaven. He healed people of sickness and disease; He discussed that God loved each person individually and all were equal before God. He knew many were misled and had no understanding of what this spiritual kingdom was like. Therefore, He said, "The harvest is plentiful but the workers are few. Ask the Lord of the harvest, therefore, to send out workers into his harvest field."[51] More-effective churches need to be started to reverse the erosion and decline of the American church.

So what is the future of the American church? If present trends continue, weekly attendance will drop to about half of the number it is now; only 10% of Americans will be attending church by 2050. The church as it stands cannot keep up with population growth or the rates of immigration. *A New Model of the Authentic Church* must be developed and implemented to address these issues and concerns.

Christian beliefs and values are disappearing from American life, and culture is filling the void with materialism, individualism, and moral relativism.[52] Less than 70% of Americans now believe in the traditional theological concept of a personal God. The mainline churches and denominations have experienced the biggest decline in their histories. Only 34% of American adults considered themselves born-again or evangelical Christians.[53]

The rise of the nones is one of the most significant developments to affect the American church in decades; it may be the most significant trend in the religious landscape in relation to the decline of the American church. The numbers of these groups called the nones, which includes atheists and agnostics, has risen since 1990 to well over 3 million. The actual numbers may be closer to 4 million.[54]

What this data shows is an overall decline in the regular attendance of church in America. What the reasons for this are probably varied and complex, but an overriding issue that has arisen when one talks to people who no longer attend church is twofold. They say the church has become irrelevant in everyday life because many people don't have the time or don't want to make the time to attend church services or participate in church activities. They also complain about money and say churches are continuously asking for money. This is a big turnoff for many. With these issues in mind, we must formulate a way for the church to become more relevant and applicable to the American public without changing its message or perhaps changing its message back to the simplicity of the gospel as portrayed by Jesus, the apostles, and the early church. We now proffer a new model for America, *A New Model of the Authentic Church.*

LESSON 1

The Decline of the American Church

To the angel of the church in Sardis write: These are the words of him who holds the seven spirits of God and the seven stars. I know your deeds; you have a reputation of being alive, but you are dead. Wake up! Strengthen what remains and is about to die, for I have not found your deeds complete in the sight of my God. Remember, therefore, what you have received and heard; obey it, and repent. But if you do not wake up, I will come like a thief, and you will not know at what time I will come to you.

REVELATION 3:1–3 (NIV)

1. What does this scripture say to you?

2. In the book *A New Model of the Authentic Church*, I am formulating a new paradigm for how church should and ought to be done in the current millennium. For us to be successful in developing this new paradigm of the Authentic Church, we must first take a cold, hard look at the status and condition of the contemporary American church. What are your initial impressions of the condition of the American church?

3. Based upon information provided in Chapter 1 about the decline of the American church, has your opinion changed? If so, why?

4. Brazil receives the most foreign missionaries of any nation in the world. And it may surprise you to find out which nation is second in the world when it comes to receiving missionaries. _____ is the second most-receiving nation for missionaries. Does that surprise you? What do you think the reasons are?

5. Look at some recent statistics on the American church.

   • Of the 250,000 Protestant churches in America, 200,000 are either stagnant (with no growth) or declining. That is 80% of Protestant churches in America.
   • Every year, 3,000 American churches close their doors.
   • Each day, 6,000 Americans leave the church.
   • Since 1950, there are one-third fewer churches in the United States.

   What does this say to you?

6. What are some of the reasons churches in America are declining, following a trend that has been occurring throughout Europe in recent years?

7. Is the church in America in need of a revival? If so, how does that revival begin?

8. Historically, Christianity started out strong in America, but has the church lost its effectiveness and relevancy in our society and culture today?

9. _____, as a label, is the largest religion in the world. Over 2 billion people can be counted as "_____." Their actual practices, beliefs, and lifestyles are another matter entirely. Comment on this.

10. Do you subscribe to the tenets of Christianity as defined as the major world religion, including beliefs in a virgin birth; the life, death, and resurrection of Jesus Christ; a personal God; the second coming of Christ; and the need to accept Jesus as one's personal savior for salvation? (This will also be referred to as "traditional Christianity.")

11. In 2010, 80% of people said they believe in God, while 12% believed in a "universal spirit." In 2006, 73% of Americans said they were "convinced God exists," and 19% said God probably exists. Do you believe there are numerous ways to gain eternal life?

12. The nonreligious population recently rose from 2% to 13–15%. Nonbelievers have mostly come from the ranks of Christian defectors. What do you think the reason for this is?

13. The vast majority of Americans do not attend church regularly. What do you think are the reasons for that?

14. Based on data accumulated over the last several decades, it appears that though the numbers in some small pockets of Christian denominations may be growing, overall, traditional Christianity is on the decline in America. The number of Christians in America has been in steady decline, while the population continues to grow rapidly. Why do you believe this trend continues?

15. Look at the level of Christian education in America today.

    • Only 25% of Americans can name the four Gospels.
    • Only 60% of Americans can list five of the Ten Commandments.
    • At least 12% of Americans think Joan of Arc was Noah's wife.

    What does this say about not only the church but Christians in general?

16. Although many Americans identify as being Christian, less than 10% affirm Christian principles such as the infallibility of the Bible, as well as other tenets of faith: receiving Christ as Savior, confessing their sins if they want to go to heaven when they die, or believing that Jesus lived a sinless life here on earth and that salvation is possible only by grace and not by works (though works would follow). They also do not affirm that God is all powerful and relevant in the world today, nor do they believe Satan exists. Why have these traditional bedrocks of the Christian faith been eroded?

17. The foundational beliefs of the Christian faith are in danger and have experienced significant drops in other areas of church and religion nationally.

    • Sunday school attendance declined 14%.
    • Volunteerism in church was down almost 30%
    • Church attendance decreased 7%.
    • Only 62% of Christians read the Bible weekly

    What does this say about Christianity in America today?

18. Saving the worst for last, we have the millennials—those thirty and under—who "are increasingly rejecting church attendance." Some church scholars suggest this generation has fallen into a black hole. Do you see this as true? What could be the reasons for this?

19. It is estimated that a staggering six of ten millennials who grew up in the church have now left it. What are the reasons for this?

20. 41% of Americans have switched their religion in their lifetime. Many have left the religion they were raised in in favor of another religion or none at all. What are the reasons for this?

21. A study led to quantifying the category of "nones" based on a survey question, "What is your religious identity?" The answer was "None." Why has this new category called the "nones" grown substantially over the last several decades?

22. A recent study by the Barna Group discovered that among Christians

    • 65% rarely or never pray with others
    • 38% almost never pray by themselves
    • 65% rarely or never attend worship services of any kind
    • 67% don't read the Bible or any other religious texts regularly

    What do these statistics tell you?

23. The Barna Group asked participants in the survey if they agreed with the following statements.

    - Absolute moral truth exists.
    - The Bible is completely accurate in all of the principles it teaches.
    - Satan is considered a real being or force, not merely symbolic.

    Most Christians do not agree with those 3 statements. Why not?

24. One survey found that 52% of all American Christians believe that "at least some non-Christian faiths can lead to eternal life." Another survey found that 29% of all American Christians claim to have been in contact with the dead, 23% believe in astrology, and 22% believe in reincarnation. Are these practices and beliefs consistent with a Christian worldview? Explain.

25. Despite an increase in immigration and population growth that has added nearly 50 million adults to the US population, almost all religious denominations have lost ground since the first American Religious Identification Survey (ARIS) survey in 1990. "More than ever before, people are just making up their own stories of who they are." They say, "I'm everything. I'm nothing. I believe in myself." Do you find this to be true with people you talk with?

26. Look at some of the key findings in the 2008 ARIS survey.

    - Many Americans claim no religion at all ("nones"). They now account for 15% of Americans, up from 8% in 1990. That category now outranks every other major US religious group except Catholics and Baptists. In a nation that has long been mostly Christian, "the challenge to Christianity...does not come from other religions but from a rejection of all forms of organized religion," the report concludes.

- Catholic strongholds in New England and the Midwest have faded as immigrants, retirees, and young job seekers have moved to the Sun Belt. Bishops from the Midwest to Massachusetts have been forced to close down or consolidate historic parishes in recent years.
- Baptists are down from 19.3% in 1990 to 15.8%.
- Mainline Protestant denominations, once socially dominant, have seen sharp declines: the percentage of Methodists, for example, dropped from 8% to 5%.

What does this tell you about traditional Christianity in America?

27. The actual number of the unaffiliated religious persons has remained about the same, between 40 and 50 million Americans. What has changed has been the number of nones; the number of those with no religious affiliation has expanded from 14 million (1990) to 34 million (2008) and continues to grow. Why do you think this is occurring?

28. Look at some additional key findings that relate to millennials.

- Oregon once led the nation in nones (18% in 1990), but in 2008, the leader, with 34%, was Vermont, where nones significantly outnumber every other group.
- From 1990 to 2008, the percentage of people who never attend religious services rose from 13% to 22%.
- Just 45% of adult respondents born after 1970 reported growing up with religiously active fathers.
- In the 1960s, about 1% of college freshmen expected to become clergy. Now, about .03% has the same expectation.

Why are so many young people declining to go to church or into the ministry?

29. Why is the Christian church losing its mass appeal?

30. Only about 18% of Americans attend church regularly—82% don't. From 2000 to 2005, overall church attendance declined in all fifty states. Even when broken down into subsets of "mainline," "Catholic," and "Evangelical," declines overwhelmed the infrequent small gains. How can we change this tide of events?

31. Why are the fastest growing groups in the country atheists and nonbelievers ("nones")? In just the 11 years from 1990 to 2001, they more than doubled, from 14 million to 29 million, from 8% of the country to 14%. There are more than twice as many nonbelievers ("nones") and atheists as there are evangelicals. Does this surprise you? If so, why?

32. Back in the 1930s and 1940s, the number of nones—those who said they were religiously unaffiliated—hovered around 5%. That number had risen to 8% by 1990. What do you think are the social reasons for this?

33. The number of people who don't consider themselves part of a religion continues to increase. Why does the trend in terms of renouncing religious affiliation continue to move up at a regular pace?

34. A third of all US adults under the age of 30 don't identify with a religion. What do you believe are some of the reasons?

35. One significant and telling fact of the condition of the American church is that in a survey conducted in 2002, of almost 1200 US churches, only 6% were growing; conversely, 94% were not or were in decline. Is this surprising? How can this trend be reversed?

36. Has the concept of "alternative fellowship"—TV, Internet, social media, and home fellowship—affected the attendance of the American church? If so, explain why. Is this good for the American church?

37. What do you think is the percentage of Americans who attend traditional Christian church services during an average week? Explain your choice.

    a.   70%
    b.   50%
    c.   30%
    d.   20%
    e.   < 20%

38. Why do you think that America's churches as a whole did not keep up with population growth from 1994 to 2004, although the country's smallest churches (1-49 attenders) and largest churches (2,000-plus attenders) did? During that period, the smallest churches grew 16.4%; the largest grew 21.5%, exceeding the national population growth of 12.2%. But midsized churches declined 1%. (A midsize church is defined as one with between 100 and 299 attenders; to put that in context, the average Protestant congregation in America is 124—declining 1%.) Why is there a disparity between church sizes and attendance?

39. What do you think of a new concept called the "church share"—where more than one church shares the same space? Different congregations worship at different times so there are no conflicts, but the space being fully used saving and pooling valuable resources.

40. The decline in attendance in the American church is a serious problem for Christianity in America. As research and studies show, church planting is the most effective means of evangelism and new church growth. More evangelism happens through church planting than through mega churches. Do you believe based on the research complied that there is a need to plant more authentic and missional churches? Does this support *A New Model of the Authentic Church* and its objective to birth small new community churches nationwide?

41. Missiologist Ed Stetzer says he is encouraged to see a renewed interest in missiology and Christology, as well as churches that are striving to change internally. "They're asking what a biblical church would look like." What would your church be and look like?

42. The future of the American church, if present trends continue, is that weekly attendance will drop to about half of the number it is now; this means that only 10% of Americans will be attending church by 2050. Can this be changed? If so, how?

43. Are Christian beliefs and values disappearing from American life? Is popular secular culture filling the void with materialism, individualism, and moral relativism? Fewer than 70% of Americans now believe in the traditional theological concept of a personal God. The mainline churches and denominations have experienced the biggest declines in their histories. Only 34% of American adults consider themselves born-again or evangelical Christians. What does this say to you as a Christian leader?

44. The reasons for this are probably varied and complex, but an overriding issue that has arisen when one talks to people who no longer attend church is twofold. They say church has become irrelevant in everyday life because many people don't have the time or don't want to make the time to attend church services or participate in church activities. They also complain about money and say churches are continuously asking for money. This is a big turnoff for many. Do you believe that these factors are affecting church attendance? If so, why?

45. Why is it that in some areas of the world outside of the United States, Christianity is experiencing explosive growth?

46. What will America's future look like without a Christological understanding of the Bible as it relates itself to a changing world and humanity?

CHAPTER 2
The Plague of the American Church

But I have this against you: You have abandoned the love you had at first. Remember then how far you have fallen; repent, and do the works you did at first. Otherwise, I will come to you and remove your lampstand from its place – unless you repent.

REVELATION 2:4–5 (HCSB)

Could this be a warning the American church should heed? Does this prophecy written thousands of years ago have any application to church life today? It may, but its words are a harsh criticism of the existing churches at the time it was written. The word *plague* is a strong word used more than 120 times in the Bible. The word is like *pestilence* in that it describes sudden outbursts of disease regarded in light of divine visitations. It is used to describe leprosy and punitive disaster in eschatological books. The synonym for this word is *disease.*[55] I believe we have allowed a debilitating disease to spread into the American church called materialism. American culture and its quest for material affluence above all else has even infected and affected the message of the gospel. We will look at what I believe is a plague and disease in the American church.

The American prosperity message is a message developed and a theology lived out in many American churches. It is very appealing to many believers in that it promises health, wealth, and prosperity as a child of God. God loves you and wants you to prosper in all areas of life in the here and now. But upon closer inspection of this gospel, it shows that it is undermining the church and its mission. In this chapter, we will look at and evaluate that message.

The American prosperity gospel argues that these diverse expressions of Christian faith-fueled abundance can be understood as a movement, for they stem from a cohesive set of shared understandings. First, the movement centered on Faith. It conceived of faith as an "activator," a power given to believers that bound and loosed spiritual forces and turned the spoken word into reality. Second and third respectively, the movement depicted faith as palpably demonstrated in wealth and health. It could be measured in both, the wallet—one's personal wealth—and in the body—one's personal health—making material reality the measure of the success of immaterial faith. Last, the movement expected faith to be marked by victory. Believers trusted that culture held no political, social, or economic impediment to faith, and no circumstance could stop believers from living in total victory here on earth.[56]

Is this what Jesus and the early church taught?

Prosperity theology is a sect of Christian beliefs and doctrine that distorts the gospel of the New Testament and undermines many of the significant teachings of Christ. The prosperity gospel is what I believe to be a displaced and destructive theology that puts a premium on achieving health, wealth, and success as the objectives of the Christian faith. It downplays pain and suffering, rejection, discipleship, and contentment in daily living while encouraging the accumulation of worldly success and a positive mental attitude.

In its most simplistic form, their message wants you to believe that God's main objective in your life is for you to experience tremendous "favor" from Him. If you have enough faith (I'm not sure how much is enough; more or less than a mustard seed) and believe whatever you aspire or desire to, you will achieve it.

In the 1990s and 2000s, it was adopted by influential leaders in the charismatic movement and promoted by Christian missionaries throughout the world, sometimes leading to the establishment of megachurches.[57]

This type of theology many times intertwines new-age self-help philosophy with Christian principles of faith morphing into this doctrine. Leaders of the movement believe and profess that sickness, poverty, spiritual corruption, and illness are curses that can be broken by faith and righteous actions.[58]

The teaching is based on nontraditional interpretations and applications of specific Bible verses taken out of context. The book of Malachi often receives special attention. While Malachi has generally been celebrated by Christians for its passages about the Messiah, teachers of prosperity theology usually draw attention to its descriptions of obedience in giving to receive financial wealth.[59]

Frequently quoted verses include,

- Malachi 3:10 (NCV): "'Bring to the storehouse a full tenth of what you earn so there will be food in my house. Test me in this,' says the Lord All-Powerful. 'I will open the windows of heaven for you and pour out all the blessings you need.'"
- Matthew 25:14–30 (NIV), the parable of the talents: "For everyone who has will be given more, and he will have abundance."

- John 10:10 (KJV): "I am come that they might have life, and that they might have it more abundantly."
- Philippians 4:19 (KJV): "My God shall supply all your need according to his riches in glory by Christ Jesus."
- 3 John 2 (KJV): "Beloved, I wish above all things that thou mayest prosper and be in health, even as thy soul prospereth."

The prosperity message is not something new to the Christian movement of the last decades.

> One prominent early figure in prosperity theology was E. W. Kenyon, educated in the 1890s at Emerson College of Oratory, where he was exposed to the New Thought movement[ix]. Kenyon later became connected with well-known Pentecostal leaders and wrote about supernatural revelation and positive declarations. His writing influenced leaders of the Nascent Prosperity Movement during the post-war American healing revival. Kenyon and later leaders in the prosperity movement have denied that he was influenced by the New Thought movement. Anthropologist Simon Coleman argues that there are "obvious parallels" between Kenyon's teachings and the New Thought movement.[60]

Many terms and concepts used by prosperity preachers today date back to Oral Roberts, a poor farmer's son turned Pentecostal preacher. In the late 1940s, Roberts claimed his Bible had flipped over to the third epistle of John, verse 2: "Beloved I wish above all things that thou mayest prosper and be in health even as thy soul prospereth." Soon, Roberts developed his famous concept of "seed faith," which is still very popular today on Christian television and from faith pulpits. It stated that if people would donate money (the seed) to the ministry offered to God, God would multiply it a hundredfold. He promised donors that if they gave to the ministry as part of a "blessing pact," God would return donations from unexpected sources. Roberts even offered to return any donation that did not lead to an equivalent or more of a return. Roberts began to recruit "partners," wealthy donors who received exclusive

---

[ix] The New Thought Religion Movement is a mind-healing movement that originated in the United States in the nineteenth century based on religious and metaphysical presuppositions. It has its roots in American Christianity. One of its followers was Mary Baker Eddy, who founded the Christian Science Movement.

conference invitations and special ministry access while he continued preaching his message to ordinary people.

Eventually, Roberts retreated into a life that revolved around private jets and country club memberships. He died on December 15, 2009,[61] but his ministries in some form continue to this day.[x]

The prosperity gospel was not bounded strictly by region; teachers of the prosperity message were from all parts of the country.

> Denominational markers did not offer many clues, since most churches claimed nondenominational status. Congregational size also proved inconclusive. While famous Faith congregations like Lakewood Church (Osteen) or The Potter's House (Jakes) crowded the list of American megachurches, countless small congregations proclaimed an equally fervent prosperity gospel. Likewise, these congregational estimates could not account for the millions of Americans who participated by watching their favorite Faith televangelists, reading their publications, or attending their conferences. Further, common sense often sent researchers in the wrong direction. The prosperity message favored theological conservatism, and yet, organizationally it was unlike other conservative movements that tended to produce mandates and institutions with iron-clad purpose. The Faith gospel lacked the semblance of this well-oiled institutional machinery, leading many observers to conclude that Faith celebrities operated as theological and institutional independents, rising, persisting, and falling haphazardly.[62]

Many appeared to be solo evangelists building their own ministries and many times their own religious empires; this included books, conventions, private jets, expansive homes, luxury living, and all the other benefits of heading a financially successful, for-profit company.

> In 2010, the Faith movement claimed millions of American followers, though estimates were hard to pin down. A recent *Time* poll found that 17% of Christians surveyed identified themselves as part of the movement, while 31% believed that God increases the riches of those who give. A full two thirds

---

[x] Though Oral Roberts was a leading force in the prosperity movement, he did much good with his ministry. He founded the City of Faith Medical and Research Center in Oklahoma, one of the world's largest health care facilities that merged medicine and prayer. He also founded Oral Roberts University, which graciously donated its law school, many of its professors, library, books, provisional accreditations, and resources to CBN University, which later became Regent University and Regent Law School of which I am a graduate.

agreed that God wants people to prosper. A Pew survey reported that 43% of all Christian respondents agreed that the faithful receive health and wealth.[63]

Many Americans have made this gospel their own.

This work goes beyond denominational history because the prosperity gospel's influence extended beyond formal church structures into what the historian Peter Williams called "extra-ecclesiastical," namely, popular religion. The prosperity gospel possessed the mass appeal of popular religion, with unmatched audiences for prosperity books, conferences, and television programming. Further, it served as a religion "of the people," as millions discovered its message outside of Sunday mornings on their televisions or in the latest paperback. Prosperity teachers fostered anti-elitism and, often, an antagonism toward "traditional" Christianity, preferring to win in the spiritual marketplace rather than the seminaries.[64]

The Internet erupted recently over the fact that televangelist and Pastor Creflo Dollar was raising funds to buy a $65 million private jet. He stated it was necessary for him to be able to commute between his church in Atlanta and New York City. Don't airlines run nonstop flights between both cities for a much cheaper rate?

Non-Christians and Christians alike were critical that the preacher felt he needed the highest-end private jet in order to spread the message of Christ. Dollar hasn't given up on his quest, recently claiming that those who criticized him just didn't understand the Bible. But Dollar is far from the first pastor to preach the "prosperity gospel … comedian John Oliver took on televangelists who promote the idea of "seed faith," which promises followers that God will richly reward them if they donate to ministries. This type of minister has infiltrated the ranks of Christianity for decades. Instead of living modestly, you might see them flying on personal jets, wearing expensive suits or residing in multi-million dollar homes. These preachers spout a mellifluous and charismatic message: God desires His followers to acquire financial riches, experience vibrant health and live comfortable lives.[65]

The board of World Changers Church International, Creflo Dollar's ministry, said it will acquire the luxury multimillion-dollar Gulfstream.

It is our belief that this ministry is called to serve people globally—to literally change the world according to the Great Commission—and our infrastructure and operational plan reflect the worldwide nature of that assignment.[66]

Is this really the message we want to show to the world we are trying to reach? I think not, nor should it be the message of the Authentic Church.

Interestingly, the prosperity message also has no ethnic barriers but rather great mass appeal. "In a recent Pew survey, 73% of all religious Latinos in the United States agreed with the statement: 'God will grant financial success to all believers who have enough faith.'"[67] This is a benchmark statement of the prosperity gospel.

"Nationally, the prosperity gospel has spread exponentially among African American and Latino congregations."[68]

"A 2008 Pew study found that 3-in-4 Latino believers—Catholic, mainline, and Evangelical—agreed with the statement: 'God will grant financial success and good health to all believers who have enough faith.'"[69]

Among mainstream, nondenominational megachurches, where much of American religious life takes place, "prosperity is proliferating" rapidly, says Kate Bowler, a doctoral candidate at Duke University and an expert in the (prosperity) gospel. Few, if any, of these churches have prosperity in their title or mission statement, but Bowler has analyzed their sermons and teachings. Of the nation's 12 largest churches, she says, three are prosperity—(Joel) Osteen's, which dwarfs all the other megachurches; Tommy Barnett's, in Phoenix; and T. D. Jakes's, in Dallas. In second-tier churches—those with about 5,000 members—the prosperity gospel dominates. Overall, Bowler classifies 50 of the largest 260 churches in the U.S. as prosperity. The doctrine has become popular with Americans of every background and ethnicity; overall, Pew (research) found that 66% of all Pentecostals and 43% of "other Christians"—a category comprising roughly half of all respondents—believe that wealth will be granted to the faithful. It's an upbeat theology, argues Barbara Ehrenreich in her new book, *Bright-Sided*, that has much in common with the kind of "positive thinking" that has come to dominate America's boardrooms and, indeed, its entire culture.[70]

The prosperity gospel is nothing more than new-age thinking and thought wrapped in New Testament language.

Theologically, the prosperity gospel has always infuriated many mainstream evangelical pastors. Rick Warren, whose book, *The Purpose Driven Life,* outsold Osteen's, told *TIME,* "This idea that God wants everybody to be wealthy? There is a word for that: baloney. It's creating a false idol. You don't measure your self-worth by your net worth. I can show you millions of faithful followers of Christ who live in poverty. Why isn't everyone in the church a millionaire?' In 2005, a group of African American pastors met to denounce prosperity megapreachers for promoting a Jesus who is more like a "cosmic bellhop," as one pastor put it, than the engaged Jesus of the civil-rights era who looked after the poor.[71]

Theological confusion takes many forms, but with this cover story, *TIME* directs us to one of the most pervasive perversions of the Christian Gospel in our times—prosperity theology. The article, written by David Van Biema and Jeff Chu …

God's promised generosity in this life and the ability of believers to claim it for themselves. In a nutshell, it suggests that a God who loves you does not want you to be broke … a higher percentage than there are Pentecostals in America—agreed that if you give your money to God, God will bless you with more money …[72]

The most famous among them—like Joel Osteen and Creflo Dollar—spread their messages through television and publishing. Osteen now dominates the field like no other, and he is front and center in the *TIME* article. Prosperity theology is fueled by the combination of Pentecostal teaching and American consumerism. Our culture of material abundance (and consumerist appetites) is fertile ground for the emergence of this distorted and corrupted teaching. Jesus never promised His disciples material security, much less material prosperity. The benefits of the Gospel of Christ are redefined in terms of material and financial blessings.[73]

The reporters quote one man who acknowledged the influence of Joel Osteen and his teaching: "I'm dreaming big–because all of heaven is dreaming big," [George] Adams continues. "Jesus died for our sins. That was the best gift God could give us," he says. "But we have something else. Because I want to follow Jesus and do what he ordained, God wants to support us. It's Joel Osteen's ministry that told me. Why would an awesome and mighty God want anything less for his children?[74]

Why would an awesome and mighty God want anything less for His children? The saddest aspect of that question is its focus on material prosperity at the expense of the limitless spiritual riches we are given in Christ. The problem with prosperity theology is not that it promises too much but that it promises too little, and its promises are false. Of even greater significance is the eclipse of the authentic gospel of Christ. The justification of sinners, a life of discipleship, is ignored as material prosperity and wealth dominate the message.[75]

So how does this prosperity gospel live up with the gospels and teachings of Christ?

> "The only way you can make Jesus into a rich man is by advocating torturous interpretations (of the Bible) and by being wholly naive historically," says Bruce W. Longenecker, a professor of religion at Baylor University, Waco, Texas. Longenecker specializes in studying the poor in the time of ancient Greece and Rome. Longenecker adds that about 90% of the people in Jesus' time lived in poverty. They were either rich or barely eking out a living.[76]

What does Jesus say on this subject matter of wealth and prosperity?

> Do not store up for yourselves treasures on earth, where moth and rust destroy, and where thieves break in and steal. But store up for yourselves treasures in heaven, where moth and rust do not destroy, and where thieves do not break in and steal. For where your treasure is, there your heart will be also … No one can serve two masters. Either you will hate the one and love the other, or you will be devoted to the one and despise the other. You cannot serve both God and Money. (Matthew 6:19–21, 24 NIV)

Jesus was clear about greed and selfishness, both of which are sins. He sternly warned religious teachers who used the Bible to enrich themselves: "Woe to you, teachers of the law and Pharisees, you hypocrites! You clean the outside of the cup and dish, but inside they are full of greed and self-indulgence" (Matthew 23:25 NIV).

While the prosperity gospel teaches that Christians should brazenly ask God for new cars, a bigger house, and nice clothes, Jesus warned, "Watch out! Be on your guard against all kinds of greed; life does not consist in an abundance of possessions" (Luke 12:15).

A well-known prosperity and faith teacher said,

> I am fully convinced—I would die saying it is so—that it is the plan of Our Father God, in His great love and in His great mercy, that no believer should

ever be sick; that every believer should live his full life span down here on this earth; and that every believer should finally just fall asleep in Jesus.[77]

... preferably in a big mansion with expensive cars in the circular driveway in a designer suit with a Rolex watch.

THE PROBLEM FOR THE PROSPERITY GOSPEL

How does the prosperity gospel talk to faithful Christians who are struggling financially or physically today?

> The prosperity gospel has some explaining to do. We are in an economic downturn and countless faithful moms and dads and (men and women) are unemployed, suffering, and going to bed worrying if there will be food on the table for the family. Countless Christians are anxious about their finances. You can see it on their faces and you can hear it in their voices and you can read it on their blogs. The problem that must be explained by proponents of the prosperity gospel is that these folks are faithful, they are trusting God, and they are still get sacked and suffering.[78]

The unfortunate must be doing something wrong or not receiving enough faith. To become prosperous, all one has to do is believe, receive, and act on God's promises. The prosperity gospel is a half-truth, perhaps less.[79] If we do not have health, wealth, and prosperity but have Christ, how can this theology ever make theological sense?

> The Faith movement seemed as American as apple pie. We have seen how it grew from religious traditions deeply rooted in the American contest and flourished both in popular and institutional forms. Phrases such as "favor," "abundant life," "positive confession," and "I'm blessed!" popped up in numerous (Christian ministries and churches), reflecting a new style of piety that had become common fare. Prosperity messages echoed in the most unlikely places, reverberating through Mennonite, Moravian, and Lutheran houses of worship. Old foes became friends. Even denominations that fiercely opposed the teachings of Oral Roberts, T. L. Osborn and other prosperity preachers borrowed a page from their playbook. Kregg Hood of the Church of Christ, an avowedly anti-charismatic denomination, penned a tithing manual,

that might as easily have been written by (a prosperity preacher): *Take God at His Word: Expect a Harvest*. Business mogul Donald Trump, supermodel Tyra Banks, and (deceased) superstar Michael Jackson called the faith teacher Paula White their personal pastor. T. D. Jakes advised American presidents, past and present. When the legendary Coretta Scott King (wife of Rev. Dr. Martin Luther King) died, prosperity celebrity (preacher) Bishop Eddie Long presided over the funeral.[80]

This gospel is not only in the United States but also in other areas of the world. In Sweden,

> Anthropologist Simon Coleman noted in his study of the Swedish prosperity movement, *The Word of Life*, the transnational Faith movement cannot be confined to a single national context. Its preachers and ideas proved to be highly mobile and played with ease on a global stage. As congregations, audiences, and leaders in disparate locations became increasingly interactive and integrated, the prosperity gospel rapidly spread as a global phenomenon.[81]

Maybe that is why Pastor Creflo Dollar needs that $65 million Gulfstream.

The American church has fallen prey to this type of message I believe because it plays on people's dreams and aspirations. People naturally want health, success, and material security, but at what expense? By adapting this dangerous type of theological thought, it distracts, manipulates, and minimizes the person and work of Jesus Christ. With this theology, as my father would say, "the church is a mile wide and an inch deep." Adherence to this type of theology has minimized the more-lofty theological concepts the Bible offers. It undermines the atoning work of Jesus Christ, the cost of discipleship, and the sufferings and persecutions the church had in the past and continues to undergo worldwide.

> The hermeneutics of the prosperity movement leaves much to be desired. Author Ken Sarles wrote of the prosperity teachers that their "method of interpreting the biblical text is highly subjective and arbitrary. Bible verses are quoted in abundance without attention to grammatical indicators, semantic nuances or literary and historical context. The result is a set of ideas and principles based on distortion of textual meaning."[82]

Faith is the "currency of heaven," these preachers claim. It gets God to move. So, the way to gain our heavenly privileges is to search within ourselves and uproot our own unbelief. There are endless lies with this theology. It results in misplaced hope, a skewed reality and wishful thinking. God never promises His followers financial wealth.[83]

St. Paul warns the church in Ephesus on this matter: "For the love of money is a root of all kinds of evil. Some people, eager for money, have wondered from the faith and pierced themselves with many griefs."[84]

John Piper, theologian, Bethlehem College and Seminary Chancellor in Minneapolis, states,

> Normal Christianity is pain … It's sorrowful, yet always rejoicing.' We can trust that God will ultimately restore what ails us—in this lifetime or in the next. If He chooses the latter, it will be for his Glory.[85]

Romans 5:3–5 (NIV) states,

> Not only so, but we also rejoice in our sufferings, because we know that suffering produces perseverance; perseverance, character; and character, hope. And hope does not disappoint us, because God has poured out his love into our hearts by the Holy Spirit, whom he has given us.[86]

Over a century ago, Charles H. Spurgeon, the famed pastor and statesman, spoke to the then-largest congregation in all American Christendom with this warning to the church on the issue of the prosperity message.

> I believe that it is anti-Christian and unholy for any Christian to live with the object of accumulating wealth. You will say, "Are we not to strive all we can to get all the money we can?" You may do so. I cannot doubt but what, in so doing, you may do service to the cause of God. But what I said was that to live with the object of accumulating wealth is anti-Christian.[87]

A further problem with the prosperity gospel is that it is not generally applicable to all peoples. Whenever I talk to people who believe in or follow the prosperity message, I ask, "How is the prosperity message relevant to people around the world who are living in poverty or in countries where they are persecuted?" This stumps them because the last message that would bring them any relevance or hope in a time of personal persecution, hunger, and death is a prosperity message.

The gospel Jesus preached about comforting the poor and persecuted and understanding their pain and suffering nevertheless remains a great hope and comfort for those who have nothing other than hope to sustain their lives. For the gospel to be meaningful and authentic, it must be transformative and applicable to anyone regardless of the color of their skin, socioeconomic status, or where they live. In regard to fulfilling these needs, the prosperity gospel lacks the power, freedom, and hope for people the gospel offers.

The Authentic Church model we will encounter in this book takes the emphasis off financial success, material blessings, fundraising, and workplace success and puts the emphasis back on building the kingdom of heaven as depicted in the Gospels and the book of Acts. Its objective is to build Christians who understand fully the whole person and work of Jesus Christ and who do not take one aspect of that work and build their own gospel around it for their own benefit. The prosperity message undermines the integrity of an Authentic Church and misleads many misguided, Christian people.

LESSON 2

The Plague of the American Church

But I have this against you: You have abandoned the love you had at first. Remember then how far you have fallen; repent, and do the works you did at first. Otherwise, I will come to you and remove your lampstand from its place—unless you repent.

REVELATION 2:4–5 (HCSB)

1. What does this scripture say to you?

2. Could this be a warning to the American church? Does this prophecy written thousands of years ago have any application to church life today? If so, how?

3. Do you believe we have allowed a debilitating disease called materialism to spread into the American church? How has that impacted the American church?

4. The American prosperity message is a message developed and a theology lived out in many American churches. Why is it so appealing to many believers? It promises each believer health, wealth, and prosperity as a child of God—aren't those good things? Since God loves you, doesn't he want you to prosper in all areas of life in the here and now? But upon closer inspection of this gospel, could it actually be undermining the church and its mission? What do you think?

5. Is the prosperity gospel a displaced and destructive theology that puts a premium on achieving health, wealth, and success as the objectives of the Christian faith? Does it downplay pain and suffering, rejection, discipleship, and contentment in daily living, while encouraging the accumulation of worldly success and a positive mental attitude?

6. Does this type of theology intertwine new-age self-help philosophy with Christian principles of faith?

7. What do these scriptures mean to you?

    •   Malachi 3:10 (NCV): "'Bring to the storehouse a full tenth of what you earn so there will be food in my house. Test me in this,' says the Lord All-Powerful. 'I will open the windows of heaven for you and pour out all the blessings you need.'"
    •   Matthew 25:14–30 (NIV), the parable of the talents: "For everyone who has will be given more, and he will have abundance."
    •   John 10:10 (KJV): "I am come that they might have life, and that they might have it more abundantly."
    •   Philippians 4:19 (KJV): "My God shall supply all your need according to his riches in glory by Christ Jesus."
    •   3 John 2 (KJV): "Beloved, I wish above all things that thou mayest prosper and be in health, even as thy soul prospereth."

8. Many religious leaders build their ministries and many times their own religious empires, including books, conferences, private jets, expansive homes, luxury living, and all the other benefits of heading a financially successful, for-profit company. Is this a biblical model?

9. A recent *Time* poll found that 17% of Christians surveyed identified themselves as part of the prosperity or faith movements, while 31% believed that God similarly increases the riches of those who give. A full two thirds agreed that God wants people to prosper. A Pew survey reported that 43% of all Christian respondents agreed that the faithful receive health and wealth. What do these findings suggest to you?

10. Does the prosperity gospel possess the mass appeal of popular religion, with unmatched audiences for prosperity books, conferences, and television programming? Further, it served as a religion "of the people," as millions discovered its message outside of their traditional outlets, for instance, Sunday mornings on television or between the covers of the latest best-selling paperback. Prosperity teachers fostered an anti-elitism and, often, an antagonism toward "traditional" Christianity, preferring to win in the spiritual marketplace rather than the seminaries. Why has this been so popular and successful?

11. What do you think of the concept "seed faith," which promises followers that God will richly reward them if they donate to ministries?

12. Barbara Ehrenreich in her new book, *Bright-Sided*, proffers that prosperity theology has much in common with the kind of "positive thinking" that has come to dominate America's boardrooms and culture. Is the prosperity gospel nothing more than new-age thinking and thought wrapped in New Testament language?

13. Pastor Rick Warren said this about prosperity theology: "This idea that God wants everybody to be wealthy? There is a word for that: baloney. It's creating a false idol. You don't measure your self-worth by your net worth. I can show you millions of faithful followers of Christ who live in poverty. Why isn't everyone in the church a millionaire?" Do you agree with his statement? If so, why?

14. Do you believe our culture of material abundance (and consumerist appetites) is fertile ground for the emergence of a distorted and corrupted teaching?

15. The saddest aspect of prosperity theology is its focus on material prosperity at the expense of the limitless spiritual riches we are given in Christ. Comment on this.

16. How does the prosperity gospel live up to the gospels and teachings of Christ?

17. How is the prosperity gospel relevant to the 90% of people in Jesus' time who lived in poverty and to the countless Christians throughout the world who live in poverty today?

18. In your opinion, what does Jesus say on this subject matter of wealth and prosperity? See Matthew 6:19–21, 24; Matthew 23:25; Luke 12:15.

19. How does the prosperity gospel talk to faithful Christians who are struggling financially or physically today?

20. If we do not have health, wealth, and prosperity but have Christ, how can the prosperity theology ever make theological or biblical sense?

21. Phrases such as "favor," "abundant life," "positive confession," and "I'm blessed!" have popped up in numerous Christian ministries and churches, reflecting a new style of piety that has become common fare. Do you hear or use these terms?

22. Do you think the American church has fallen prey to this type of message because it plays on people's dreams and aspirations?

23. Do you agree that Christianity at times is sorrowful, yet always rejoicing? That we can trust that God will ultimately restore what ails us—in this lifetime or in the next? That if he chooses the latter, it will be for his glory?

24. What is your impression of Romans 5:3–5 as it relates to the prosperity message?

25. Over a century ago, Charles H. Spurgeon, the famed pastor and statesman, spoke to the then-largest congregation in all American Christendom with this warning to the church on the issue of the prosperity message. "I believe that it is anti-Christian and unholy for any Christian to live with the object of accumulating wealth. You will say, 'Are we not to strive all we can to get all the money we can?' You may do so. I cannot doubt but what, in so doing, you may do service to the cause of God. But what I said was that to live with the object of accumulating wealth is anti-Christian." Comment on this.

26. How is the prosperity message relevant to people around the world who are living in poverty or in countries where people are persecuted?

27. Can the prosperity gospel be generally applicable to all people in all parts of the world?

28. For the gospel to be meaningful and authentic, it must be transformative and applicable to anyone regardless of the color of their skin, their socioeconomic status, or where they live. Should the American church reject the prosperity gospel for a gospel more in line with that of the apostles and the early church?

CHAPTER 3

A New Reformation

And Jesus went into the temple of God, and cast out all them that sold and bought in the temple, and overthrew the tables of the moneychangers, and the seats of them that sold doves, And said unto them, It is written, My house shall be called the house of prayer; but ye have made it a den of thieves.

MATTHEW 21:12–13 (KJV)

When we look at the American church, we see an institution that has had significant challenges of relevancy and transparency over the last several decades. The questions we need to ask are, Is the church relevant in society today? Has it lost its effectiveness and distinctiveness because of its pursuit of financial well-being? How similar is it to or distant from the Authentic Church depicted in the book of Acts or the early church?

We must ask whether this has occurred before and continues to this day. Has the church been corrupted and lost its way? Has money, ignorance, and pride corrupted the American church? The Authentic Church is a new way to do church in America, one that is transformative and challenging to the way church is done. It re-images a beckon call of the original church pictured in the book of Acts and the early church. What this proposes is a new reformation of the American church.

In this chapter, I will propose that the American church in particular needs a new reformation. Something significant happened in October almost 500 years ago that is relevant to the church today. What lessons can and should be learned from history?

October is the beginning of the harvest season, and at the end of the month, many will celebrate All Saints Day, and many others will celebrate the secular version called Halloween. It is important to understand how these seemingly different holidays share commonality. One is pagan, and the other a sacred holiday celebrated by the church. In recent times, it appears that the sacred has been swallowed up by the pagan. How did this happen? How could this happen? To further understand this, we will look at something very significant that happened in the history of the church on Halloween 1517.[xi]

> Halloween (October 31) is celebrated by millions each year with costumes and candy. Halloween's deepest roots are decidedly pagan, despite its Christianized name. Its origin is Celtic and has to do with summer sacrifices to appease Samhain, the lord of death, and evil spirits. Those doing the pagan rituals believed that Samhain sent evil spirits abroad to attack humans, who could escape only by assuming disguises and looking like evil spirits themselves. Christians tried to confront these pagan rites by offering a Christian alternative (All Hallows' Day) that celebrated the lives of faithful Christian saints on November 1. In medieval England the festival was known as All Hallows, hence the name Halloween (All Hallows' eve) for the preceding evening.[88]

Whether this was a wise thing for the church to do remains questionable.

There's a curious connection between Halloween and Reformation Day, and it's more than just proximity on the calendar. Why did Martin Luther nail his famous 95 Theses to the Wittenberg church door on (Halloween) October 31, 1517? Was he confronting two religious observances that promoted false saintliness and exploited people's fear of judgment and purgatory? Was he trying to reroute the direction of the church back to its original concepts and tenets of its faith and practice?[89]

> All Hallows' Day or All Saints Day (November 1) was first celebrated on May 13, 609, when Pope Boniface IV dedicated the Pantheon in Rome to the Virgin Mary. The date was later changed to November 1 by Pope Gregory III, who dedicated a chapel in honor of all saints in the Vatican Basilica. In 837, Pope Gregory IV (827–844) ordered its church-wide observance. Its origin lies earlier in the common commemorations of Christian martyrs. Over time these celebrations came to include not only the martyrs, but all saints. During the Reformation the Protestant churches came to understand "saints" in its New Testament usage as including all believers and reinterpreted the feast of All Saints as a celebration of the unity of the entire Church.[90]

[xi] On October 31, 2005, Toms River Community Church, *A New Model of the Authentic Church*, was incorporated. Almost 500 years later, we are still trying to recapture and recreate the Authentic Church.

The proponent of the Reformation was Martin Luther (not to be confused with civil rights leader Rev. Dr. Martin Luther King, Jr.). He was born in Eisleben, Germany, in 1483, and became one of Western civilization's most significant historical figures. Luther spent his early years in relative anonymity as a monk and scholar. In 1517, he wrote the 95 Theses attacking the Catholic Church's practices of selling indulgences to absolve sin.[91]

> Reformation Day (October 31) commemorates Luther's posting of his 95 Theses on the door of the Castle Church in Wittenberg, Germany on October 31, 1517. This act triggered the Reformation, as they were immediately translated and distributed across Germany in a matter of weeks. The Protestant Reformation's main theme was the rediscovery of the doctrine of justification—that is, salvation by grace alone through faith alone in Christ. (Gal. 2:21)[xii] It was also a protest against the corruption within the Roman Catholic Church. The century before the Reformation was marked by widespread dismay with corruption of the leaders in the Roman Catholic Church and with its false doctrines, biblical illiteracy, and superstition. Monks, priests, bishops, and popes in Rome taught unbiblical doctrines like the selling of indulgences, the treasury of merit, purgatory, and salvation through good works.[92]

Many of these practices are still going on today but packaged in a more contemporary way. Luther believed in the simplicity of Christ's teachings.

> God receives none but those who are forsaken, restores health to none but those who are sick, gives sight to none but the blind, and life to none but the dead. He does not give saintliness to any but sinners, nor wisdom to any but fools. In short: He has mercy on none but the wretched and gives grace to none but those who are in disgrace. Therefore no arrogant saint, or just or wise man can be material for God, neither can he do the work of God, but he remains confined within his own work and makes of himself a fictitious, ostensible, false, and deceitful saint, that is, a hypocrite (Luther W. A. 1.183ff).[93]

What may have sparked Luther's response was that earlier that year, in 1517, Pope Leo X made an unconventional move. Pope Leo wanted to rebuild St. Peter's Basilica in Rome, but he

---

[xii] "I do not frustrate the grace of God: for if righteousness come by the law, then Christ is dead in vain. (Galatians 2:21 KJV).

did not want to spend his considerable personal wealth to do so. This is not surprising, seeing as (Pope) Leo was a member of the wealthy Medici banking family, which dominated Florence.[94]

The pope was more banker than pastor.

Pope Leo's solution was therefore to begin offering indulgences in exchange for donations to the basilica's renovation. While these monetary donations could technically be considered pious works by some, Luther saw them simply as payments. In Luther's eyes, the church was exploiting the poor by selling them salvation. He witnessed peasants giving up their life savings to buy indulgences for dead relatives in the hope of saving them from purgatory. All the while, the church grew richer on the backs of the poor.[95] Though the practice of selling indulgences is no longer practiced under that title or name, just watch a few moments of Christian television and you will see that some are still selling salvation. Luther knew that theologically and scripturally, selling indulgences was impossible to justify. This had to be purged out of the church to make it holy and pure.

Along with his criticisms of indulgences, Luther also reflected on popular attitudes about the "St. Peter's scandal"[xiii] in the 95 Theses. He wrote, "Why does not the pope, whose wealth today is greater than the wealth of the richest Crassus, build the basilica of St. Peter with his own money rather than with the money of poor believers?"[96]

I wonder whether this practice of raising money, peddling indulgences, is used in a new way to obtain revenue for the American church just packaged differently. Luther was trying to stop the church from engaging in practices he considered unchristian. The practice of extorting money from the poor and needy with a promise of absolution was not right then and it is not right now.

Luther picked up the teachings echoed by St. Augustine who in 340–430 had emphasized the dominance of the Bible rather than church officials as the ultimate religious authority. He also believed that humans could not reach salvation by their own acts but that only God could bestow salvation by His divine grace. In the Middle Ages, the Catholic Church taught that salvation was possible through good works or works of righteousness. Luther came to share St. Augustine's two central beliefs that formed the basis of Protestantism. The Catholic Church's practice of granting indulgences to provide absolution became increasingly corrupt. Indulgence selling had been banned in Germany, but the practice continued.[97] Money and religion never mix well.

An indulgence is a monetary payment to the church for remission of punishment of

---

[xiii] To pay for increasing building costs of St. Peter's Basilica, popes peddled indulgences. Absolution was bartered for building funds, infuriating Martin Luther and other Reformation figures and culminating in the division of the Christian West into Protestants and Catholics.

sins. Luther's problem with the church's practice of selling indulgences was that for him, an indulgence amounted to nothing more than a get-out-of-purgatory-free card. The church had been in the practice of granting indulgences in exchange for good works and acts of piety for many centuries, but granting indulgences for money was something new and a practice Luther found abhorrent.[98] Let us now explore the content of the 95 Theses and their relevance to the Authentic Church.

> The 95 Theses, which would later become the foundation of the Protestant Reformation, were written in a remarkably humble and academic tone, questioning rather than accusing. The overall thrust of the document was nonetheless quite provocative. The first two of the theses contained Luther's central idea, that God intended believers to seek repentance and that faith alone, and not deeds, would lead to salvation. The other 93 theses, a number of them directly criticizing the practice of indulgences, supported these first two.[99]

Luther's 95 Theses propounded two central beliefs; one, the Bible is the central religious authority, and two, humans can achieve salvation only by their faith in Christ and not by their deeds. These two central beliefs sparked the Protestant Reformation. Though these ideas had been advanced before, Martin Luther codified them at a moment in history that was ripe for religious reformation.[100] I believe now the time is ripe for an American reformation.

> Committed to the idea that salvation could be reached through faith and by divine grace only, Luther vigorously objected to the corrupt practice of selling indulgences. Acting on this belief, he wrote the "Disputation on the Power and Efficacy of Indulgences," also known as "The 95 Theses," a list of questions and propositions for debate (and change).[101]

Luther hung the document on the door of the church to announce the ensuing academic discussion around it that he was organizing.[102] What happened was more like a long but powerful chain reaction than a sudden explosion. It started on Halloween/All Saints' Eve, October 31, 1517, when Luther formally objected to the way one friar was preaching on plenary indulgence.[103]

Luther questioned whether the church had the authority to grant such indulgences. He believed the only true path to salvation lay through faithfulness to Christ and his teachings, not through adherence to the ideologies and dogmas of the Catholic Church, and certainly not by paying monies for the remission of sins.[104]

A sampling of the 95 Theses Martin Luther nailed on the church door at Wittenberg are relevant to today's church and shed light on many of its practices. Luther recognized that the church must be a representative and a conduit for the gospel of Christ, not a prosperous financial organization.

Here are excerpts from the 95 Theses in which Luther accused the church of many things.

- 27. They preach only human doctrines who say that as soon as the money clinks into the money chest, the soul flies out of purgatory.
- 28. It is certain that when money clinks in the money chest, greed and avarice can be increased; but when the church intercedes, the result is in the hands of God alone.
- 31. The man who actually buys indulgences is as rare as he who is really penitent; indeed, he is exceedingly rare.
- 32. Those who believe that they can be certain of their salvation because they have indulgence letters will be eternally damned, together with their teachers.
- 35. They who teach that contrition is not necessary on the part of those who intend to buy souls out of purgatory or to buy confessional privileges preach unchristian doctrine.
- 42. Christians are to be taught that the pope does not intend that the buying of indulgences should in any way be compared with works of mercy.
- 43. Christians are to be taught that he who gives to the poor or lends to the needy does a better deed than he who buys indulgences.
- 45. Christians are to be taught that he who sees a needy man and passes him by, yet gives his money for indulgences, does not buy papal indulgences but God's wrath.
- 48. Christians are to be taught that the pope, in granting indulgences, needs and thus desires their devout prayer more than their money.
- 50. Christians are to be taught that if the pope knew the exactions of the indulgence preachers, he would rather that the basilica of St. Peter were burned to ashes than built up with the skin, flesh, and bones of his sheep.
- 51. Christians are to be taught that the pope would and should wish to give of his own money, even though he had to sell the basilica of St. Peter, to many of those from whom certain hawkers of indulgences cajole money.
- 54. Injury is done to the Word of God when, in the same sermon, an equal or larger amount of time is devoted to indulgences than to the Word.
- 62. The true treasure of the church is the most holy gospel of the glory and grace of God.[105]

What did it mean to fully understand the purpose and work of Christ and the church collectively? Look at what transpired in Luther's life when this occurred.

The dark clouds of false theology were moved back and for the first time Luther could see the pure rays of the gospel light shining upon his face. Luther recalls this moment:

Though I lived as a monk without reproach, I felt that I was a sinner before God with an extremely disturbed conscience. I could not believe that he was placated by my satisfaction. I did not love, yes, I hated the righteousness of God who punishes sinners, and secretly, if not blasphemously, certainly murmuring greatly, I was angry with God, and said, "As if, indeed, it is not enough, that miserable sinners, eternally lost through original sin, are crushed by every kind of calamity by the law of the Decalogue, without having God add pain to pain by the gospel and also by the gospel threatening us with his righteousness and wrath!" Thus I raged with a fierce and troubled conscience. Nevertheless, I beat importunately upon Paul at that place, most ardently desiring to know what St. Paul wanted.

At last, by the mercy of God, meditating day and night, I gave heed to the context of the words, namely, "In it the righteousness of God is revealed, as it is written, "He who through faith is righteous shall live." 'There I began to understand that the righteousness of God is that by which the righteous lives by a gift of God, namely by faith. And this is the meaning: the righteousness of God is revealed by the gospel, namely, the passive righteousness with which merciful God justifies us by faith, as it is written, "He who through faith is righteous shall live." Here I felt that I was altogether born again and had entered paradise itself through open gates."[106]

This was Luther's lightbulb moment (though the lightbulb would go out in other of his writings on the Jews)[xiv]; it was not through the acts of buying indulgences from the church that one could earn salvation in Christ. In that corrupt practice, how much money one had to give equated with how much absolution from sin one could gain. Of course, the poor could

---

[xiv] Martin Luther in (1543) wrote "On the Jews and Their Lies," which was clearly anti-Jewish and anti-Semitic. He suggested, "Jews are truly stupid fools," full of lies, conceit, and blasphemy and that books and Torahs should be burned along with synagogues. This came to fruition on November 9, 1938—Kristallnacht. The theology of this subject matter on the Jews and Israel clearly undermines the good Martin Luther wrote about in 1517 on the Reformation.

not buy much, so they would wallow in sin. Luther learned that only through recognition of who and what we are before Christ can we be justified by our faith; we obtain remission of our sins and salvation.

The Reformation he started has never ceased. In fact, the practice of questioning traditions and of examining the teachings of the scriptures for oneself emerged as a new form of Christianity, different and distinct from the Catholic and Orthodox traditions that dominated the Christian religion for nearly 1,500 years. This I propose is what the American church needs to do now—look at itself in the mirror to see if it is in line with what Christ taught. Is it the Authentic Church as depicted in Acts?

This is an example of what Jesus would think of indulgences, money, and prosperity being preached in his house, the church. While Christians celebrate Jesus' birth and the events around his crucifixion (Holy Week starting with Palm Sunday and ending on Easter), they give much less attention to a clear sign of his religious activism—the overturning of the money changers' tables at the temple in Jerusalem. This was much the same way that the selling of indulgences was taking place after the time of Christ. Jesus in turn was posing in radical fashion a reformation that changed the way religious practice was done. He would try to banish these ungodly and evil practices from religious life that were rooted in greed and money. Can we discern any truth from the cries of the reformers and of Jesus?

The cleansing of the temple narrative tells of Jesus expelling the merchants and the money changers from the temple and occurs in all four canonical Gospels of the New Testament.[107]

> Just as in the days of Martin Luther and John Calvin, our churches have ceased to understand the fullness of the Gospel of Jesus Christ. We have failed to live into the power of the Holy Spirit that resides within each and every one of us. We have grown enamored with our positions of power and privilege in American society, and in so doing, have forsaken those whom Christ himself has called us to honor the most."[108] So, what can we learn from the Scriptures about Jesus overturning the tables of the money changers? Let us examine the quote I opened this chapter with more closely.

> Jesus entered the temple area and drove out all who were buying and selling there. He overturned the tables of the money changers and the benches of those selling doves. "It is written," he said to them, "My house will be called a house of prayer," but you are making it a den of robbers." [109]

> William R. Herzog II, Professor of New Testament Interpretation at the Andover Newton Theological School in Massachusetts, drawing on a range of scholarly and biblical sources, proposes that, "with the technological advances

in ancient agrarian societies (the plow, draft animals, etc.), came surplus yields, and the temple became a sneaky and seductive way for rulers to extract this additional output from the peasant base, i.e. workers would hand over their hard-earned surplus-produce to the temple for the purported sake of pleasing or appeasing the gods."[110]

The Temple had become a lot more than a religious temple. It had become a tax collection agency and a bank ... With that fat treasury, the Temple had entered the banking business and regularly made loans, primarily to poor people. Poor people were the victims not only of a flat tax, but also high-interest loans.[111]

As depicted in the Gospels, Jesus and His disciples travel to Jerusalem for Passover where Jesus expels the merchants and money changers from the temple, accusing them of turning the temple into a den of thieves through their commercial and financial activities. In the Gospel of John, Jesus refers to the temple as "my Father's house," thus making a claim to being the Son of God. This narrative occurs near the end of the synoptic Gospels (Mark 11:15–19, Matthew 21:12–17, and Luke 19:45–48) and near the start of the Gospel of John (John 2:13–16). Some scholars believe that these accounts refer to two incidents given that the Gospel of John also includes more than one Passover.[112] This is not the most important question to ask, but rather, why would Jesus do something so radical and out of character? There is only one viable explanation—he was opposed to the very core of His being as to what the religious leaders and money changers had turned His place of worship into. The temple tax was nothing more than men taking advantage of others by putting hindrances before the free access to God by way of an indulgence.

Upon entering the temple, Jesus saw the money changers along with merchants who were selling animals for sacrifice. Many people brought coins from their hometowns, most bearing the images of Roman emperors or Greek gods, something the temple authorities considered idolatrous. The high priest accepted only Tyrian shekels for the annual half-shekel temple tax because these coins contained a higher percentage of silver, so money changers exchanged their worthless coins for these valuable shekels. Of course they extracted a profit, sometimes much more than the law allowed.

Jesus was so filled with anger at the desecration of the holy place that He took some cords and wove them into a small whip. He ran about knocking over the tables of the money changers, spilling coins on the ground. He drove the exchangers out of the area along with the men selling animals. He also prevented people from using the temple court as a shortcut. As he cleansed the temple of greed and profit, Jesus quoted Isaiah 56:7: "My house shall be called a house of prayer, but you make it a den of robbers" (Matthew 21:13 ESV). The disciples and others were in awe of Jesus' authority in God's sacred place. His followers recalled a passage from Psalm 69:9: "Zeal for your house will consume me" (John 2:17 ESV). The common people were impressed by Jesus' teaching, which caused the chief priests and scribes to fear his popularity. They began to plot a way to destroy Jesus.[113]

Jesus' actions were an open rebuke of a nation and their spiritual state indicated by their apparent disregard of the sacredness of the house of God and the pursuit of money. It was a precursor, a warning of the judgment that was to be visited upon them because of their apostasy, greed, and unbelief.[114]

> The abuse which our Lord was rebuking (greed and unbelief) had arisen from what was at first a mere matter of convenience for worshipers. The sale of sacrifices in a place adjacent to the Temple, and the exchange of foreign money for the sacred coins with which the Temple tax could be paid, (may have been) innocent enough; but little by little the traffic had crowded into the very court of the Temple; it was accompanied by disorder, greed, dishonesty, and extortion, until the place of worship had become, as Christ declared, "a house of merchandise."[115]

As we study and learn from history and how people were taken advantage of and how much the church had become an institution for revenue making, we recognize that the church needed a correction or reformation to return it to its core mission of sharing the love and redemptive work of Christ.

So this question must be asked, has the same thing occurred in society and the church today? Almost two thousand years later at another important prophetic fulcrum in history, the world is possessed by an enthusiasm for money changing. Commerce and finance have thoroughly captured the heart of society, and many churches and so-called Christian ministries have become obsessed with the false notion that wealth accumulation or prosperity is the essence of human existence. At the precise time that the world's focus should be "looking up, for our redemption draweth nigh" (Luke 21:28), much of the American church and society at large have been caught up in an accelerating practice of money changing, greed, prosperity, and indulgence buying.[116] The church appears to be no different from what it was during the time of Christ and the Reformation.

The apostle Paul reminds us,

> People who want to get rich fall into temptation and a trap and into many foolish and harmful desires that plunge men into ruin and destruction. For

the love of money is a root of all kinds of evil. Some people, eager for money, have wandered from the faith and pierced themselves with many griefs." (1 Timothy 6:9–10) That was happening already in his day.[117]

One of the key phrases that emerged out of the Reformation was, "Reformed and Reforming." This means that the Christian church was always meant to be undergoing spirit-led, scripturally based reformation and listening to the voice of God as we move forward in history.[118]

The Reformation theology also produced concepts that have relevance to our daily living and the Authentic Church. The principles of the Reformation stated were these.

SOLA SCRIPTURA: SCRIPTURE ALONE

> For Luther the church was the creation of the Bible, born in the womb of Scripture. "For who begets his own parent?" Luther asked. "Who first brings forth his own maker?" He held a high view of the inspiration of the Bible, calling it once "the Holy Spirit book."[119]

We must recapture in our lives the significance, relevance and importance of Holy Scripture.

SOLA CHRISTO: CHRIST ALONE

In this area, we must more fully understand the person and work of Jesus Christ as one and the same. He is the center point of our faith and practice. To more fully understand the person and work of Jesus Christ is to better understand the fullness of his work for humanity.

> Stated positively, each *sola* affirms the centrality of Jesus Christ, Christ *alone*. First, Luther proclaimed that Christ is the sole content of Scripture and the principle for selectivity within Scripture. Famously he criticized the Epistle of James because it did not proclaim Christ sufficiently in his view: "Whatever does not teach Christ is not apostolic, even though St. Peter or St. Paul does the teaching," he wrote. "Again, whatever preaches Christ would be apostolic even if Judas, Annas, Pilate and Herod were doing it!" Secondly, Christ is the center of Luther's doctrine of justification by faith: through Christ's substitutionary death on the cross, God acted to redeem fallen humanity. In his *Large Catechism*, Luther wrote, "We could never come to recognize the Father's favor and grace were it not for the Lord Christ, who is a mirror of the Father's heart."[120]

SOLA GRATIA: GRACE ALONE

It is not to be a human endeavor that we are made righteous before God but rather His righteousness is dispensed to us in the form of grace.

> Luther however, saw the human will as completely enslaved by sin and Satan: we think we are free, but we only reinforce our bondage by indulging in sin. Grace releases us from this enslaving illusion and leads us into "the glorious liberty of the children of God." God wants us to love him freely, Luther said. But that is only possible when we have been freed from captivity of Satan and self.[121]

SOLA FIDE: FAITH ALONE

The only conduit through which we can receive the blessings of God is faith. It is impossible to please God without faith.

> God accepts Christ's righteousness, which is alien to our nature, as our own. Though God does not actually remove our sins, God no longer counts them against us. We are at the same time righteous and sinful ("simul justus et peccator," as Luther put it) Luther called this a "sweet exchange" between Christ and the sinner: "Therefore, my dear (friend), learn Christ and him crucified; learn to pray to him despairing of yourself, saying "Thou, Lord Jesus, art my righteousness and I am thy sin. Thou hast taken on thyself what thou wast not, and hast given to me what I am not."[122]

The Authentic Church must be able to look at itself objectively and implement a new reformation. This will not be easy; unnecessary programs will have to be ended, and finances, budgets, and fundraising will have to be curtailed. We must go back to the simplicity and authenticity of the gospel, reach out to all people with the Good News of Christ, feed the poor, free those oppressed, and bring life to the spiritually dead.

The gospel is free salvation. It was paid for by Christ; no one can buy it. The church is not established to be profitable financially but to be profitable spiritually, not charge and raise money for the next program, church building, or excessive pastoral salaries. The church must realize it cannot buy or sell its way into heaven via indulgences. It must return to the way Christ wanted the church to be and the directives He gave through His parables and teachings.

If Christ were physically here today, would He go into churches, overturn the tables of money, and cast out those who had been transacting business? The church is to be the bride of Christ, not a prostitute.

The thrust of Reformation theology is to sanitize the church from these corrupt practices. The church, Christ's bodily representative on earth, directs us to do good, heal the sick, minister to those in need, and feed and clothe the poor. The church had become so corrupted that the same church that directs us to help and support the poor and neglected preys on them.[123] Not a lot has changed since the Reformation of the 1500s.

The Reformation was a process of reform, correction, confrontation, and change that took place for God's glory. Many people who led and participated in it should be remembered for what they accomplished. Ultimately, we should honor them for what they did for Christ—not to heap recognition or fame on them.[124]

We must never forget this, and we must be forever grateful that something greater than carved pumpkins, black cats, and mutilated zombies took place on October 31. We should remember Luther and recognize that the Reformation actually started in the preaching of men long before Luther came on the scene. It also started before St. Augustine. It started in the preaching of Paul as he served as a "reformer" in his own day—preaching the true gospel and eventually dying for the Christ who died for him.[125] Even before that, Jesus challenged the religious leaders of His time and began a spiritual reformation that has no end. The Authentic Church needs to do the same today.

LESSON 3
A New Reformation

And Jesus went into the temple of God, and cast out all them that sold and bought in the temple, and overthrew the tables of the moneychangers, and the seats of them that sold doves, And said unto them, It is written, My house shall be called the house of prayer; but ye have made it a den of thieves.

MATTHEW 21:12–13 (KJV)

1. What does this scripture say to you?

2. Has the church lost its effectiveness and distinctiveness because of its pursuit of financial well-being?

3. Is today's American church similar to or distant from the Authentic Church depicted in the book of Acts or the early church?

4. Has the American church been corrupted and lost its way? Has money, ignorance, and pride corrupted the American church?

5. Does the American church need a new reformation?

6. Something significant happened in October 1517, almost 500 years ago, that is relevant to the church today. What lessons can and should be learned from history?

7. Why did Martin Luther nail his famous 95 Theses to the Wittenberg church door on (Halloween) October 31, 1517? Was he confronting two religious observances that promoted false saintliness and exploited people's fear of judgment and purgatory? Was he trying to reroute the direction of the church back to its original concepts and tenets of its faith and practice?

8. The Protestant Reformation's main theme was the rediscovery of the doctrine of justification—that is, salvation by grace alone, through faith alone in Christ (Galatians 2:21). What do you think of the Reformers' concepts? Is that applicable to the American church?

9. The century before the Reformation was marked by widespread dismay with the corruption of leaders in the Roman Catholic Church and with false doctrines, biblical illiteracy, and superstition. Monks, priests, bishops, and popes in Rome taught unbiblical doctrines like the selling of indulgences, the treasury of merit, purgatory, and salvation through good works. Many of these practices are still going on today but packaged in a more contemporary way. Do you see this in the modern American church and Christian television?

10. During the Reformation period, Pope Leo wanted to rebuild St. Peter's Basilica in Rome. Even though Pope Leo was a member of the wealthy Medici banking family, which dominated Florence, he did not want to spend his considerable personal wealth to do so. To raise money, Pope Leo's solution was to offer indulgences in exchange for donations to the basilica's renovation. Does this go on today in the American church in different forms?

11. In Luther's eyes, the church was exploiting the poor by attempting to sell them salvation. He witnessed peasants giving up their life savings to buy indulgences for dead relatives in the hope of saving them from purgatory. All the while, the church grew rich on the backs of the poor. Though the practice of selling indulgences is no longer practiced under that title or name, just watch a few moments of Christian television, and you will see that some are still selling salvation. Do you agree or disagree?

12. Is this practice of raising money (i.e., peddling indulgences) just a newly packaged way to obtain revenue for the American church?

13. A sampling of the 95 Theses Martin Luther nailed on the church door at Wittenberg are relevant to today's church and shed light on many of its practices. Luther recognized that the church must be representative of and a conduit for the gospel of Christ, not a prosperous financial organization. What do you think?

14. Consider these objections Luther made, and see if they can apply today.

    - 27. They preach only human doctrines who say that as soon as the money clinks into the money chest, the soul flies out of purgatory.
    - 28. It is certain that when money clinks in the money chest, greed and avarice can be increased; but when the church intercedes, the result is in the hands of God alone.

- 32. Those who believe that they can be certain of their salvation because they have indulgence letters will be eternally damned, together with their teachers.
- 35. They who teach that contrition is not necessary on the part of those who intend to buy souls out of purgatory or to buy confessional privileges preach unchristian doctrine.
- 43. Christians are to be taught that he who gives to the poor or lends to the needy does a better deed than he who buys indulgences.
- 45. Christians are to be taught that he who sees a needy man and passes him by, yet gives his money for indulgences, does not buy papal indulgences but God's wrath.
- 50. Christians are to be taught that if the pope knew the exactions of the indulgence preachers, he would rather that the basilica of St. Peter were burned to ashes than built up with the skin, flesh, and bones of his sheep.
- 51. Christians are to be taught that the pope would and should wish to give of his own money, even though he had to sell the basilica of St. Peter, to many of those from whom certain hawkers of indulgences cajole money.
- 54. Injury is done to the Word of God when, in the same sermon, an equal or larger amount of time is devoted to indulgences than to the Word.
- 62. The true treasure of the church is the most holy gospel of the glory and grace of God.

Are there any similarities in the American church to the practices outlined by the original 95 Theses? If so, explain.

15. The Reformation, the practice of questioning traditions and of examining the teachings of the scriptures for oneself, emerged as a new form of Christianity, different and distinct from the Catholic and Orthodox traditions that dominated the Christian religion for nearly 1,500 years. I propose this is what the American church needs to do now to look at itself in the mirror and see if its image is in line with what Christ taught. Is it the Authentic Church as depicted in the Gospels and the book of Acts or more like the church during the time of the Reformation?

16. Jesus expelled the merchants and money-changers from the temple, accusing them of turning the temple into a den of thieves through their commercial and financial activities. Does this have any application in the church today?

17. While doing this, was Jesus in turn posing in radical fashion a reformation that changed the way religious practice was done? Was he attempting to banish these ungodly and evil practices from religious life that were rooted in greed and money? Can we discern any truth from Jesus and the Reformers on this issue?

18. Just as in the days of Martin Luther and John Calvin have our churches ceased to understand the fullness of the gospel of Jesus Christ. We have failed to live in the power of the Holy Spirit that resides within each and every one of us. We have grown enamored with our positions of power and privilege in American society, and in so doing, have forsaken those whom Christ himself has called us to honor the most. So, what can we learn today from the scriptures about Jesus overturning the tables of the money-changers and the lessons of the Reformers?

19. Was the overturning of the money-changers' tables at the temple in Jerusalem, much the same way that the selling of indulgences was taking place after the time of Christ? Does this continue in some form today?

20. Why would Jesus do something so radical and out of character?

21. Were Jesus' actions an open rebuke of a nation and its spiritual state indicated by its apparent disregard of the sacredness of the house of God in the pursuit of money? Was it a precursor, a warning of the judgment that was to be visited upon them because of their apostasy, greed, and unbelief?

22. Has the same thing occurred in society and the church today?

23. Has the American church and society at large been caught up in an accelerating practice of money changing, greed, prosperity, and indulgence buying? Is the church any different from what it was during the time of Christ and the Reformation?

24. The principles of the Reformation were:

   • Sola Scriptura: Scripture Alone
   • Sola Christo: Christ Alone
   • Sola Gratia: Grace Alone
   • Sola Fide: Faith Alone

   Have we applied, and should we apply, these to the modern church?

25. The church is not established to be profitable financially but to be profitable spiritually, not to charge and raise money for the next program, church building, or excessive pastoral salaries. Do you agree?

26. If Christ were physically here today, would he go into churches, overturn the tables of money, and cast out those who had been transacting business?

27. The thrust of Reformation theology is to sanitize the church from these corrupt practices. Do we need to revisit those same issues today?

28. The Authentic Church must be able to look at itself objectively and implement a new reformation. This will not be easy; unnecessary programs will have to be ended. Finances, budgets, and fundraising will have to be curtailed. We must go back to the simplicity and authenticity of the Gospel, reach out to all people with the Good News of Christ, feed the poor, free those oppressed, and bring life to the spiritually dead. The gospel is free salvation. It was paid for by Christ; no one can buy it. What do you think?

CHAPTER 4

Tentmaking: The Model of St. Paul

After these things Paul departed from Athens and went to Corinth. And he found a certain Jew named Aquila, born in Pontus, who had recently come from Italy with his wife Priscilla (because Claudius had commanded all the Jews to depart from Rome); and he came to them. So, because he was of the same trade, he stayed with them and worked; for by occupation they were tentmakers.

ACTS 18:1–3 (NKJV)

In this chapter, I will explain what I believe *A New Model of the Authentic Church* entails in practical formation and application. It is not a new model or paradigm; it has been in place for centuries but has been almost completely lost or forgotten. If we recapture this model of church and leadership, it will free the church from the financial chains and spiritual bondages it has put on itself and help restore it to its true and original purpose. It will encourage those with a deep calling to build an Authentic Church and discourage those who are not called for ministry or those who pursue ministry as a job rather than a calling to get out of the ministry and allow the Authentic Church to be rediscovered.

This model and its characteristics can and should be applied to institutional churches as well as noninstitutional denominations. The example I will use as a foundation for the actual and practical building of the church is the model of St. Paul, the tentmaker. Why do we believe Paul continued to do physical labor when he was such a brilliant scholar, theologian, and religious leader? We know his education and credentials were excellent and the necessity for him to actually do such hard, physical labor (tentmaking) certainly could have affected his ability in time and manner to preach the gospel and build the church. There must have been a spiritual reason for Paul to continue doing physical labor while steadfastly embarking on building not only tents but also the kingdom of God.

By laboring with his hands, Paul was preaching the Word. He set an example that spoke against the sentiment that by preaching the gospel, a minister was excused from hard physical labor or work. Paul knew that if ministers neglected work, they could become feeble. He desired to teach young ministers that by working outside ministry, they would stay grounded, humble, and relevant in society and be an example to the unbelieving world.[126, xv]

Paul recognized that physical labor was part of the education he was giving to other leaders. But he was wise and perceptive enough to realize that his teaching would lack vitality if he didn't keep all parts of the human machinery (body, mind, and spirit) exercised in use.[xvi]

In light of the above, I will say something that may offend some in the pastorate, but I feel compelled to give my opinion based on having been in the pastorate for over a decade while still holding down full-time employment as a trial attorney. Based on observation, I feel many pastors have an easy job and too much time on their hands. I know this may be contrary to statistics about pastors leaving the ministry because of burnout, but many pastors I know have very flexible schedules that allow them a tremendous amount of freedom for downtime and leisure. I am not saying that all pastors have easy jobs or significant amounts of leisure time, but many do, especially those with small churches.

There is no logical or reasonable argument why pastors of small congregations should be allowed to deplete scarce church resources to be paid full-time salaries when they could be working full or part-time jobs outside the ministry while still fulfilling their ministry obligations as the apostle Paul did. In this chapter, which contains the thesis or new paradigm of the Authentic Church, we will examine and discuss these issues.

We pastors and lay ministers need to ask ourselves how we can balance work, family, and ministry. The apostle Paul asked himself following the death, resurrection, ascension, and appearance of Jesus Christ, How can I birth and sustain new ministries? Do I revert to one aspect of my life at the cost of another? Do I have to work in addition to ministry? The question is why Paul spent so much time doing manual labor when he did not have to do it while engaged in full-time ministry. The question should concern us because in the twenty-first century, we need far more Paul-type tentmakers than ever before.

Before we examine Paul's example and his teachings, consider briefly these benefits of having an occupation outside of ministry as Paul did and apply these benefits to today's church and world. This concept is significant for *A New Model of the Authentic Church*.

Combining work and ministry would:

[xv] His labor to support himself, his ministry, and others should have been commended rather than regarded as belittling to his position as a minister of the gospel.

[xvi] I do not propose the form of muscular Christianity popularized in the Victorian British Empire by Charles Kingsley that suggests Christians should work with their hands and keep their bodies physically fit as well as spiritually fit.

- allow new ministries to be birthed without the need for large budgets,
- conserves funds of operating and new churches,
- multiply ministry personnel without affecting the church's budget,
- allow churches to have larger staff, ministries, and people to further reach the community in evangelism and mission,
- provide ministers and ministries that are integrated into the workplace and society while building the kingdom of heaven,
- separate those who are really called by God rather than those looking for a job or career,
- allow a freedom of ministry in that you are not solely dependent financially on church offerings,
- not put undue pressure on small churches to support salaried pastors and benefit packages,
- lessen red tape and administrative costs to focus on important missional objectives,
- enable churches to be free from debt and incurring loans to pay overhead expenses, and
- allow a freedom of expression to not do and say the things people want to hear for fear of losing tithes and offerings.

I will use the term *tentmaker* to mean missions-committed Christians who support themselves financially while being involved in full or part-time ministry. This enables them to make Jesus Christ known on the job as well as in their free time and ministry. They may be in full-time ministry even when they have full or part-time jobs, allowing them to integrate work and ministry. They follow Paul's model of tentmaking for the same reasons he did. In this chapter, we will challenge the conventional thought of looking at ministry as another paying position; we will examine it as a calling from God that must be accomplished in the best possible way in order to reestablish the Authentic Church.

I am amazed at the lack of attention to Paul's model of tentmaking. We cannot continue the missional work of the church without a new generation of such tentmakers. The word *tentmaker* has been co-opted, which is why Paul's example and teachings on this unique approach have gone largely ignored. A major reason for this misuse of the term is the common misunderstanding that Paul had church support and made tents only during financial emergencies. Another possible explanation is that Paul's model may be too difficult for people to ascribe to because it goes against their self-interests and conventional concepts of church building.

I hope to prove that this misunderstanding is a myth and that there were profoundly significant reasons why Paul used this model successfully throughout his ministry. To get the whole picture, we must examine relevant passages and correlate them, especially Paul's letters and the events in Acts. These passages interpret and limit each other. Therefore, we must ask some basic questions.

1. How much manual labor did Paul actually do?
2. How much financial support did he receive from church or donor gifts?
3. Why did he work when he did not have to?
4. Did this foster integration of ministry and culture?
5. What was Paul's tentmaker strategy?
6. How effective was this model?
7. What practical implications does Paul's tentmaking have for us as we enter a new millennium?
8. Can we successfully replicate Paul's model of ministry, and will it dramatically affect the topography of the American church today?[127]

PAUL'S MISSIONARY JOURNEYS

Did Paul work while on his first missionary journey? In 1 Corinthians 9:6, Paul asks, "Are Barnabas[xvii] and I the only ones who cannot refrain from working for a living?" This suggests strongly that they worked while on the first missionary journey, the only time the two traveled together. They must have supported themselves by working as they traveled through Cyprus and Galatia and continued to do so after they formed separate teams.[128] This seems to suggest that Paul and Barnabas were the only ones in ministry who were still working at the time. Was Paul more effective in his ministry because of rather than in spite of his work? Are there elements in the pressures of everyday work that make Paul's ministry more relevant and applicable to ordinary life? The success he had and the lasting effect of his ministry fosters this point.

On the second missionary journey, did Paul do manual labor in Philippi? (2 Corinthians 11:12 was written from Philippi). Both of Paul's letters to the Thessalonians say that he worked day and night, that is, early morning and late-afternoon shifts while taking the usual Mediterranean siesta during midday.[129]

"After leaving Philippi, Paul went to Thessalonica, on the seacoast. The history of his

---

[xvii] Barnabas, born Joseph, was an early Christian and one of the prominent Christian disciples in Jerusalem. He and Paul the apostle undertook missionary journeys together and defended Gentile converts against the Judaizers. They traveled together making more converts (ca. 45–47) and participated in the Council of Jerusalem (ca. 50).

work there is recorded in the first and second chapters of First Thessalonians. He labored in the gospel, working with his hands."[130]

> As apostles of Christ, we could have been a burden to you … Surely you remember our toil and hardship as we worked night and day in order not to be a burden to anyone while we preached the gospel of God to you. (1 Thessalonians 2:6–9)

This short portion of scripture describes how committed Paul was to his tentmaker model, yet this model is grossly ignored or overlooked in the American church today. *A New Model of the Authentic Church* recaptured this in practical form to infuse the church like the early church.

On his third missionary journey, Paul spends almost three years in Ephesus. Acts 19 gives a poignant description of Paul preaching in his work clothes. His audience is likely similarly dressed. It is written that people listening to him preach took away his apron and the sweat rag from his brow in the hope of using them as healing agents for ailing friends.[131] God worked extraordinary miracles even with the work clothes Paul wore. People would carry away towels and aprons Paul used to wipe the sweat off his brow during work, and amazingly, these were taken to the sick, and they were healed (Acts 19:11–15).

Finally, even during Paul's farewell meeting with his elders, he reminds them that he had earned his own support with his own hands and that he expects them to continue his example (Acts 20:33–35).[132] Has the American church followed his example?

Here is a beautiful picture of the model of St. Paul: dressed in his work clothes, laboring all day in the hot sun, building, driving tent stakes, pulling the ties, and lifting the tent's canvas roof. Making tents and putting them up is not easy. Then after laboring all day, he begins to teach and preach still in his work clothes whenever and wherever he is. This is a telling example of how the gospel can be made real, relevant, and integrated into society through one devoted disciple's example. A ministry that is not restricted to buildings, churches, or synagogues but in society. This is the authentic missional purpose of the church. This is the message in *A New Model of the Authentic Church* and is based on the Apostle Paul's example: those in the workforce should labor both for themselves and for the Lord.

How can anyone with shabby clothes and blistered hands who works as a carpenter or tentmaker also be an apostle or prophet? Well, Paul and Jesus did, so why can't we?

Paul was very clear and at times forceful that there was one standard for many of the other so-called church apostles and himself. In 1 Corinthians 9:1–16, Paul substantiates by what authority he is in fact an apostle. He was commissioned directly by the Lord in Acts 9; we read of his encounter with the risen Lord and his commissioning. In light of that, he wondered why he was not treated like some of the other apostles. He didn't garner the respect others had; maybe that was because he did so much manual labor. He didn't receive church-sponsored support as the others did, so he had to continue to work. He didn't receive the food and drink the other apostles benefited from consistently. This could be why Paul was so different from and more effective than the other so-called super apostles.

When you study the letters and writings of Paul, you begin to understand why he believed that self-supported ministries were so important to the life of the minister and the ministry and the growth of the church.

There must have been considerable discussions and talk about why Paul did so much manual labor and the self-supporting model of his ministry. At times, because he was human, he must have felt he was a second-class minister because he wasn't treated as were others who were similarly situated. Paul wrote, "But I do not think I am in the least inferior to the 'super-apostles.' I may not be a trained speaker, but I do have knowledge. We have made this perfectly clear to you in every way" (2 Corinthians 11:5–6). Could this statement be attributed to the people in the church who looked down on Paul's manual labor? Why did he labor while in ministry while others such as Peter did not and were told not to by Jesus?[xviii]

In light of these directives, Paul continued to build the church while building tents. He believed it was incumbent upon him to deliver the gospel free of charge. He addressed this subject further in the same chapter where he indicated to the church at Corinth, "Was it a sin for me to lower myself in order to elevate you by preaching the gospel of God to you free of charge?" (2 Corinthians 11:7).

Paul never burdened a church or group to fully support his ministry. That is clearly different from if he had been in need and people supplied him things freely. He was sure that he kept himself "from being a burden to anyone" (2 Corinthians 11:9).

Paul says that he and Barnabas have just as much right to financial support as others. Paul is proving his own right to financial donor support. Paul says three times in the same chapter (1 Corinthians 9) that he has never made use of his right to financial support. That must include all three journeys and probably the period before and after. Then he gives his reasons

---

[xviii] Jesus had called Peter from his fishing business to give all his time to be fishers of men. When Peter briefly returned to his business, Jesus asked him to promise three times that he would not go back to fishing for fish. (Luke 5:1–11; John 20:21) Two decades later, Peter and his wife still received support for their missionary travels while Paul did not. But one must remember that when Peter was called, he was not involved in ministry; he was one of the original disciples who would spend the next three years learning and traveling with Jesus. This may have been an exception to the general rule. The time the original disciples spent with learning the precepts of the kingdom of God with Jesus was such a brief and exceptional period, and so much needed to be accomplished for the future of the church that full-time ministry may have been indispensable.

for insisting on self-support when he could have lived on donor support.[133] There must be a spiritual, practical or theological reason Paul did this.

How many American pastors or missionaries have ascribed to Paul's model? Probably very few; it is a difficult model to implement and live by, but as Paul points out, the benefits are substantial. Would the results of his ministry been as significant if he didn't work and had not been involved or integrated into society? Knowing this makes one wonder if Paul's preaching and worldview were affected by the type of work he chose. Additionally, Paul did not have to tell people what they wanted to hear to receive their financial support; he was free to preach the gospel unfettered by concerns about losing finances or offending supporters. It is a real question one must ask themselves: if they are in paid ministry, can they be unconditionally honest and forthright? Can they preach the gospel as intended, or will financial constraints force them to mold it in a way that makes it more easy, palatable, and profitable?

One of the most damaging myths or obstacles that the tentmaking model has to overcome today is the image it conjures up in the secular world and to an increasing extent the church. The phrase *bivocational minister* usually paints a mental picture of a retired or relatively uneducated pastor serving a church that is rural, small, dying, or all three. Perhaps someone with limited formal training and licensed by a local church but not ordained by a denomination working at a full-time, nonministry job while serving a church that is limping along and cannot afford a "real" pastor. Dennis Bickers, a bivocational minister, mentions the perceptions of bivocational ministers.

> The churches we lead are often smaller churches with few resources. Many of them have plateaued or are in decline. A large number of us serve with little or no formal theological training. Bivocational ministry is looked at by some as "second-class" ministry performed by people who don't have the gifts to serve a larger church.

Many seminary graduates may not consider bivocational ministry because of such stigmas. Positions that require tentmaking are often viewed as consolation prizes for candidates who have been passed over by more-desirable churches.[134] Much stress and anxiety take place around young seminary graduates seeking full-time, paid pastorates. In this shrinking economy and with the dwindling number of churches and attendance, the current model will become more difficult to sustain. Out of necessity, we may have to revert to the tentmaker model.

Over the next several decades, young seminary graduates should not worry about pursuing full-time, paid pastoral jobs but set their sights on obtaining full-time jobs that will provide for them and their families and allow them to start, build, and be part of a ministry without depleting valuable church resources. Seminary students and graduates are properly trained and gifted with the vocational skills to build ministries. However, all too often, they rush into a job or position that may not be right for them or their families just to be able to pay their bills including student loans. I suggest they do something different, something that will make them more effective in society and ministry without draining the resources of churches. They can do this, as Paul did, by working full- or part-time to continue to be integrated in society while building the kingdom of God in their ministry positions.

FULL-TIME PAID MINISTERS

With that in mind, let us now look at the cold, hard facts about paid ministry in America. According to a recent report in the Religious News Service, a new survey finds that large churches in the Southern United States tend to pay their senior pastors the highest salaries. That (is consistent) with one of the conclusions on churches and finances released by the Leadership Network, a Dallas-based church think tank, and the Vanderbloemen Search Group, a Houston-based executive search firm for churches and ministries. A total of 727 churches in the U.S. and Canada with attendance ranging from 1,000 to more than 30,000 answered questions. That's more than double the number of congregations featured in previous studies. The survey found that 14% of large churches have a financial bonus structure for their top leader (much like a CEO or COO of a large financial corporation).[135]

And one in five of the big congregations finds a way to collect money in addition to passing the proverbial offering plate.

The report says that the average senior pastor in U.S. churches today makes more than $80,000 a year plus benefits. When you add in benefits such as retirement, life insurance, health insurance, continuing-education allowances, and favorable tax benefits, the base salary increases substantially and closes in on six figures for the average senior pastor. Pastors who hold a higher academic degree are paid up to $30,000 more per year than pastors without any postsecondary education. The statistics come from the 2009 Compensation Handbook for Church Staff, an annual analysis of compensation packages at churches across the country. It was recently reported that 4,800 U.S. churches representing about 11,000 employees were surveyed by the Your Church Media Group at Christianity Today International. Compensation is highest in suburban churches with suburban senior pastors making an average of 50% more than do their rural counterparts. The pay is lower in metropolitan areas, small towns, and rural communities.[136]

The size of U.S. churches tells us a lot about the necessity of full-time, paid pastors. The median church in the United States has only 75 regular congregants in worship on Sunday mornings. The majority of U.S. churches having 75 people in attendance for worship on Sunday should not necessitate full-time, paid, pastoral services.[137] Researchers measured the median church size—the point at which half the churches are smaller and half the churches are larger—rather than the average, 186 attendees reported by a USCLS survey.[138] That average is an inflated number due to the influence of very large churches. But while the United States has a large number of very large churches, most people attend smaller churches. The National Congregations Study estimated that the smaller churches (under 499) draw 94% of those who attend church services regularly.

Meanwhile, only 2.41% of churchgoers attended the largest of congregations (1,000+ regular congregants). Now, seeing and understanding the raw data, we can implement the model of St. Paul to effectively transform and revolutionize the way we do church today! Look at the statistics that support the evidence that 94% of all churches have fewer than 499 congregants and 59% have fewer than 99 congregants.[139]

APPROXIMATE DISTRIBUTION OF U.S. PROTESTANT AND OTHER CHRISTIAN CHURCHES BY SIZE (BASED ON NCS STUDY AND EXCLUDING CATHOLIC/ORTHODOX)

Attendance	Number	Weekly Worshipers	Percent
7–99	177,000	9 million	59%
100–499	105,000	25 million	35%
500–999	12,000	9 million	4%
1,000–1,999	6,000	8 million	2%
2,000–9,999	1,170	4 million	.4%
10,000 plus	40	7 million	.01%
Totals (approx.)	300,000	56 million	100%

The majority of U.S. churches that accounts for 34 million weekly worshipers have attendance of only 7-499 people, which make up over a quarter of a million of all U.S. churches. These are the categories of attendance that must be looked at and revisited in terms of tentmaking and *A New Model of the Authentic Church.*

A New Model of the Authentic Church is relevant for denominations that are continuing to lose members and can no longer sustain those expenses. Mainline Protestant denominations continued to decline according to the 2012 Yearbook of American and Canadian Churches. The United Methodist Church, the Evangelical Lutheran Church in America, the Presbyterian Church USA, and the United Church of Christ all reported decreases in membership in 2011. For several years, the Southern Baptist Convention, a conservative evangelical denomination, also showed a decrease. In addition, the Roman Catholic Church reported a decrease of less than 1%.[140]

Counterintuitively, it appears that membership and attendance may be in decline in many Christian denominations though salaries continue to rise. Even in the largest churches, the model of Paul as pastor and tentmaker is still applicable to much of the ministry staff and pastors. Although it may be necessary to have some paid pastors and ministers when churches are that big, the question is, how many? We could still have the same amount of dedicated pastoral staff without them being full-time, paid employees. This will keep the number of staff the same and relieve the church of additional expenses including incurring debt, payroll, and others. Churches large and small should look for ways to integrate their church leaders into society via the workforce while they minister.

According to a newly released survey conducted by the Barna Research Group, Protestant churches of America are more numerous and are raising record amounts of cash each year but attendance remains mired at its lowest point in the past decade. Eventually, with a decline in attendance, finances will also decline. The study revealed that the compensation packages of the average pastor rose nearly 9% from 1999 levels. While the average number of adults attending services at Protestant churches during a typical week remains stuck at 90, the same total was measured in the prior year's study. This reflects a 10% decline from the 1997 level (100 adults) and a 12% drop from 1992.

Church attendance was highest in the south, where churches had an average of 100 adults in attendance, while the lowest figures were recorded in the Northeast and West, each region averaging 80 adults. The Midwest fell in the middle category, with 90 adults participating in church services during a typical week. The survey also revealed an intriguing anomaly. While churches affiliated with a charismatic denomination attract an average of just 80 adults, churches that are charismatic but not aligned with a charismatic denomination attract more adults than the national average or the norm for charismatic churches overall. Those churches—a combination of mainline, independent, and evangelical congregations—average 150 adults per week, nearly 90% more than denominational charismatic churches.[141]

This statistic is vital for showing how this range of church size would fit well into Paul's model of tentmaking. I believe that using Paul's tentmaking model, 1,000 new effective, relevant, sustainable, and Authentic Churches could be developed throughout America. Given the sizes of small congregations, it would not be possible for a pastor to have a compensation package and still be able to meet the overhead costs of the church.[xix]

So now that we are armed with this raw data, it's time to dialogue on this model of

---

[xix] Pastoral compensation is a mixture of salary and benefits such as housing allowance, car allowance, insurance, and retirement contributions. Current laws make it advantageous for pastors to receive part of their compensation as housing and auto allowances thereby reducing their taxable income. There has been a 19% increase in compensation packages since 1992—significant in dollars but still lagging inflation during that period.

ministry presented by St. Paul. Should most pastors be paid? I think in some cases yes but in most cases no. Should pastors be required to work outside church to support themselves? Yes in most cases, no in others. Look at some of these sobering statistics about the state of the modern pastorate.

- 58% of all pastors' marriages will end in divorce.
- 1,500 pastors leave the ministry every month in the United States.
- 80% feel unqualified.
- 78% feel their seminaries did a poor job of educating them.
- The saddest statistics of all are that eight in ten pastors will leave the profession after ten years and the average stay for a pastor at one church is three years.[142]

A BIBLICAL APPROACH AND ANALYSIS OF WHETHER PASTORS SHOULD BE PAID

It has been said that most marriages fail because of financial reasons. What if pastors were more integrated into society by holding down full- or part-time work while they minister? It would take the pressure off them to fully rely on the ministry and not be as prone to burnout and divorce if life were more balanced and integrated. There are practical as well as spiritual and theological reasons for St. Paul's model. Though dozens of references in the Old Testament show the Levitical priesthood were paid out of the tithes and offerings, that was their primary means of making a living since they were not allowed to own property. (The Levitical priesthood system is not in effect in the American church.) We will restrict our discussion to New Testament scriptures about whether a pastor or elder, which they are sometimes called, should be paid or not. In 1 Timothy 5:17–18 (ESV), Paul tells Timothy to let the elders who rule well be considered worthy of double honor, especially those who labor in preaching and teaching. For the Scripture says, "You shall not muzzle an ox when it treads out the grain," and, "The laborer deserves his wages." Where Paul says "You shall not muzzle an ox when it treads out the grain" is an Old Testament Law of mercy where animals that labored deserved to eat from what they provided, and so the same principle was felt equally important for elders or pastors. Every elder is a teacher and every pastor is technically an elder and so the term elder can be used interchangeably with the word pastor.[143]

Because this scripture suggests that those who teach should get some form of remuneration, it doesn't mean they should be paid a full salary, housing, car allowances, and health and retirement benefits. It seems obvious that some pastors should be paid, but most churches are so small and their membership is so poor that a full-time salary and benefits are hard to provide.[xx][144] Some of the fault may lay with members of the congregation who do not give any money or so little that what they give must be used exclusively to keep the lights on and the doors of the church open. But it seems obvious from the New Testament that pastors should be paid. As Paul says in 1 Corinthians 9, "Do we not have the right to eat and drink?" (v. 4), "Or is it only Barnabas and I who have no right to refrain from working for a living?" (v. 6), "Who serves as a soldier at his own expense?" (v. 7). "Does not the Law say the same? For it is written in the Law of Moses, 'You shall not muzzle an ox when it treads out the grain.' Is it for oxen that God is concerned?" (vv. 8–9), and if pastors have "sown spiritual things among you, is it too much if we reap material things from you? If others share this rightful claim on you, do not we even more?" (vv. 11–12). "The Lord commanded that those who proclaim the gospel should get their living by the gospel" (v. 14). That should settle this issue.[145] Paul argued that he was an apostle and qualified for that title because he saw the Lord and built churches as commissioned by Christ. He made a defense that he had the right to be considered an apostle and to have a wife as others did during their missionary work.

He also used the example of a soldier who should not have to do so at his own expense or a farmer who plants a vineyard who should be able to eat his grapes. But in light of all those reasons to be able to obtain financial support biblically based, he forgoes that because as he writes,

> I would rather die than have anyone deprive me of this boast. Yet when I preach the gospel, I cannot boast, for I am compelled to preach. Woe to me if I do not preach … in preaching the gospel, I may offer it free of charge, and so not make use of my rights in preaching it.[146]

A New Model of the Authentic Church advocates for more pastors to adopt this example of St. Paul and not make use of that right; they should preach freely so others will be blessed freely.

[xx] **Church Statistics, 1992–2000**	**2000**	**1999**	**1992**
Adult attendance at Protestant churches	90	90	102
Annual church operating budget ($000)	115	110	82.1
Median pastoral compensation package ($000)	38.2	35.2	32.0**

** Though some of the data is conflicting, it is apparent that the church is in decline and pastors' salaries at even small churches are rising and account for a large percentage of the churches' operating budgets.

GROWTH OF INDEPENDENT CHRISTIAN MINISTRIES: FERTILE GROUND FOR THE BIRTH OF THE AUTHENTIC CHURCH

One of the most insightful statistics that supports this new paradigm I am proposing is the growth of independent Christian ministries. These ministries are not supported financially by larger denominations and do not have large budgets and plentiful physical or financial resources, but they are nevertheless being birthed and growing. Most of the ministers are volunteers or bivocational.

This statistic is important to foster the birth of new churches using the model of St. Paul. This independent and largely "unsung group of Christians is eclipsing the traditional mainline Protestants."[147] Independent evangelicals are projected to grow 15.8% by 2025 to 437 million—that's 50 million more than traditional mainstream Protestants.

These churches don't answer to any central hierarchy. Such independents have already outstripped the traditional mainline Protestants according to Gordon-Conwell, which estimates their numbers at 377 million. It's not easy for religion reporters to write about this nonconforming group. As a result, the old mainline churches continue to get the big headlines.

> The Episcopalians and Presbyterians "pause, amid their frantic renovations, and consider not just what they would change about historic Christianity, but what they would defend and offer *uncompromisingly* to the world. Absent such a reconsideration, their fate is nearly certain: they will change, and change, and die."[148]

You can see it in poll results from Pew Research to the Barna Group; you can hear it preached about from the pulpit and more quietly discussed in church focus groups, but agreement is widespread: church attendance is declining in most Christian sects; even the oldest and most conservative are losing ground in America.[149] What can we do? The answer for me lies in the model of St. Paul and *A New Model of the Authentic Church*. It makes me believe the model of St. Paul and tentmaking is so important. I strongly advocate for this type of model for the American church because the simplicity of ministry along with the simplicity of the New Testament church have gotten lost in the centuries since its inception. When Jesus preached, it was in a no-frills atmosphere. Many times, He preached in people's houses, for example, when they brought the crippled man through the roof of the house in Mark 2:2–12 (NIV).

> A few days later, when Jesus again entered Capernaum, the people heard that he had come home. They gathered in such large numbers that there was no

room left, not even outside the door, and he preached the word to them. Some men came, bringing to him a paralyzed man, carried by four of them. Since they could not get him to Jesus because of the crowd, they made an opening in the roof above Jesus by digging through it and then lowered the mat the man was lying on. When Jesus saw their faith, he said to the paralyzed man, "Son, your sins are forgiven" ... He got up, took his mat and walked out in full view of them all. This amazed everyone and they praised God, saying, "We have never seen anything like this!"[150]

Jesus did not need an expensive church structure or programs to meet people where they were. He had church wherever He felt it was needed. No budgets, no salaries, no administration, no stained glass or altar—just meeting the needs of people with love.

Luke 5:1–3 (NIV) reads,

One day as Jesus was standing by the Lake of Gennesaret, the people were crowding around him and listening to the word of God. He saw at the water's edge two boats, left there by the fishermen, who were washing their nets. He got into one of the boats, the one belonging to Simon, and asked him to put out a little from shore. Then he sat down and taught the people from the boat.[151]

Jesus taught on the plain in the Sermon on the Mount in Matthew 5:1–2 (NIV).

Now when Jesus saw the crowds, he went up on a mountainside and sat down. His disciples came to him, and he began to teach them.[152]

There was simplicity in the way He conducted His ministry; there was no need to over-administrate it or have large budgets. When the disciples needed to add support or ministry staff, they did so by adding deacons. Were they paid at the time? The Bible is silent on this subject. Today, we seem to over-administrate things and make them more complicated than they ought to be especially when it comes to church administration practices and programs.

Churches with paid ministers have become too costly and have fallen victim to the economy. We have to look at the model of St. Paul because by being tentmakers, that will take pressure off the church and disperse it into society. When you have small churches with numerous volunteers who shoulder the responsibility of church functions, you have a model found in the book of Acts (when the disciples gave and sold all they had). This is the genius of having ministries like Paul's that support the operation and expense of their own ministries.

It is difficult to understand how preaching the gospel and sustaining ministries became so complex and costly, but they did.

This new model places the responsibility to set the example on those who lead and minister, not the other way around. This is done by having the ministers work in the business world in society and as contributors to both church and society.[xxi] Paul thought this concept was so important to reach the masses and keep the church and ministries relevant. "Each one should remain in the same situation which he was in when God called him."[153] This keeps the minister relevant in everyday life and makes the church more stable financially while allowing the church to remain economy-proof and relevant. If things get tight financially, churches can adjust without the added burden of salaries, health insurance, and payroll expenses; in this way, they will become more operational and in effect recession proof.

In today's economy, you see many churches whether start-ups or existing churches close their doors because of an inability to pay large salaries, staffs, and mortgages. If we can solve that problem, we can start more churches by using this model that is effective and durable even through difficult financial times. The time is right for a new model of church, the Authentic Church, to be birthed.

To further complicate matters, I ask three questions of those pastoring churches or leading ministries. Are you doing this because you are getting paid? Would you do this work without getting paid? That may eliminate a substantial portion of pastors and potential pastors. The last question is, would you do this if you had to pay? Paul did this in his model of ministry. That clearly would leave only a few very dedicated pastors. Too many ineffective and uncommitted pastors is a major problem in the American pastorate today. Look at how God dealt with this issue when Gideon had too many men not committed or prepared. Judges 7:2–7 (NIV) states,

> The Lord said to Gideon, "You have too many men for me to deliver Midian into their hands. In order that Israel may not boast against me that her own strength has saved her, announce now to the people, "Anyone who trembles with fear may turn back and leave Mount Gilead." So twenty-two thousand men left, while ten thousand remained. But the Lord said to Gideon, "There are still too many men. Take them down to the water, and I will sift them for you there. If I say, "This one shall go with you," he shall go; but if I say, "This one shall not go with you," he shall not go." So Gideon took the men down to the water. There the Lord told him, "Separate those who lap the water with

---

[xxi] Can you imagine a model of church in which the senior pastor works outside the church and tithes a substantial part of his or her income to the church? What a role reversal for the American pastorate.

their tongues like a dog from those who kneel down to drink." Three hundred men lapped with their hands to their mouths. All the rest got down on their knees to drink. The Lord said to Gideon, "With the three hundred men that lapped I will save you and give the Midianites into your hands. Let all the other men go, each to his own place."[154]

Those 300 are the ones that the American church needs to transform the church—those who are committed no matter what the cost without looking for anything in return.

Jesus was involved in work as well as ministry. We can look to our Savior and see His involvement with an everyday job. Mark 6:1–3 (NIV) states,

Jesus left there and went to his hometown, accompanied by his disciples. When the Sabbath came, he began to teach in the synagogue, and many who heard him were amazed. "Where did this man get these things?" they asked. "What's this wisdom that has been given him, that he even does miracles! Isn't this the carpenter? Isn't this Mary's son and the brother of James, Joseph, Judas and Simon? Aren't his sisters here with us?" And they took offense at him.[155]

If Jesus and Paul worked and had jobs while in ministry, ought not the pastors of the American church follow suit?

Using the model of Paul as a tentmaker is a significant and a foundational component to reviving and transforming the American church. For there to be more missionally minded churches and ministries, we need more men and women called and equipped to do the work of the Lord. Those who have employment and are able to have their needs met financially are in a good position to start or begin a ministry without financially draining the ministry.

One question often asked with start-up churches or ministries is, when can I begin to work full-time in the ministry? The real question is, how long will it take to create a ministry so prosperous and abundant that I can leave my other job and be paid for it full-time? We need to redefine what church is and how we do it. The former is not the proper question; ministry is a full-time, life commitment. St. Paul's model of the tentmaker will encourage more lay ministers and future pastors to begin their ministries and allow ministries and churches to grow and develop without the need for substantial resources or the accompanying financial pressure. This model will encourage many grassroots ministries to be birthed, and the results may be surprising. Look at what St. Paul did part-time as a bivocational minister: he built the church and changed the world for Jesus Christ.

This new paradigm of the Authentic Church may undermine traditional thoughts of church. It will certainly unveil or shine light on how church is done today and question whether pastors or ministers ought or need to be paid full-time salaries. This paradigm will ensure that only those who really want to be in the pastorate for the right reasons are there. It will elevate the energy and competency in the pastorate and vet out those who are in it for the wrong reasons or should not be in it at all.

The church has waddled in mediocrity far too long; it is time to develop *A New Model of the Authentic Church* that Jesus and Paul, a carpenter and a tentmaker, set as an example.

Lesson 4
Tentmaking: The Model of St. Paul

After these things Paul departed from Athens and went to Corinth. And he found a certain Jew named Aquila, born in Pontus, who had recently come from Italy with his wife Priscilla (because Claudius had commanded all the Jews to depart from Rome); and he came to them. So, because he was of the same trade, he stayed with them and worked; for by occupation they were tentmakers.

ACTS 18:1–3 (NKJV)

1. What does this scripture say to you?

2. Why did Paul continue to do physical labor when he was such a brilliant scholar, theologian, and religious leader? His education and credentials were excellent and the necessity for him to actually do such hard, physical labor (tentmaking) certainly could have affected his ability in time and manner to preach the gospel and build the church. Do you think there may be spiritual reasons why Paul continued doing physical labor while steadfastly embarking on building not only tents but also the kingdom of God?

3. Do you believe many full-time pastors have an easy job and a lot of free time on their hands?

4. Do you believe, at least in small churches, pastors have very flexible schedules that allow them freedom for downtime and leisure?

5. Do you believe that pastors of small congregations should be allowed to deplete scarce church resources to be paid full-time salaries when they could be working full- or part-time jobs outside the ministry while still fulfilling their ministry obligations as the Apostle Paul did?

6. If necessary, how can we balance part- or full-time work, family, and ministry?

7. Can I birth and sustain new ministries if I still need to work?

8. Should pastors and leaders work in addition to ministry?

9. Why do you think Paul spent so much time doing manual labor while engaged in full-time ministry?

10. Briefly, list 4 benefits of having an occupation outside of ministry as Paul did.

   1. _____
   2. _____
   3. _____
   4. _____

11. What do you think the term "tentmaker" means? Does it reference missions-committed Christians who support themselves financially while being involved in full- or part-time ministry?

12. How much manual labor did Paul actually do?

13. How much financial support did Paul receive from the church or donor gifts?

14. Why did Paul work when he did not have to?

15. Did this foster integration of ministry and culture?

16. What was Paul's tentmaker strategy?

17. How effective was this model?

18. What practical implications does Paul's tentmaking have for us as we enter a new millennium?

19. Can we successfully replicate Paul's model of ministry? If so, will it dramatically affect the topography of the American church today?

20. Did Paul work while on his first missionary journey? See 1 Corinthians 9:6.

21. What do you think? Was Paul more effective in his ministry because of rather than in spite of his work?

22. Are there elements in the pressures of everyday work that make Paul's ministry more relevant and applicable to ordinary life?

23. On the second missionary journey, did Paul do manual labor in Philippi? See 2 Corinthians 11:12.

24. Did Paul work when he went to Thessalonica? See 1 Thessalonians 2:6–9.

25. On his third missionary journey, Paul spent almost three years in Ephesus. Did he work while there? See Acts 19:11–15.

26. Do you think the American church has followed Paul's example? See Acts 20:33–35.

27. *A New Model of the Authentic Church* is based on the Apostle Paul's example that those in the workforce should labor both for themselves and for the Lord. Is that possible in today's age?

28. The question that will be raised against those who pursue the tentmaker model will be, "How can anyone with shabby clothes and blistered hands who works as a carpenter or tentmaker also be an apostle or prophet?" What do you think of that charge? See 1 Corinthians 9:1–16.

29. Would the results of Paul's ministry have been as significant if he didn't work and had not been involved with or integrated into the society work force?

30. Were Paul's preaching and worldview affected by the type of work he chose?

31. Because Paul worked, he did not have to tell people what they wanted to hear to receive their financial support; he was free to preach the gospel unfettered by concerns about losing finances or offending supporters. What do you think of this?

32. If ministers are in full-time paid ministry, can they be unconditionally honest and forthright with those who support the ministry?

33. Can they preach the gospel as intended, or will financial constraints force them to mold it in a way that makes it easier, more palatable, and more profitable?

34. The phrase "bivocational minister" usually paints a mental picture of a retired or relatively uneducated pastor serving a church that is rural, small, dying, or all three. What do you think of this?

35. In this shrinking economy and with the dwindling number of churches and decline in attendance, the current model will become more difficult to sustain. Out of necessity, we may have to revert to the tentmaker model. What do you think?

36. A total of 727 churches in the United States and Canada with attendance ranging from 1,000 to more than 30,000 were surveyed. The survey results found that 14% of large churches have a financial bonus structure for their top leader (much like a CEO or COO of a large financial corporation). Is this consistent with the early church?

37. The report says that the average senior pastor in US churches today makes more than $80,000 a year plus benefits. When you add in benefits such as retirement, life insurance, health insurance, continuing-education allowances, and favorable tax benefits, the base salary increases substantially and closes in on six figures for the average senior pastor. Pastors who hold a higher academic degree are paid up to $30,000 more per year than pastors without any postsecondary education. Is this necessary in small or starting churches, and can this be sustained?

38. The size of US churches tells us a lot about the necessity of full-time paid pastors. The median church in the United States has only 75 regular congregants in worship on Sunday mornings. If the majority of US churches have 75 people in attendance for worship on Sunday, do they need full-time paid pastoral services?

39. The National Congregations Study estimated that the smaller churches (under 499) draw 94% of those who attend church services regularly. Meanwhile, only 2.41% of churchgoers attended the largest of congregations (1,000+ regular congregants). What does this say in relation to the "tentmaker model"?

40. What about the statistic that 94% of all churches have fewer than 499 congregants and 59% have fewer than 99 congregants?

41. The majority of US churches, which account for 34 million weekly worshipers, have an attendance of only 7–499 people, which make up over a quarter of a million of all US churches. These are the categories of attendance that must be looked at and revisited in terms of tentmaking and *A New Model of the Authentic Church*. Why?

42. Do you agree that some pastors should be paid but that most churches are so small and their membership so poor that a full-time salary and benefits are hard to provide?

43. Should both large and small churches look for ways to integrate their church leaders into society by requiring them to hold down full- or part-time work while they minister?

44. In your opinion, should all pastors be paid?

45. Should pastors be required to work outside the church to support themselves and the ministry?

46. *A New Model of the Authentic Church* advocates for more pastors to adopt the example of St. Paul and not make use of any right to be paid; it asserts that they should preach freely so others will be blessed freely. What do you think of this novel concept?

47. One of the most insightful statistics that supports this new paradigm I am proposing is the growth of independent Christian ministries. These ministries are not supported financially by larger denominations and do not have large budgets and plentiful physical or financial resources. Do you believe that this new model is more, or less, sustainable than older models of the church?

48. Can you imagine a model of church where the senior pastor works outside the church then tithes a substantial part of his or her income to the church where they pastor? What a role reversal for the American pastorate. Comment on this.

49. When the disciples needed to add support or ministry staff, they did so by adding deacons. Were they paid at the time?

50. Paul thought this concept was very important to reaching the masses and keeping the church and ministries relevant. He wrote, "Each one should remain in the same situation which he was in when God called him." This keeps the minister relevant in everyday life and makes the church more stable financially while allowing the church to remain economy-proof and relevant. What do you think?

51. There are three questions that should be asked and answered for those pastoring churches or leading ministries. First, are you doing this because you are getting paid?

52. Second, would you do this work without getting paid?

53. Third, would you do this work if you had to pay?

54. If Jesus and Paul worked and had jobs while in ministry, ought not the pastors of the American church follow suit?

55. Those who have employment and are able to have their needs met financially are in a better position to start or begin a ministry without financially relying on the ministry. One question often asked of pastors or young seminarians leading start-up churches or ministries is, "When can I begin to work full-time in the ministry?" The real question is, "How long will it take to create a ministry that is financially stable so that I can leave my other job and be paid for it full-time?"

56. What are your thoughts as to what St. Paul did part-time as a bi-vocational minister?

57. With Paul's tentmaking model, 1,000 new, effective, relevant, sustainable, and Authentic Churches could be developed throughout America. What do you think?

CHAPTER 5

Understanding Prophets Have No Honor in Their Hometowns

Now Philip was from Bethsaida, the hometown of Andrew and Peter. Philip found Nathanael and told him, "We have found the One Moses wrote about in the Law (and so did the prophets): Jesus the son of Joseph, from Nazareth!" "Can anything good come out of Nazareth?" Nathanael asked him. "Come and see," Philip answered.

JOHN 1:44–46 (HCSB)

If you are called to start a ministry or an Authentic Church where you were born, raised, or reside, this is an issue you will most likely confront. The challenges and difficulties you will face will take place while developing your ministry and occur throughout its life. There is an old saying, "The closest ones to you hurt you the most." We will see how this plays out in the ministry of the Authentic Church.

Wounds from friends can hurt much more deeply than those from enemies. Such wounds ache, throb, and are slow to heal. The rejection usually comes unexpectedly therefore making the pain worse. We have all experienced rejection whether it was being picked last for a game at recess, being turned down for a date, not getting a job, or being ridiculed for our faith—rejection from anyone hurts. One thing brings us hope in the midst of any rejection—knowing our Savior was rejected too even by his closest friends.[156]

In this chapter, we will look at some of the situations and circumstances that may happen to you when you are beginning a ministry or beginning a work in the place where you grew up or reside. It raises interesting questions about ministry and presents unique challenges. We have heard in the scriptures that we are to "grow where we are planted."[157] We are also encouraged by the apostle Paul to remain in the line of work we were in when we received the Lord.

Each one should remain in the situation which (they were) in when God called (them). Were you a slave when you were called? Don't let it trouble you—although if you can gain your freedom, do so. For he who was a slave when he was called by the Lord is the Lord's freedman; similarly, he who was a free man when he was called is Christ's slave. You were bought at a price; do not become slaves of men. Brothers, each man, as responsible to God, should remain in the situation God called him to.[158]

This is further support of the tentmaker paradigm and the Authentic Church model we discussed in the previous chapter. This supports the proposition that in many instances, God wants you to grow where you are planted. There was tension and rejection in the life and the ministry of Jesus and the prophets when they ministered to family, friends, and the people of their hometown. It has been reported that Jesus never traveled more than 200 miles from his hometown. Those who were most familiar with the prophets and Jesus rejected them many times.

The biblical prophets knew what rejection was. Not only did they possess a religious insight that was unique, but the insight was the gift through which God spoke to others. Still the people often rejected both the religious message and the insightful prophet. This was probably because of the way they understood the power of the prophetic word. Since it was considered the word of God, no human could prevent it from accomplishing what it described. If the people did not want to hear that powerful word, their only recourse was to silence the one proclaiming it.[159]

Hence, prophets often faced persecution, rejection, and even death. Although you may not face persecution or the threat of physical harm in America,[xxii] you will feel acute emotional, personal, and spiritual misunderstanding and rejection often by people closest to you.[xxiii]

What a way to start a ministry? Look at Ezekiel's call to ministry by God.

[xxii] But in other parts of the world, persecution and death are commonplace.

[xxiii] CNN reports that "(2015) was the most violent for Christians in modern history, rising to "a level akin to ethnic cleansing," according to a new report by Open Doors USA, a watchdog group that advocates for Christians. In total, the survey found that more than 7,100 Christians were killed in 2015 for "faith-related reasons," up 3,000 from the previous year (2014)." The group has a very narrow definition of Christian persecution as "any hostility experienced as a result of one's identification with Christ."

Ezekiel was informed of his future rejection at the time of his call to ministry: "Hard of face and obstinate of heart are they to who I am sending you." The people of Nazareth to whom Jesus spoke were no better than the ancient Israelites. They rejected Jesus, saying: "Where did this man get all this? In other words: Who does (he) think he is? They knew him: "is he not the carpenter?"[160]

The questions they posed were not asked out of interest; they were issued from cynical people trying to bring him down a peg. "Because of their hard-heartedness and rigid skepticism, Jesus was not able to perform many mighty deeds for these people of his own hometown."[161] Jesus was not welcomed in many places he lived and preached. Many times, He had to flee for his life. This started at his birth, and continued through much of his ministry life.

Jesus' parents had fled to Egypt after they had been warned by God that King Herod would attempt to murder (their Son) and every child under two years of age. So they fled to Egypt in order to save Jesus. Later the family returned from Egypt after God told them that King Herod had died and directed them to return to Israel. When the family returned, they settled in Nazareth, a city in the northern part of Israel in a region known as Galilee. Consequently, Nazareth became Jesus' hometown. There He grew up from a child into an adult and then started His ministry. Early in Jesus' ministry He relocated His family (apparently after His father had died), from Nazareth to Capernaum. His sisters remained in Nazareth, perhaps because they were already married.[162]

An incident in Jesus' hometown gives a rare insight into his work prior to becoming a traveling preacher. The context is that Jesus' hometown friends and acquaintances can't believe that this familiar local boy has become a great teacher and prophet. In the course of their complaints, they say, "What deeds of power are being done by his hands! Is not this the carpenter, the son of Mary and brother of James and Joseph and Judas and Simon, and are not his sisters here with us?" This is the only passage in the Bible to directly state Jesus' trade. (In Matthew 13:55, Jesus is called "the carpenter's son," and Luke and John do not mention his profession.).[163]

This stony reception at the very beginning of Jesus' ministry foreshadowed the kind of rebuffs that lay ahead of him. It must have been particularly stinging, coming from the people of Nazareth, the very people who should have welcomed him with open arms. But they were not welcoming. Rather, "they took offense at him." Jesus simply responded: "A prophet is not without honor except in his native place and among his own kin and his own house." These words have echoed down through the ages, strengthening others who have offered their religious insights, only to be spurned.[164]

How do we minister in our hometown or develop a ministry with people we know and are familiar with us? We may be rejected or not accepted by them. The saying "Familiarity breeds contempt" is attributed to the ancient philosopher Publius the Syrian. Perhaps Phillips Brooks, the American Episcopal clergyman, clarified the true point of the saying when he revised it to "familiarity breeds contempt, only with contemptible things or among contemptible people." The people in Jesus' hometown thought they really knew Him, but their hatred for Him says nothing about Jesus and everything about them; they did not expect their Savior to come from among them. They did not expect a carpenter to lead them to the Promised Land. When the people perceived that even His closest friends and family rejected Him, they were more offended by Him. His familiarity stood as a stumbling block to their belief.[165]

William Barclay, a Church of Scotland minister and professor, suggests that nothing can be done if the atmosphere is wrong. People cannot be healed spiritually if they refuse to be healed. An atmosphere of coldness and indifference will prohibit understanding the message of the best sermon. There can be no peacemaking in the wrong atmosphere. If people come together to hate, they will hate. If people refuse to understand, they will misunderstand. If people see only their own point of view, they will see no other. Alternatively, if people love Christ and seek to love one another, even those most widely separated can come together in Him. There is laid on us the tremendous responsibility to help the work of Christ; we can open the door wide to Him or shut it in His face.[166]

Why did this occur to Jesus and others, and how can we handle similar situations in our own ministries?

> Francois Mauric wrote in his life of Jesus: It is baffling to record that, for a period of thirty years, the Son of Man did not appear to be anything other than a man. Those who lived with him thought they knew him. He fixed their tables and chairs. They ate and drank with his extended family. When he stepped outside the role they had fixed for him, they put him down as just a workman.[167]

In Luke 4:1–13, the temptation of Christ is a section that is titled the public ministry of the Son of Man. Luke 4:14 reads,

Jesus returned to Galilee in the power of the Spirit, and news about him spread through the whole countryside. He taught in their synagogues, and everyone praised him. He went to Nazareth, where he had been brought up, and on the Sabbath day he went into the synagogue, as was his custom. And he stood up to read. The scroll of the prophet Isaiah was handed to him. Unrolling it, he found the place where it is written: "The Spirit of the Lord is on me, because he has anointed me to preach good news to the poor. He has sent me to proclaim freedom for the prisoners and recovery of sight for the blind, to release the oppressed, to proclaim the year of the Lord's favor."

Then he rolled up the scroll, gave it back to the attendant and sat down. The eyes of everyone in the synagogue were fastened on him, and he began by saying to them, "Today this scripture is fulfilled in your hearing." All spoke well of him and were amazed at the gracious words that came from his lips. "Isn't this Joseph's son?" they asked. Jesus said to them, "Surely you will quote this proverb to me: 'Physician, heal yourself! Do here in your hometown what we have heard that you did in Capernaum.' "I tell you the truth," he continued, "no prophet is accepted in his hometown."[168]

Jesus proclaims He was there to preach the Good News to the poor, free, the prisoners and heal the sick, possessed, and oppressed. He begins to explain the thought processes the hearers of that Good News would go through as they decided to accept or reject Him and His work. It seems those who listened to Him wanted to continue in their unbelief and opposition to the ministry of Jesus but at the same time wanted the benefits of His ministry. This is especially evident when they say to Him, "Do here in Nazareth what we have heard you have done in other places such as Capernaum."[169] Jesus would not and could not because of their obstinate attitudes of disbelief.

After this exchange, Jesus told them He would not perform any of the miracles He had done in Capernaum in Nazareth. Luke 4:28–29 (NIV) states, "All the people in the synagogue were furious when they heard this. They got up, drove him out of the town, and took him to the brow of the hill on which the town was built, in order to throw him down the cliff."[170]

Here again, they had it in their hearts to kill Jesus, but He walked right through the crowd and went on His way. This is one of the most overlooked miracles Jesus performed. Was He able to walk through the crowd in a physical or metaphysical sense like a ghost, or did the crowd part for His exit like the Red Sea had parted? We do not know for sure, but the result was miraculous much like what we see in John 20:26, when Jesus appeared to walk through one of the doors after His resurrection.

Many believe that was the first time Jesus appeared in Nazareth. There would be a second time. On the second occasion, it is believed that Jesus healed two blind men and cast a demon out of a man who could not speak or hear. Ironically, the same Pharisees who pleaded with Jesus to perform miracles during his first visit responded by accusing Jesus of performing miracles by demonic power. Let's recap: Jesus visits the city of Nazareth two times. On the first visit, He enters the synagogue quoting Isaiah 61:1–2 and declares He is the Messiah. For that, the people attempt to kill Him by throwing Him off a cliff. But Jesus escapes. So why in the world did Jesus return to Nazareth?[171]

> Jesus walked this earth as the Son of God, yet we find two occasions in the New Testament where he was actually astonished. He was astounded, first at the lack of belief (in Him) in his hometown (critical astonishment) and second at the faith of the Capernaum centurion (admiration).[172]

When the centurion in Capernaum asks Jesus if he would heal his servant who is lying in terrible pain, Jesus states, "I will go and heal him." The centurion replied, "Lord, I do not deserve to have you come under my roof. But just say the word, and my servant will be healed."[173] When Jesus heard this, he marveled and said in Matthew 8:10 (NIV), "I tell you the truth, I have not found anyone in Israel with such great faith."[174] This is being astounded in a positive way.

Mark 6:1–6 (NIV) states,

> Jesus left there and went to his hometown, accompanied by his disciples. When the Sabbath came, he began to teach in the synagogue, and many who heard him were amazed. "Where did this man get these things?" they asked. "What's this wisdom that has been given him, that he even does miracles! Isn't this the carpenter? Isn't this Mary's son and the brother of James, Joseph, Judas and Simon? Aren't his sisters here with us?" And they took offense at him. Jesus said to them, 'Only in his hometown, among his relatives and in his own house is a prophet without honor.' He could not do any miracles there except lay his hands on a few sick people and heal them. And he was amazed at their lack of faith.[175]

The issue this chapter raises is a very practical one that you may experience in your attempts to bring the Authentic Church to your hometown: how will you be received by your family, friends, and people in your community if you attempt to build a ministry among them? Based on the passages in the Bible we just examined about Christ's ministry, I'd like to forewarn you that it may not be any different for you than it was for Him.

We must realize the challenges we will face and be encouraged by the work of others who have experienced these attitudes of rejection and distain and yet completed their work. So why did those more familiar with Jesus seem less inclined to benefit or even receive His ministry? We can look to modern psychology and human nature for those answers.

> The present research shows that although people believe that learning more about others leads to greater liking, more information about others leads, on average, to less liking. Thus, ambiguity—lacking information about another—leads to liking, whereas familiarity—acquiring more information—can breed contempt. This "less is more" effect is due to the cascading nature of dissimilarity. Once evidence of dissimilarity is encountered, subsequent information is more likely to be interpreted as further evidence of dissimilarity, leading to decreased liking. The authors (of the study)[xxiv] document the negative relationship between knowledge and liking in laboratory studies and with pre-and postdate data from online daters, while showing the mediating role of dissimilarity.
>
> Familiarity leads to liking; familiarity breeds contempt. The first proposition is supported by decades of research in psychology, whereas the second is supported by everyday experience: the disintegration of friendships, the demise of business relationships, and the prevalence of divorce ... We propose that the relationship between knowledge and liking within individuals is in fact negative: that more information about any one person leads, on average, to less liking for that person. We further suggest that this relationship is due to the lure of ambiguity."[176]
>
> "Everything looks perfect from far away" Lyrics from "Such Great Heights" by Ben Gibbard and James Tamborello.[177]

The conclusions of these studies indicate that though people believe knowing leads to liking, knowing more means liking less. That was the case with Jesus and the prophets and most likely the attitude you will encounter in your ministry.

[xxiv] Study completed by Michael I. Norton, Harvard Business School; Jeana H. Frost, Medical Information Systems Unit, Boston University; Dan Ariely, Sloan School of Management, Massachusetts Institute of Technology. *Journal of Personality and Social Psychology* by the American Psychological Association.

When you make that profession of faith or that proclamation you are a Christian and decide to start a work, ministry, or church, you must realize there will be adversity, conflict, and rejection. These components are necessary in the process of strengthening your ministry and the Authentic Church and will probably have the long-term effect of not allowing your ministry to be undermined by adversity but be strengthened by it. The work the Lord has called you to do includes partaking to some degree in His suffering.

Second, you may (and most likely will) be rejected by your family, friends, acquaintances, and people in your hometown because of the principles of familiarity. They will ask, Why all of a sudden are you doing this? Why are you special? They will insist you are no different from them, and they will resent your attempts—as they see it—to elevate yourself to a higher or holier position than theirs. You will have to work through that. If we are strong and resolved, adversity works in a positive way to keep us in conformity and communion with the image and ministry of Christ. That will give us the proper attitude to move forward with humility, vigor, and constancy and confirm our calling to ministry. As members of an Authentic Church, we must be Christlike and not think of ourselves as better than anyone else but rather hold others in higher esteem.

Third, you will not be the only one who has experienced rejection and adversity while in ministry. We can look through the Old and New Testaments and look at many of the prophets, the apostle Paul, and Jesus and see they met adversity. In ministry, I am reminded of the apostle Paul when he wrote, "Alexander the metalworker did me a great deal of harm. The Lord will repay him for what he has done."[178] If Paul and Jesus were not spared adversity and rejection, we cannot think that we in our ministry or the Authentic Church will be spared.

The fourth point is that we must continue to carry on in the face of adversity and rejection and continue to pursue the will of God in our lives and ministries. Though rejection and adversity appear to be negatives that cause pain and heartache to the individual and possibly even short-term damage to the ministry, in the long term, adversity, rejection, circumstances, and trials will strengthen the ministry and the work. It can be used as a refining fire for the Authentic Church. If things going on in the Authentic Church are not appropriate or consistent biblically, this adversity and rejection from the outside may be warranted. It acts as a corrective measure for us and the Authentic Church.

Last is that God's purpose in your life and the life of the Authentic Church will not be frustrated to the point of exhaustion and expiration if you are doing God's will and do not give up. Life has adversity; Jesus was affirmed as a prophet, the Son of God and yet was without honor in his hometown. "In view of that reality, He could not perform any miracles in Nazareth except for healing a few sick people. The people of Nazareth were apparently plagued by unbelief and paid little attention to the claims of Jesus."[179]

At first glance, one might get the impression that Jesus' miraculous power was utterly dependent on peoples' faith to work. That is, however, not the meaning of this verse. It is not that Jesus was unable to perform miracles in Nazareth; it was that Jesus could not do miracles there in the sense He would not do so in view of the pervasive unbelief in that city. Because of Nazareth's rejection of the person and work of Jesus Christ, He went to other cities whose people responded positively to Him and received Him. We have no evidence that Jesus returned to Nazareth.[180] You will face these same challenges in your ministry.

If you are called to build a ministry or Authentic Church in your community, it is better to understand what it will take and the opposition you may face before it occurs. Take comfort in the words of the Apostle Paul.

> Dear friends, do not be surprised at the painful trial you are suffering, as though something strange were happening to you. But rejoice that you participate in the sufferings of Christ, so that you may be overjoyed when his glory is revealed. If you are insulted because of the name of Christ, you are blessed, for the Spirit of glory and of God rests on you.[181]

After reading this chapter, you may wonder, *why would anyone want to start a ministry in his or her hometown if even Jesus tried to do this and was rejected and misunderstood?* You will not face as much opposition and rejection as the Son of God faced, but you will face some. Nonetheless, your hometown may be the only place you can start a ministry. If that is the case, at least you are now prepared for the work.

LESSON 5

Understanding Prophets Have No Honor in Their Hometowns

Now Philip was from Bethsaida, the hometown of Andrew and Peter. Philip found Nathanael and told him, "We have found the One Moses wrote about in the Law (and so did the prophets): Jesus the son of Joseph, from Nazareth!" "Can anything good come out of Nazareth?" Nathanael asked him. "Come and see," Philip answered.

JOHN 1:44–46 (HCSB)

1. What does this scripture say to you?

2. If you are called to start a ministry or an Authentic Church where you were born, raised, or reside, an issue you will most likely confront is rejection. How will you deal with that?

3. There is an old saying, "The closest ones to you hurt you the most." Are you prepared for this to occur in your ministry?

4. We have heard in the scriptures that we are to "grow where we are planted." We are also encouraged by the Apostle Paul to remain in the line of work we were in when we received the Lord.

    > Each one should remain in the situation which (they were) in when God called (them). Were you a slave when you were called? Don't let it trouble you—although if you can gain your freedom, do so. For he who was a slave when he was called by the Lord is the Lord's freedman; similarly, he who was a free man when he was called is Christ's slave. You were bought at a price; do not become slaves of men. Brothers, each man, as responsible to God, should remain in the situation God called him to.

    Will you be able to minister effectively in the sphere of influence in which God has placed you?

5. There was tension and rejection in the life and the ministry of Jesus and the prophets when they ministered to family, friends, and the people of their hometown. How will you be able to cope with the same challenges?

6. Look at Ezekiel's call to ministry by God. Ezekiel was informed of his future rejection at the time of his call to ministry: "Hard of face and obstinate of heart are they to who I am sending you." What a way to start a ministry! Would you begin a ministry knowing that is what you will encounter?

7. Jesus was not welcomed in many places he lived and preached. He even had to flee for his life. Why?

8. Jesus' hometown friends and acquaintances couldn't believe that this familiar local man had become a great religious teacher and prophet. In the course of their complaints, they said, "What deeds of power are being done by his hands! Is not this the carpenter, the son of Mary and brother of James and Joseph and Judas and Simon, and are not his sisters here with us?" Why was this a problem for them?

9. How can we minister in our hometown or develop a ministry with people who know us and are familiar with us? If this is what we face, should we not even attempt it?

10. Phillips Brooks, the American Episcopal clergyman, clarified the point by saying, "familiarity breeds contempt, only with contemptible things or among contemptible people." What did he mean?

11. Why did this happen to Jesus and other prophets, and how can we handle similar situations in our own ministries?

12. When people step outside the role others have fixed for them, you must expect rejection. Comment on this.

13. Jesus said to them, "Surely you will quote this proverb to me: 'Physician, heal yourself! Do here in your hometown what we have heard that you did in Capernaum.' I tell you the truth," he continued, "no prophet is accepted in his hometown." What implication does this have for you?

14. The issue this lesson raises is a very practical one that you will experience in your attempts to bring the Authentic Church to your hometown: How will you be received by your family, your friends, and people in your community if you attempt to build a ministry among them? What are your thoughts?

15. Several studies indicate that though people believe knowing leads to liking, knowing more means liking less. That was the case with Jesus and the prophets and is most likely the attitude you will encounter in your ministry. Do you agree with those conclusions?

16. When you make a profession of faith or a proclamation that you are a Christian and decide to start a work, ministry, or church, you must realize there will be adversity, conflict, and rejection. Are you prepared?

17. What if you are rejected by your family, friends, acquaintances, and people in your hometown because of the principles of familiarity while building the ministry? Will you continue?

18. You can take comfort in knowing that you are not the only one who has experienced rejection and adversity while in ministry. Many have before you. Will it help you to know that?

19. Are you ready to continue and carry on in the face of adversity and rejection and pursue the will of God in your life and in ministry?

20. If you are doing God's will, God's purpose in your life and the life of the Authentic Church will not be frustrated to the point of exhaustion and expiration. Do not give up. Are you ready for the great challenges and rewards?

21. Why would anyone want to start a ministry in his or her hometown if even Jesus tried to do this and was rejected and misunderstood?

CHAPTER 6

I Am Barabbas

"What is truth?" Pilate asked. With this he went out again to the Jews and said, "I find no basis for a charge against him. But it is your custom for me to release to you one prisoner at the time of the Passover. Do you want me to release 'the king of the Jews'?" They shouted back, "No, not him! Give us Barabbas!"

JOHN 18:38–40 (NIV)

This message is perhaps not preached in churches often enough though I think it encapsulates my personal theology and Christology best. This subject may embody the whole thesis of the Bible found in the person and work of Jesus Christ. You can say everything about the Bible and God's plan for humanity's redemption in nearly one word, *Barabbas*.

I'd like to share with you the deeper and more profound story of Barabbas, whose life was spared in exchange for the death and crucifixion of Jesus. John 18:28–40 deals with Barabbas, about whom we know very little. He was arrested by Roman authorities for insurrection, rebellion against a government authority, and murder. It is probably safe to say the murder he was charged with was the killing of a Roman citizen or Roman soldier during his act of rebellion or revolt.[182] "Whether we condemn or justify his actions however, he was found by the governing authorities in Rome to be guilty, and he was sentenced to die … and his manner of death was crucifixion."[183]

The day of Barabbas's crucifixion was to be very different from what he could have anticipated: he would have an encounter with Jesus, and his life would never be the same. The only reason we know his name at all is that Barabbas (name meaning "son of the father") was to have died on the same day that Jesus of Nazareth (Son of the Father) was arrested, tried, and condemned to death. When the path of the son of the father crossed that of the Son of the Father, the great exchange took place for humanity. In that moment, Jesus exchanged His sinless life for that of a sinner and for all sinners. He would become sin and death in place for all humanity. He would take the place of Barabbas, die on the cross, and take our place. This exchange provides a valid and vital message for the Authentic Church as to the significance of Jesus dying in the place of Barabbas. We would come to understand that I am Barabbas, you are Barabbas, and we are Barabbas!

Barabbas was a representative of all humanity in whose place Jesus died. Barabbas may be one of the most fortunate people ever. He was scheduled to die yet was spared, released, and given new life. Let's look at what scripture says about Barabbas.

> In Matthew 27:16: At that time they had a notorious prisoner, called Barabbas. He is not an ordinary prisoner; he has a reputation that precedes him. Whether that reputation was for good behavior or bad, depends on which side you were on.
>
> In Mark 15:7: Barabbas had led an insurrection. Therefore Barabbas was in prison with other insurrectionists who had committed murder during the uprising. The word insurrection means "a rising against a civil or political authority." He was a rebel against the government that claimed to be instituted and ordained by God. Like many others, he had a problem submitting to this particular governing authority.
>
> In Luke 23:19: Barabbas had been thrown into prison for an insurrection in the city, and for murder. It was not that he was falsely accused or was in jail for a righteous reason; he was there as a result of participating in acts of violence and evil.
>
> In Luke 23:25, he is again identified: He had released the man who had been thrown into prison for insurrection and murder, the one they asked for, and surrendered Jesus to their will. We have another characterization of Barabbas, that he was also a robber and thief. These are some of the characteristics and personality traits that we have in Barabbas. He was a notable prisoner, robber, murderer, thief, insurrectionist, a troublemaker and he was in jail for all of the above and deserved death.[184]

When the crowd was asked to pick between the two, there was a stark contrast between the person and work of Barabbas (a violent, murderous man inspired by other men) and Jesus (a loving, peaceful man sent by God). The crowd was choosing between two approaches to liberation—one enacted through physical force in the natural world and the other by the unseen spiritual force in the kingdom of God. Jesus and Barabbas were mutually exclusive.

The crowd's choice demonstrates the deceptiveness of sin and death prevalent in the world since the Garden of Eden and the Fall. The path that looks right and seems to be in concert with the world is actually against God. St. Augustine states, therefore, that we choose not the Savior but the murderer, not the Giver of Life but its destroyer. C. S. Lewis wrote, "There is no neutral ground in the universe, every square inch, every split second is claimed by God and counterclaimed by Satan."[185] Each one of us faces the same challenge Pilate and the crowds had.

> According to the Gospels, it was customary for the Romans to release a Jewish prisoner during the Passover festival The Roman governor Pontius Pilate tried to use this custom as an excuse to release Jesus. But the crowd in the courtyard demanded that a prisoner named Barabbas be freed instead, and Pilate eventually gave into the pressure. Thus Barabbas was released and Jesus was crucified.[186]

We must examine why the crowd chose Barabbas instead of Jesus. Barabbas is depicted in so many ways as an ugly, revolting figure. He was an insurrectionist, revolting against the Roman government. He was a thief, robber, and murderer. He did not appear to have any redeeming qualities, and yet the crowds thought it was important he be released rather than Jesus. Maybe this is more of a commentary of society's ills and poor ethical choices; it may even be human nature lashing out in frustration. Jesus taught love, forgiveness, and understanding. He came to heal, to release those who were oppressed; He was loving, kind, and generous in all situations and always considered the plight of humanity in all He did. Maybe it is fortunate for us that Barabbas was released so Jesus became the unblemished lamb led to death in Barabbas's and our place.

Understanding that Barabbas was an important political or rebel leader would explain why the crowd shouted for his release because any leader in the fight against the hated Romans would be very popular with the common people. Jesus was also very popular with the common people for a while.

> When he entered Jerusalem on Palm Sunday, he was greeted by large excited crowds. Many people believed that he was the long-awaited Messiah, who with God's help would overthrow all oppressive rulers and establish a new eternal Kingdom of God.[187]

Barabbas was trying to physically overthrow the government while Jesus was trying to overthrow the government in a spiritual way.

If Jesus and Barabbas were both very popular, why did the crowd call for Jesus to be crucified and Barabbas to be released? (One) explanation is that the crowd (may have been) dominated by employees of the Jewish religious authorities. Their servants and henchmen would have been in the courtyard, and (may have) composed a significant part of the gathering there. Also, because Jesus was arrested late at night and brought before Pilate early the next morning, most of his followers probably didn't know where he was, or what was happening to him. His closest followers had apparently gone into hiding out of fear of arrest. Thus the Jewish leaders could have told their servants and henchmen to shout for Barabbas to be released, and the rest of the crowd could have then joined in. This explanation is supported by Mark 15:11, which says that the "chief priests stirred up the crowd to have Pilate release Barabbas instead." But why did the Jewish leaders want Jesus to die instead of Barabbas? The answer is that many of the common people believed that Jesus was the Messiah, and this made him a threat to their authority.[188]

The Jews asked Pilate to condemn Jesus to death without due process. At first, Pilate refused to do this. Though they asked Pilate to condemn an innocent man, they refused to go into the Gentile court. How ready we are to "Strain out the gnat but swallow a camel."[189] We worry about the smallest matters while neglecting the more important.

Pilate comes before them and the so-called sham trial begins. Pilate interrogates Jesus and finds no crime; he tells the Jews to handle it themselves; they want His death but had no jurisdiction to do this, so it was imperative that they fabricate charges so the Roman government would take jurisdiction of the criminal prosecution and have Him killed.

Jesus' first crime, they allege, is that He called Himself the King of the Jews. Pilate expects Jesus to say no. He was not claiming to be the leader of a political or seditious rebellion but acknowledged that was who and what He was. Jesus' weapon of choice is not a sword but truth and love. The revelation of God is the Word. Pilate wants to release Jesus, so he compromises and has Jesus tortured, scourged, and beaten, but that doesn't satisfy the crowd. Pilate found Jesus not guilty of any crime.

Jesus' second alleged crime is that He called Himself the Son of God. Was He an imposter or the Divine made man? Jesus never denied He was the Son of God. This was not persuasive to Pilate either. Pilate found Him not guilty.

His third alleged crime was that He claimed to be king. Those accusing Jesus said they had only one king, Caesar. They had successfully found the charge that would allow them to obtain the death penalty against Jesus. They brought Jesus out for crucifixion and released

Barabbas. In the end, the people, the religious authorities, and the government all chose Barabbas over Jesus.

"The Roman tradition, to appease the crowds, was to show mercy once a year. It was an attempt to control the mobs, by being able to say in an uprising, 'But look what we have done for you!'"[190] It's obvious to see the change in public opinion. The crowds that had shouted Jesus' praise on Palm Sunday—the day we celebrate His arrival into Jerusalem as Messiah and King—were now shouting for His execution. How fast public perceptions and opinions change. Their opinions swayed so far that they requested that this scoundrel, this horrible person named Barabbas be set free while Jesus be tortured and crucified. You and I are indeed Barabbas; in a spiritual sense, Jesus took the place of Barabbas for our eternal benefit. In a spiritual sense, each of us is a type of Barabbas, and it is our punishment that Jesus assumed.

This first great exchange took place for all humanity: Jesus willingly died in place of a sinner. Here you have Barabbas, who deserved death, replaced by Jesus, who deserved life. This is what I call the first fruits of the great spiritual exchange. Jesus gave His life for another, Barabbas. Jesus took on the blame for sin and death and substituted Himself for Barabbas and everyone else. This is the beginning of a spiritual reconciliation between God and man that will transform all humanity.

Matthew Henry's commentary on John 18:28–30 states,

> Thus he was treated as a malefactor, being made sin for us. The crowds and the Roman government went through great lengths to have Jesus killed. How could these groups put someone to death who had done so much good in the world, and then be willing to throw the odium upon the Roman government in order to make that more acceptable to the people and save themselves from reproach.[191]

Romans 6:23 (NIV) states, "For the wages of sin is death."[192] Some people may say, "I certainly am not capable of committing murder, sedition, or robbery as Barabbas did." Maybe we haven't done that physically, but many of us have wished harm and hatred to our neighbors. We shouldn't fool ourselves; we all fall short of the glory of God and need to be forgiven of our sins. This great exchange between Jesus and Barabbas was the first fruits of our sin, corruption, and separation from God being forgiven and exchanged for righteousness, redemption, and reconciliation before God. Galatians 5:19–21 (NIV) states,

> The acts of the sinful nature are obvious: sexual immorality, impurity and debauchery; idolatry and witchcraft; hatred, discord, jealousy, fits of rage,

selfish ambition, dissensions, factions and envy; drunkenness, orgies, and the like. I warn you, as I did before, that those who live like this will not inherit the kingdom of God.[193]

And Jeremiah 17:9 (NIV) reads, "The heart is deceitful above all things and beyond cure. Who can understand it?"[194] Can we say to ourselves that we are better than Barabbas? We are spiritually similar to Barabbas; we are caught in sin, death, and separation from God. We have been involved in rebellion against God. When Jesus first demonstrated His love toward humanity in sacrificing Himself for somebody who was not worth being sacrificed for in the eyes of all, He did it for Barabbas, you, and me. That is why I say I am Barabbas, you are Barabbas, we are Barabbas! We should not have such a high opinion of ourselves as it relates to the way we live and the way we are and our relationship with God and others.

Romans 5 holds one of the most important applications of this exchange between Barabbas and Jesus. "You see at the right time when we were still powerless, Christ died for the ungodly. Very rarely will anyone die for an unrighteous person, though for a good person, someone might possibly die."[195] God demonstrated His love for us in this while we were still sinners; Christ died for us.

We have no idea how Barabbas felt about the situation; scripture leaves us no clues about that. We can surmise he was very happy to be spared a brutal death and to be reunited with his family, friends, and partners in crime. How do you react to the sacrificial and substitutionary death of Jesus like or unlike Barabbas? More important, how do you respond to the person and work of Jesus Christ?

> We know that Jesus died for us, that He took our place, but it doesn't seem to affect us much. We still try to do all the things we want to do without considering God's opinion about them. We try to get all the things we want, not considering what God wants for us. We know Jesus died for us, but to live for Him is too much. Once again, we show how much alike we are with the scoundrel, the notorious criminal Barabbas.[196]

You may wonder what application this theological exercise has to *A New Model of the Authentic Church* I propose. It forms the theology and more important the Christology of a proper understanding of the person and work of Jesus Christ.

LESSON 6

I Am Barabbas

"What is truth?" Pilate asked. With this he went out again to the Jews and said, "I find no basis for a charge against him. But it is your custom for me to release to you one prisoner at the time of the Passover. Do you want me to release 'the king of the Jews'?" They shouted back, "No, not him! Give us Barabbas!"

JOHN 18:38–40 (NIV)

1. What does this scripture say to you?

2. This subject may embody the whole thesis of the Bible found in the person and work of Jesus Christ. You can say everything about the Bible and God's plan for humanity's redemption in nearly one word: *Barabbas*. Barabbas (name meaning "son of the father") was to die on the same day that Jesus of Nazareth (Son of the Father) was arrested, tried, and condemned to death. When the path of the "son of the father" (Barabbas) crossed that of the Son of the Father (Jesus), the great exchange took place for all humanity. In that moment, Jesus exchanged his sinless life for that of a sinner and for all sinners. He would become sin and death in place for all humanity. What do you think about this great exchange?

3. Was Barabbas a representative of all humanity in whose place Jesus died?

4. The crowd was choosing between two approaches to liberation—one enacted through physical force in the natural world and the other by the unseen spiritual force in the kingdom of God. Jesus and Barabbas were mutually exclusive. Why do you think the crowd chose Barabbas instead of Jesus?

5. C. S. Lewis wrote, "There is no neutral ground in the universe, every square inch, every split second is claimed by God and counterclaimed by Satan." Is that true?

6. Barabbas was trying to _____overthrow the government, while Jesus was trying to _____overthrow the government.

7. Why did the Jewish leaders want Jesus to die instead of Barabbas?

8. What was Jesus' first alleged crime? Was he found guilty?

9. What was Jesus' second alleged crime? Was he found guilty?

10. What was Jesus' third alleged crime? Was he found guilty?

11. The crowds that had shouted Jesus' praise on Palm Sunday—the day we celebrate his arrival into Jerusalem as Messiah and King—were now shouting for his execution. Why the turn of events?

12. Are we any better than Barabbas?

13. What do you think it means when I say, "I am Barabbas, you are Barabbas, and we are Barabbas"?

14. Do you agree that I am Barabbas, you are Barabbas, we are Barabbas?

15. Do you understand the person and work of Jesus Christ? If so, explain in your own words.

16. What application does this theological lesson have to *A New Model of the Authentic Church*?

CHAPTER 7

What the American Church Is Not Building—Disciples

And when he had called the people unto him with his disciples also, he said unto them, Whosoever will come after me, let him deny himself, and take up his cross, and follow me. For whosoever will save his life shall lose it; but whosoever shall lose his life for my sake and the gospel's, the same shall save it. For what shall it profit a man, if he shall gain the whole world, and lose his own soul? Or what shall a man give in exchange for his soul? Whosoever therefore shall be ashamed of me and of my words in this adulterous and sinful generation; of him also shall the Son of man be ashamed, when he cometh in the glory of his Father with the holy angels.

MARK 8:34–38 (KJV)

The spirit of exceptionalism has been quoted by many in politics and other areas when describing American culture and its status in the world. Recently, a president was quoted as saying, "I believe in American exceptionalism."[197] It means that a country, culture, or society has arrived and accomplished things in an extraordinary way; it need not conform to a principle or moral norm because it has proven itself by achieving excellence. How that excellence is measured is unclear. But the American church has become exceptional at building multimillion-dollar institutions and ministries though it has largely failed in the true objective of the church—to develop disciples.

One of the great challenges of the American church and the Authentic Church is to evangelize in a way that increases the number of true disciples. Early in my theological education, I thought that evangelism and making disciples were one and the same; I thought a Billy Graham Crusade was the way to do evangelism and make disciples. As I developed a better understanding of the task of sharing the gospel, evangelism, I learned that the making of disciples is dramatically different from what I had thought. I came to realize that one must grow out of the other.

While Webster's Dictionary describes a disciple as "a pupil or follower of any teacher or school of religion, leaning, art, etc.," a Christian disciple follows Jesus Christ. A Christian disciple is one who loves God with everything one has. A Christian disciple, by God's grace, becomes more and more like Christ through a life of faith and obedience.[198]

When we look at the New Testament Gospels, we see that those who followed Jesus truly were His disciples. Because of their love for Christ, many left their jobs, homes, and security to walk with Him as He ministered to people throughout Palestine. They had the benefit of walking with Christ in the flesh.[199]

Discipleship and following Christ are used synonymously. The canonical Gospels, Acts, and Epistles urge disciples to be imitators of Jesus Christ or of God himself. Being an imitator requires obedience exemplified by moral behavior. With this biblical basis, Christian theology teaches that discipleship entails transformation from some other World view and practice of life into that of Jesus Christ, and so, by way of Trinitarian theology, of God himself."[200]

If the closest relationships of a disciple's life conflict with the claims of Jesus Christ, then our Lord requires instant obedience to Himself. Discipleship means personal, passionate devotion to a Person—our Lord Jesus Christ. There is a vast difference between devotion to a person and devotion to principles or to a cause. Our Lord never proclaimed a cause—he proclaimed personal devotion to Himself. To be a disciple is to be a devoted bond servant motivated by love for the Lord Jesus. Many of us who call ourselves Christians are not truly devoted to Jesus Christ.[201]

So is making disciples and developing discipleship relevant in the church today? Has the church been successful in making or attracting disciples of Christ? The answer is no.

More than one-quarter of American adults have left the faith in which they were raised in favor of another religion or no religion at all. The survey finds that the number of people who say they are unaffiliated with any particular faith today (16.1%) is more than double the number who say they were not affiliated with any particular religion as children. Among Americans ages 18–29, one in four say they are not currently affiliated with any particular religion. The Landscape Survey confirms that the United States is on the verge of becoming a minority Protestant country; the number of Americans who report that they are members of the Protestant denomination stands at barely 51%. This would be the first time in American history that Protestants would be less than 50%.[202]

In light of the decline of religious commitment, the questions are, What has become of discipleship and following Jesus? Why is there a lack of commitment to the example of Christ and His directives in the church? Why don't people attend church?

Across age and denomination, the top two reasons unchurched Americans say they do not think attending church is important were always the same; 40% say, "I find God elsewhere" and 35% say, "Church is not relevant to me personally."[203] We have failed as the church to build disciples and honor the directive of Christ to make disciples.

The church is called to make disciples, but there seems to be a discipleship deficit in evangelicalism.[204] There certainly is a place for evangelism collectively in the church and individually in our lives, but there must be a better understanding that while we are called to evangelize and share the gospel as directed by the Great Commission, that is not the final objective. Mark 16:15 (NIV) states, "Go into all the world and preach the good news to all creation." Matthew 28:18–20 (NIV) reads,

> All authority in heaven and on earth has been given to me. Therefore go and make disciples of all nations, baptizing them in the name of the Father and of the Son and of the Holy Spirit, and teaching them to obey everything I have commanded you.

We must begin to evangelize and more important make disciples. Evangelism is important, but it has been misunderstood and simplified in the church today. What does it really mean to call oneself a Christian? True disciples of Jesus discipline themselves to love God above all else. A disciple must be confident that his or her salvation lies in the efficacy of Christ's death and resurrection. A disciple demonstrates love for God, neighbor, fellow disciples, and enemies. A disciple is one who knows how to read, study, memorize, and meditate on the Word of God. A true disciple of Jesus is a person of prayer. A disciple is one who obeys the commands of God in a lifestyle that honors Christ.[205] A true disciple puts God first and others ahead of himself or herself.

Originally, the word *Christian* was a derogatory term. Many people today have the wrong idea of what a Christian is maybe because of how they act and interact with society. Many people think Christians pray, read the Bible, go to church, live by the Golden Rule, and keep the Ten Commandments. Even if you did all that, you still wouldn't be a Christian. It is more than that. You must be a disciple.[206] While every disciple is a believer, not every believer is a disciple. The Christian experience of the believers in the first-century church may seem radical to many in the church today, but for the early believers, it was normal Christianity. These men and women empowered and motivated by the Holy Spirit turned the world upside down for the sake of Christ.[207] They were true disciples of Jesus Christ in word and deed.

So what does it mean to follow Jesus? Is it enough to go to church a few times a month or a few times a year? Read your Bible once in a while? Pray when you are in a predicament? Talk to friends about Jesus? Wear a "What Would Jesus Do?" bracelet or a cross? This seems to be the level of commitment many American Christians have. We need to look at what Jesus said about the cross, about following Him, and about what role the Authentic Church should play in making disciples.

In a letter from Dietrich Bonhoeffer[xxv] to Eberhard Bethge from Tegel Prison dated April 30, 1944, Bonhoeffer explained how being held in a concentration camp brought clarity to him about true discipleship.

> You would be surprised, and perhaps even worried by my theological thoughts and the conclusions that they lead to; and this is where I miss you most of all, because I don't know anyone else with whom I could so well discuss them to have my thinking clarified. What is bothering me incessantly is the question what Christianity really is, or indeed who Christ really is, for us today ... We are moving toward a completely religionless time; people as they are now simply cannot be religious anymore. Even those who honestly describe themselves as "religious" do not in the least act up to it, and so they presumably mean something quite different by "religious"[208]
>
> For Bonhoeffer, all true theology begins in prayer and is centered on Jesus Christ. Bonhoeffer could point to this one who was born in a crib and died on a cross, and say, "This man is God for me." Bonhoeffer, unlike prevailing liberal theologians, refused to separate the Jesus of history from the Christ of faith. We meet the risen Christ who is present in the church's proclamation, he insisted. But the present Christ is none other than the historical Jesus who taught and healed, forgave sinners, and died on a cross. As the incarnate One,

---

[xxv] Dietrich Bonhoeffer, born in 1906, was a German Lutheran pastor and theologian who spoke out critically against the policies and practices of Adolf Hitler and the Third Reich. He was a leader of the Confessing Church, which stood in opposition to the Nazi-supported German Christian Church movement. Bonhoeffer was eventually arrested for his activities in an attempted assassination of Adolf Hitler and his opposition to his policies. He was executed by the Gestapo on April 9, 1945.

Christ demonstrates God's love for the world. As the crucified One, Christ discloses God's judgment upon humanity's sin. As the risen One, Christ reveals God's will for the renewal of humanity. Like spokes that go out from the hub of a wheel, everything in Bonhoeffer's theology radiates from Christ the center. He is the center of human existence, of history, and even of nature.[209]

In Matthew 8:18–22 (NIV), we see this principle being expanded.

> When Jesus saw the crowd around him, he gave orders to cross to the other side of the lake. Then a teacher of the law came to him, and said, "Teacher, I will follow you wherever you go." And Jesus replied, "Foxes have holes and birds of the air have nests, but the Son of Man has no place to lay his head." Another disciple said to him, "Lord, first let me go and bury my father." But Jesus said to him, "Follow me, and let the dead bury their dead."[210]

Jesus seems to have this unique way to underline the urgency of those who want to follow Him. They must stop everything, immediately go when called by the Holy Spirit, and begin following Him no matter what the cost. Whatever they are doing must be put in its proper priority, and the call to follow Christ must be heard and acted on.

Matthew 5:11 (NIV) says, "Blessed are you when people insult you, persecute you, and falsely say all kinds of evil against you because of me. Rejoice and be glad because great is your reward in Heaven, for in the same way they persecuted the Prophets, who were before you."[211]

In this parable, Jesus is saying there is a cost associated with being a disciple. Just as others before us, the apostles, and prophets were persecuted, we may experience similar treatment. If we choose to follow Jesus, we will be persecuted and encounter resistance and rejection.

In the verse I used at this beginning of this chapter, I made it clear I feel it is difficult and frightening to be a disciple and follow Christ. Review what Jesus said is required of those who follow.

> Then he called the crowd to him along with his disciples and said: "If anyone would come after me, he must deny himself and take up his cross and follow me. For whoever wants to save his life will lose it, but whoever loses his life for me and for the gospel will save it. What good is it for a man to gain the whole world, yet forfeit his soul? Or what can a man give in exchange for his soul? If anyone is ashamed of me and my words in this adulterous and sinful generation, the Son of Man will be ashamed of him when he comes in his Father's glory with the holy angels."[212]

How does the logic of the cross work? It seems offensive and illogical to us. How can we gain life from losing life? Does that make any sense? The wisdom of this world would have us believe that we need to look out for ourselves. People in our society are most likely quite shocked by Jesus' question: for what will it profit a whole person to gain the world and forfeit his or her soul or life? Is not gaining the whole world so deeply ingrained into us and our society that it's our life's objective? We have turned that into a means of salvation, a god, or a fundamental creed or to replace Christ and Christianity. This is Jesus' answer to the message of pursuing all the things, except for himself.[213] Pick up your cross and follow me.

Jesus continues this kingdom principle in Matthew 6:19 about more elements of discipleship.

> Do not store up for yourselves treasures on earth where moth and rust destroy and where thieves break in and steal. But store up for yourselves treasures in Heaven, where moth and rust do not destroy. For where your treasure is, there your heart will be also.[214]

Theologian and Bible commentator Adam Clarke wrote, "If Jesus Christ had come into the world as a mighty and opulent man, clothed with earthly glories and honors, he would have had a multitude of followers, and most of them hypocrites."[215] This is why most of the American church is making hypocrites, not disciples.

Jesus gave a warning to all who would follow him.

1. **Let them deny themselves**. It was bad enough that the disciples would learn Jesus would suffer, be rejected, and die on the cross. Jesus told them they may be called to do the same in their daily living.
2. **Everyone knew what the cross signified**. The unrelenting instrument of death by the Roman government, the cross, had no other purpose other than to inflict pain and death and to humiliate the person in the process.
3. **Jesus equates denying of Himself with taking up our own crosses**. Those who carried the cross knew they couldn't save themselves and knew the painful process that lay ahead. They would suffer the punishment of taking up their own crosses.

Can we follow Jesus and take up our own crosses? Look at the daily paper and read about ordinary people taking the call of discipleship to Christ seriously. You can never live life fully until you are buried spiritually with Christ.

Followers of Christ have been transformed into His disciples by their passion to follow

Him many times at great personal cost. Look at what may be expected when you become a believer in Christ and a disciple. Jesus said,

> If the world hates you, keep in mind that it hated me first. If you belonged to the world, it would love you as its own. As it is, you do not belong to the world, but I have chosen you out of the world. That is why the world hates you.[216, xxvi]

People around the world have made the decision to follow Christ and be His disciples. The kingdom and the Authentic Church need people committed to what Jesus directed. In America today, we have a comfortable Christianity, whereas in many other places in the world, becoming a Christian is a life-and-death decision. It is a decision between understanding the distinction between expensive grace and cheap grace.

A version of cheap grace that is comfortable in modern American Christianity has now become rampant in the American church. Cheap grace means justifying sin without any change in your life, for example, preaching about forgiveness and love without changing the way you live and act through repentance. We can take communion each week and month without a true acknowledgement of confession of our sin and our condition before God and what it means to be in true communion with Christ. We can rely on the grace of Christ while not following His example or Him. Cheap grace means no type of personal sacrifice or understanding of the true implications of the cross and Christ's sacrifice in our daily lives. It means we take things for granted. It means we don't join in solidarity with others who are suffering persecution and are displaced and broken and most of all those who suffered death because of their faith. Worst of all, we don't join in or share the triumph, joy, and liberation Christ humbly provided us.

Costly grace is the perfect example of Jesus. He lived a sinless life and brought Good News to all even unto death, when He took the place of a murderer, insurrectionist, robber, and thief—Barabbas—and died on the cross. Costly grace was personified when a sinless Jesus died in our place on the cross at Calvary. It was personified when Jesus prayed for us, fasted for us, healed us, and sacrificed for us by being spit on, whipped, pierced, and ultimately hung on the cross. He said, "Father, forgive them, for they do not know what they are doing."[217] Being a disciple is overcoming difficult and sometimes tragic circumstances in life to look forward for life eternal.

[xxvi] So allegiance to Christ is enmity to the world and the system of exceptionalism. When you become a disciple of Christ, you may suffer in personal relationships, in the workplace, even with the people closest to you—your spouse, siblings, and friends. There is a cost to being a follower and disciple of Christ. It may cost you economically, emotionally, and physically, but the spiritual gains will last into and through eternity.

Why were the lives of the great saints, martyrs, and apostles not easy? In America today, we have this philosophy of Christianity that we should be healthy, wealthy, and wise and life should be easy. When I read the New Testament, I see that Jesus, the apostles, and the disciples paid a tremendous cost; it was the same in the Old Testament with the saints who followed God. What is it about discipleship and suffering for Christ that was welcome then but so unwelcome in today's American Christianity? Through numerous trials, persecutions, separations, and suffering, the apostle Paul developed this perspective.

> To keep me from becoming conceited because of these surpassingly great revelations, there was given to me a thorn in my flesh, a messenger of Satan, to torment me. Three times I pleaded with the Lord to take it away from me. But he said to me, "My grace is sufficient for you, for my power is made perfect in weakness."[218]

Samuel Rutherford said, "The cross of Christ is the sweetest burden that I ever bore. It is a burden to me such as wings are to a bird or sails are to carry me forward to my harbor."[219]

> In every Christian's heart there is a cross and a throne, and the Christian is on the throne till he puts himself on the cross; if he refuses the cross, he remains on the throne. Perhaps this is at the bottom of the backsliding and worldliness among gospel believers today. We want to be saved, but we insist that Christ do all the dying. No cross for us, no dethronement, no dying. We remain king within the little kingdom of Man's soul and wear our tinsel crown with all the pride of a Caesar; but we doom ourselves to shadows and weakness and spiritual sterility.[220]
>
> It is good to learn early, that suffering and God are not a contradiction … for the idea that God himself is suffering … has always been one of the most convincing teachings of Christianity. I think God is nearer to suffering than to happiness, and to find God in this way gives peace … and a strong and courageous heart. (Dietrich Bonhoeffer)[221]

So what was Jesus thinking when He was being rejected by those He loved? What was He thinking when He was doing God's will for humanity but was the ultimate sacrifice for us? In one way, that moment was a crisis for Jesus when He was being prepared to be crucified. Whatever Jesus might have been thinking, He knew an inescapable cross lay ahead. The problem confronting Jesus was this: with the cross looming, had He had any effect at all? Had he achieved anything? Had anyone discovered who He really was? Had He made true disciples? If He had lived, taught, and moved among these men and women for three years and no one had glimpsed the Spirit of God upon him, all His work was for nothing. There was only one way He could leave a message with people—write it on someone's heart. In that moment, Jesus put all things to the test. He asked His disciples what people were saying about Him, and they shared with Him the popular rumors and reports. Then came a breathless silence. He asked the question that meant so much: "Who do you say that I am?"[222]

Suddenly, Peter realized what he had always known deep down in his heart. This was the Messiah, the Christ, the Anointed One, the Son of God.[223] And with that answer, Jesus knew He had affected people and made clear who He was; any and all suffering He went through and would go through would be beneficial to humanity; He had made disciples.

Jesus called ordinary people like you and me. He saw some fisherman, Simon and his brother, and said, "Follow me." They left their nets and followed Him. Then He saw James and his brother John. He called them and said, "Follow me." They left the boat and followed Jesus. Then Jesus saw a tax collector named Matthew, and He said to Matthew, "Follow me."[224] He got up and followed Jesus. Jesus called each one publicly to get up and follow Him. When they were called to action to be His disciples, they knew not what their future held. They did not know if wealth or worldly success would follow, but they desired spiritual success, eternal life, and conformity to the person who had called them. Being a disciple means to put your life second to following Jesus.

Dietrich Bonhoeffer wrote, "When Christ calls a man, he bids him come and die ... Cheap grace is the deadly enemy of our church. We are fighting today for costly grace."[225]

The Authentic Church must be concerned with building disciples, not the number of converts or how much money ends up in the collection plate. It must evoke a transformational change in attitude and belief that begins to replicate the life of Christ in our lives individually and in the life of the Authentic Church collectively.

LESSON 7

What the American Church Is Not Building—Disciples

And when he had called the people unto him with his disciples also, he said unto them, Whosoever will come after me, let him deny himself, and take up his cross, and follow me. For whosoever will save his life shall lose it; but whosoever shall lose his life for my sake and the gospel's, the same shall save it. For what shall it profit a man, if he shall gain the whole world, and lose his own soul? Or what shall a man give in exchange for his soul? Whosoever therefore shall be ashamed of me and of my words in this adulterous and sinful generation; of him also shall the Son of man be ashamed, when he cometh in the glory of his Father with the holy angels.

MARK 8:34–38 (KJV)

1. What does this scripture say to you?

2. The spirit of exceptionalism has been quoted by many in politics and other areas when describing American culture and its status in the world. Recently, a president was quoted as saying, "I believe in American exceptionalism." What do you believe this to mean?

3. Has the American church become exceptional at building multimillion-dollar institutions and ministries but largely failed in the true objective of the church, which is to _____? One of the great challenges of the American church and the Authentic Church is to _____ in a way that increases the number of true disciples.

4. While *Webster's Dictionary* describes a disciple as "a pupil or follower of any teacher or school of religion, leaning, art, etc.," a Christian disciple follows Jesus Christ. A Christian disciple is one who loves God with everything one has. A Christian disciple, by God's grace, becomes more and more like Christ through a life of faith and obedience. Are you a disciple of Christ?

5. Discipleship means personal, passionate devotion to a person—our Lord and Savior Jesus Christ. Is there a difference between devotion to a person and devotion to principles or to a cause?

6. Is making disciples and developing discipleship relevant to the church today? Has the church been successful in making or attracting disciples of Christ?

7. In light of the decline of religious commitment, what has become of the meaning of discipleship and following Jesus? Is there a lack of commitment to the example of Christ and his directives on discipleship in the church?

8. The top two reasons unchurched Americans say they do not think attending church is important are always the same: 40% say, "I find God elsewhere," and 35% say, "Church is not relevant to me personally." Have we failed as the church to build disciples and honor the directive of Christ to make disciples?

9. There is a place for evangelism collectively in the church and individually in our lives, but there must be a better understanding that while we are called to evangelize and share the gospel as directed by the Great Commission, the final objective is to make disciples. Do you agree with this?

10. Refer to these scriptures to see what they mean and how they apply to the lesson:

   Mark 16:15

   Matthew 28:18–20

11. What do you think it really means to call oneself a Christian?

12. Many people think Christians pray, read the Bible, go to church, live by the Golden Rule, and keep the Ten Commandments. Is that what a Christian does?

13. While every disciple is a believer, not every believer is a disciple. Explain the difference.

14. In your own words, what does it mean to follow Jesus?

15. In a letter from Pastor Dietrich Bonhoeffer to Eberhard Bethge from the Nazi-controlled Tegel Prison dated April 30, 1944, Bonhoeffer explained how being held in a concentration camp with the Jews brought clarity to him about true Christian discipleship. He wrote this:

> You would be surprised, and perhaps even worried by my theological thoughts and the conclusions that they lead to; and this is where I miss you most of all, because I don't know anyone else with whom I could so well discuss them to have my thinking clarified. What is bothering me incessantly is the question what Christianity really is, or indeed who Christ really is, for us today…We are moving toward a completely religionless time; people as they are now simply cannot be religious anymore. Even those who honestly describe themselves as "religious" do not in the least act up to it, and so they presumably mean something quite different by "religious."

What are your thoughts on this?

16. Let us review what Jesus said is required of those who follow.

> Then he called the crowd to him along with his disciples and said: "If anyone would come after me, he must deny himself and take up his cross and follow me. For whoever wants to save his life will lose it, but whoever loses his life for me and for the gospel will save it. What good is it for a man to gain the whole world, yet forfeit his soul? Or what can a man give in exchange for his soul? If anyone is ashamed of me and my words in this adulterous and sinful generation, the Son of Man will be ashamed of him when he comes in his Father's glory with the holy angels."

Jesus seems to have a unique way of underlining the urgency for those who want to follow him. They must stop everything, immediately go when called by the Holy Spirit, and begin following him no matter what the cost. Whatever they are doing must be put in its proper priority, and the call to follow Christ must be heard and acted on. See Matthew 5:11. Is this approach practical in today's world?

17. Can you explain how the logic of the cross works?

18. Jesus continues this kingdom principle in Matthew 6:19. In this verse, Jesus gives a warning to all who would follow him.

- Let them deny themselves.
- Everyone knew what the cross signified.
- Jesus equates denying of himself with taking up our own crosses.

What do you think of these 3 statements?

19. In America today, we have what I call "comfortable Christianity"; whereas in other places in the world, becoming a Christian is a life-and-death decision. It is a decision that shows understanding of the distinction between expensive grace and cheap grace. What are your thoughts on this?

20. Can you identify an example of "cheap grace" in the American church?

21. Can you identify an example of "costly grace" in the American church?

22. Do you agree that being a disciple of Christ is overcoming difficult and sometimes tragic circumstances in life but looking forward to life eternal?

23. In America today, we have this philosophy in Christianity that we should be healthy, wealthy, and successful in life, and it should be easy. Is that discipleship?

24. What is it about discipleship and suffering for Christ that was welcome in the early church and around the world but is unwelcome in today's American Christianity?

25. There is a saying, "In every Christian's heart there is a cross and a throne, and the Christian is on the throne until he puts himself on the cross; if he refuses the cross, he remains on the throne." Comment on this.

26. Dietrich Bonhoeffer wrote, "It is good to learn early, that suffering and God are not a contradiction…for the idea that God himself is suffering…has always been one of the most convincing teachings of Christianity. I think God is nearer to suffering than to happiness, and to find God in this way gives peace…and a strong and courageous heart." Do you agree with this?

27. When Jesus first called his disciples, they knew not what their future held. They did not know if wealth or worldly success would follow; but instead, they were led directly to desire spiritual success, eternal life, and conformity to the person who had called them. Being a disciple means to put your life second to following Jesus. Have you done this?

28. Dietrich Bonhoeffer wrote, "When Christ calls a man, he bids him come and die..." What does this mean?

29. The Authentic Church must be concerned with building disciples, not the number of converts or how much money ends up in the collection plate. Is this a radical departure from Christianity in America today?

CHAPTER 8

The Dirty Little Secret of the American Church[xxvii]

Whosoever causes one of these little ones who believe in Me to sin, it would be better for him if a millstone were hung around his neck, and he were drowned in the depth of the sea.
MATTHEW 18:6 (NKJV)

One of the most problematic aspects of the American church that is not talked about and is treated as a dirty little secret in the confines of the American church is Protestant clergy sex abuse. Many people do not realize that the Protestant church like the Catholic Church has a widespread problem across all denominational lines. Many people tend to think because the Catholic Church has been very publicly accused of harboring child sexual abusers and relocating cardinals, archbishops, bishops, and priests once it was determined they were abusers that sexual abuse is exclusive to the Catholic Church.

The Catholic Church has certainly garnered most of the attention in the papers over the last two decades in this respect. However, sexual abuse is not exclusive to the Catholic Church. "Statistics reveal that one in every four women and one in every six boys will be sexually abused before the age of eighteen."[226] Sexual abuse is so prevalent in society that the church should be a safe haven from those casualties; instead, it more often than not acts like a fox guarding the hen house.

We read in the newspapers and see on television that the Catholic Church has taken the brunt of the bad publicity as it relates to the sexual abuse of children that culminated in several large lawsuits in Boston, Philadelphia, and California. The Catholic Church has also taken a beating in the courts of public opinion as former altar boys, members of youth athletic

---

[xxvii] This chapter was originally a paper entitled "Suffering in Silence" submitted to Dr. Deborah van Deusen Hunsinger for her class entitled "Trauma and Grace: Toward Healing and Resilience" at Princeton Theological Seminary.

leagues, and ordinary parishioners come forward with horrible stories of sexual abuse that in many cases lasted for years.[227] Unknown to many in the American church are the significant and egregious acts by Protestant clergy that have failed to generate the same level of outrage in public opinion. Why?

When we look at the Catholic Church, we see a huge institution that is centralized in America and globally through the Vatican. All Catholic priests go through the same training and adhere to a chain of command in the Catholic Church that ends in allegiance to the pope. A 1990 study by the Freedom from Religion Foundation shows that sexual abuse and pedophilia by clergy is prevalent in Protestant denominations as well as in the Catholic Church. Surprisingly, in America, there are more reported cases of sexual abuse among Protestant clergy than among Catholic clergy. During one period, there were approximately two members of the clergy arrested per week for sex crimes against children in North American churches. Surprisingly, almost 60% of those arrested were not Catholics but Protestants.[228] In this chapter, we will ask, Why is sexual abuse in the American church not discussed? Why have we overlooked Protestant sexual abuse in the churches and publicized and decreed with outrage the Catholic Church sex abuse scandal? It is time that the American church becomes the Authentic Church by looking at itself in the mirror and ridding its churches of this horrific conduct to make it the church Christ envisioned.

When we talk about sexual abuse in the churches, it is easy to point out that unlike the Protestant churches, which are broken up into several subcategories in the denominations, the Catholic Church is a centralized religious institution. Thus, it is easier for the Catholic Church to codify and accumulate statistics of sexual abuse throughout the denomination. The greater difficulty is in tracking and reporting sexual abuse that possibly goes on in a Baptist church as compared to a Methodist or a Lutheran church because Protestant churches have no centralized reporting.

Why then does the Catholic Church seem to get such terrible press with sexual abuse when sexual abuse may be more rampant in the Protestant denominations? One of the commonly held myths is that because Catholic priests are celibate, they are more inclined to be sexual abusers or homosexuals than those who are not celibate. There is no data to support the idea that priests who are celibate are at a higher risk of being sexual abusers than those who are married.

Another possible reason the Catholic Church garners more publicity for sexual abuse than do the Protestant denominations may be that the Catholic Church is a historic, affluent, and wealthy institution and one of the largest landholders in the world. According to *Business Insider*, the Catholic Church owns 110 acres that constitute Vatican City and roughly another 177 million acres of various lands worldwide. They rank number three of the top landowners worldwide.[229] Sexual-abuse lawsuits against the Catholic Church are many times more lucrative and sensational and generate considerable press. Sexual-abuse lawsuits in general may not garner as much press as do Catholic cases. Also, the Catholic Church allocates the necessary resources to defend itself and resolve these cases unlike many Protestant denominations. The other issue may be that there are far more Protestants in America than there are Catholics, and it is easier to blame the minority for bad conduct.

Whatever the reason, it is time we realize that sexual abuse is not limited to the Catholic Church; it is a problem in the American church. The American church has to come to grips with sexual abuse for it to become the Authentic Church Christ founded.

It is important to understand what victims of sexual abuse go through. According to one victim of sexual abuse, though I still become caught in fear and anger, each day I become more aware of the power I possess to choose love. The most powerful words given to me during this painful process of healing came from Martin Luther King, Sr.: "No matter what you do to me, I will not give you the power to make me hate."[230]

Those words are significant and powerful especially for those who have been sexually abused or suffered trauma in their lives. Many victims of childhood sexual abuse have so much pain and anger that they have difficulty functioning in everyday life. Because the trauma is so deep and painful, many victims remain silent, suffer in silence, or lash out in hate and rage due to deep and unhealed wounds.

Neuroscience has taught us, "We can never erase or completely work through a traumatic experience because it remains encoded in our neurophysiology (and) there is no such thing as working something through once and for all."[231] These are very problematic findings that lead us to believe many victims of sexual abuse and trauma have to live with this all their lives.

It is important that we understand what the word *trauma* means—wound.

> [It] has come to describe an extremely distressing and harrowing personal or communal experience that exceeds our normal abilities to cope. Traumatic experiences can leave us feeling overwhelmed, emotionally flooded, disoriented, unsure of ourselves, no longer able to trust others or our ability to perceive reality correctly. Experiences of trauma can result in what has become known as post-traumatic stress disorder or what Judith Herman more accurately calls "complex post-traumatic stress disorder" because "the responses to trauma are best understood as a spectrum of conditions rather than as a single disorder."[232]

Understanding this diagnosis is very important. It is a shame that the church of Christ is causing people pain, anxiety, and hurt instead of healing.

Data on sexual-abuse victims tell us that the trauma involved is difficult for the victim to understand and process. Children who have experienced sexual abuse often try to repress their memories of it to function normally.

> Child victims of sexual abuse face secondary trauma in the crisis of discovery. Their attempts to reconcile their private experiences with the realities of the outer world are assaulted by the disbelief, blame and rejection they experience from adults. The normal coping behavior of the child contradicts the entrenched beliefs and expectations typically held by adults, stigmatizing the child with charges of lying, manipulating or imagining from parents, courts, and clinicians.[233]

> Most persons who have been traumatized remember their traumatic experiences relatively clearly. They've never forgotten them, and they have no doubt about what happened. For others, like the woman whose exploration of her anxiety led to a revelation of childhood sexual molestation, matters are not so clear. These persons may have gone for years—even decades—without remembering various traumatic childhood experiences. Then, seemingly out of nowhere, images suggestive of traumatic experience start coming to mind.[234]

> Although the concept is controversial, *repression* can play a role in not remembering traumatic events. When we deliberately avoid trying to think about something—often making matters worse—we are employing *suppression*. In contrast, repression is an automatic, nonconscious process that inhibits emotionally painful thoughts and memories from being elaborated in consciousness.[235]

Many victims of sexual abuse have used these mental coping techniques daily not realizing they were causing more emotional damage.

> Sadly, trauma does not necessarily end when the traumatic situation is long past. Many traumatized persons continue to re-experience the trauma wherever memories of the event are evoked. Along with the memories come painful emotions and the sense of helplessness.[236]

> Many persons are blindsided by flashbacks that have been triggered out of the blue by some reminder of trauma. Not uncommonly, the triggers are hard to identify, compounding fear with bewilderment. Traumatic memories also intrude into sleep in the form of nightmares. Flashbacks and nightmares

can be direct replicas of the traumatic experience. Some traumatic events are remembered and relived with crystal clarity, in full detail, accompanied by a coherent sense of what happened. These are prototypical personal event memories, albeit with a traumatic intensity of emotion.[237]

Unfortunately, many victims of sexual abuse experience these phenomena on a regular basis.

These are some of the significant ramifications for those who have experienced this type of trauma and abuse. Many of these victims are never able to forget or get over the trauma. Many times, the victims do not have the resources to find competent and capable counseling, pastoral care, or medical care to come to a healing place with regard to the abuse they have suffered. Many thus continue this vicious cycle of abuse long after the abuse has stopped.

> A century ago, Freud labored to understand the causes of debilitating symptoms, including anxiety, depression, suicide attempts, painful physical sensations, and eruptions of intense emotions associated with images of hallucinatory vividness. He had worked with 18 patients with such symptoms and concluded that in *every instance* (emphasis in original), the symptoms were connected with sexual trauma in early childhood.[238]

Almost every victim of sexual abuse I have worked with as a lawyer, advocate, and pastor had issues of anxiety, depression, suicidal thoughts and actions, painful physical sensations, alcohol abuse, drug abuse, and vivid hallucinations or flashbacks. These are commonplace for those who have been sexually abused, and many times, they live for years in silence with these effects.[xxviii]

The traumatic events and abuse disrupt an individual's secure base and destroys the basic trust humans need to function. It also deeply disturbs physiological regulation. Often, a kind of double whammy results: the traumatic experience generates hyperarousal (fear, panic, pain), and when the individual is then abandoned or neglected after being injured and aroused, that compounds the negative effects of the experience.[239] Many victims of clergy sexual abuse feel abandoned by the church, its leaders, and ultimately God.

The initial discovery of research for sexual abuse as it relates to clergy or church disclosed

---

[xxviii] As a trial lawyer, I have handled over a hundred sexual-abuse cases in my career. I was able to handle one of the largest sex abuse cases in the country (J.F., E.J., B.S., C.S., G.T., R.W., J.B., S.B., C.S., S.D., J.J., B.D., K.E., J.B., M.B., W.M., C.D., A.B., AND D.S. v. The Lutheran Church of America, et al.). Most of my career I have advocated for victims of abuse and I have seen first-hand the significant psychological toll it takes on their lives.

that a majority of offenders regularly attend church. Other studies have suggested "that the majority of offenders are fundamentalists"[240] or come from highly traditional, fundamental, devout, authoritarian families who are most at risk to commit sexual abuse. Statistics demonstrate that abusers are usually well known to the victim as evidenced by the fact that approximately 75–85% of offenders know their victims. Often, the abuser is a trusted family member, friend, or child-care provider.[241] Sexual abuse is often an act of convenience, opportunity, power, and control.

Statistically, fewer male victims of sexual abuse will come forward and disclose their abuse to authorities or guardians or engage in any kind of public attention or public reporting: "8% [of male victims] compared to the 92% who are female"[242] Statistics demonstrate that while approximately 90% of female victims come forward, less than 10% of male victims come forward and report. Moreover, somewhere between "50–80% of all child abuse is considered unreported";[243] thus, the exact number of male victims is unknown. In the majority of cases, male victims try to forget about the sexual abuse and keep it to themselves. Whatever the underlying psychological reasons are, they many times even deny the abuse occurred. Victims who were passive in the abuse may in fact equate the passivity with homosexuality.[244] It is unfortunate that these young victims of sexual abuse often have deep-rooted psychological and emotional problems along with substance-abuse problems later in life.

Sexual abuse of anyone is strictly prohibited in the Old and New Testaments.

> [God] created sex to be an act of mutual love between adults and to distort the gift of sex to sexually abusing children was clearly not within the design that God had intended. Sexual abuse interrupts a child's delicate process of emotional, social, and sexual maturation.[245]

We have scriptural directives from Jesus in Matthew 18:6 (NIV): "If anyone causes one of these little ones—those who believe in me—to stumble, it would be better for them to have a large millstone hung around their neck and to be drowned in the depths of the sea."[246] Other translations of the King James Bible say, "But who shall offend one of these little ones which believe in me, it were better for him that a millstone were hanged about his neck, and that he were drowned in the depth of the sea."[247] The Holman Christian Bible says, "But whoever causes the downfall of one of these little ones who believe in me—it would be better for him if a heavy millstone were hung around his neck and he were drowned in the depths of the sea!"[248]

These prohibitions given by Jesus Christ show how much He loves children and how society and the church ought to protect these innocent lives. There is so much at stake when these children are abused at young ages; their futures may be devastated and destroyed. This can and will cause their lives to be disrupted mentally and for the children to stumble and fall into abuse, addiction, and sin through no fault of their own.

Due to the sexual abuse perpetrated against them, that trauma could become the norm for children as they grow up and struggle with many psychological, physical, and mental issues by dealing with the abuse. The ramifications of one who harms one of these children or causes him or her to stumble Jesus equates to the worst of the worst. This raises a very interesting question: why did Jesus suggest such a significant penalty—drowning—for those who have sexually abused children? He wanted to stress the evil inherent in sexual abuse.

> We do not know if the Jews punished criminals by drowning the perpetrator, though it's suggested that it was practiced in some cases; but by other nations this penalty was commonly used. Among the Romans, Greeks and Syrians, it was certainly the practice. The punishment seems to have been reserved for the greatest criminals; and the size of the stone would prevent any chance of the body rising again to the surface and being buried by friends—a consideration which, in the minds of heathens, greatly increased the horror of this kind of death.[249]

That underlines how early societies responded to those who had sexually abused children. As we have indicated earlier, "many studies have concluded that around one in four women and one in six men have been victims of sexual violence or abuse at some point in their lives which equates to about 20% of the church."[250] One out of five in the pews of our churches may have been sexually abused.

> The findings of the June 2014 IMA World Health[xxix] survey revealed that nearly three quarters of church leaders are not aware of the level of sexual violence and victimization experienced within their congregations. The same study showed that slightly more than half of pastors surveyed were not familiar with resources available and how to treat the victims of sexual abuse.[251]
>
> We cannot assume that we can avoid this topic simply by making sure our doctrines are right, our values conservative, and our people sheltered from the

---

[xxix] IMA World Health is an international nonprofit healthcare service organization. The faith-based charity specializes in procuring and distributing medical supplies and services to underdeveloped nations. IMA states its purpose is to "provide healthcare … without bias, to vulnerable and marginalized people in the developing world;" Directory of Community Services.

world. If we are not addressing this issue, it is only because we are ignoring what is going on in our communities, and all too often in our pews.[252]

Clergy sexual abuse has and continues to be the church's dirty little secret.

Boz Tchividjian, the founder of GRACE (Godly Response to Abuse in the Christian Environment), a Christian-based organization whose mission is to recognize, prevent, and respond to child abuse, agrees. Mr. Tchividjian "believes that an understanding of the subject within the church lays the foundation for protection and healing from sexual abuse."[253] Recognition of the problem and addressing the problem is the first step in bringing healing and change. He stated,

> Most people in the church do not know enough about the subject. We need to start conversations by reaching outside of our world to understand the issue. When we have a better grasp of the dynamics of sexual abuse, this will help the church develop and transform a culture that is safer for children and a safe place for abuse survivors.[254]

A study on clergy sexual abuse and the Catholic Church done by the John Jay College of Criminal Justice in New York revealed some startling facts.

> About 4% of U.S. priests ministering from 1950–2002 were accused of sexual abuse of a minor, according to the first comprehensive national study of the issue. The study said that 4,392 clergymen—almost all priests—were accused of abusing 10,667 victims, with 75% of the incidents taking place between 1960 and 1984. During the same time frame there were 109,694 priests … Sex-abuse related costs totaled $573 million, with $219 million covered by insurance companies. It noted, however, that the overall dollar figure is much higher than reported; 14% of the Dioceses and religious communities did not provide financial data and the total did not include settlements made after 2002, such as the $85 million agreed to by the Boston Archdiocese.[255]

Unfortunately, there were no comparable studies in the Protestant churches.

What the American church is dealing with is a very significant problem of sexual abuse, it also has to deal with the victims themselves and the ramifications sexual abuse has on the community at large. In 2014, the Vatican released statistics for the first time as to how its priests accused of raping and molesting children had been disciplined. Vatican statistics showed that

"848 priests have been defrocked[xxx] and another 2,572 given lesser sanctions over the past decade."[256] The committee from the Vatican has self-reported that they "adjudicated these sex abuse cases globally, and that there has been approximately, since 2004, more than 3,400 credible cases of abuse had been referred to the Vatican, including 401 cases in 2013 alone."[257]

The Catholic Church has taken steps to curtail and stop sexual abuse of minors and has shown some transparency in gathering data and sharing data, but many others and I believe it is still grossly underreported. The Vatican's U.N. ambassador in Geneva, Archbishop Silvano Tomasi, said,

> Over the last decade 848 priests had been defrocked, or returned to the lay state by the pope. Another 2,572 were sentenced to a lifetime of penance and prayer or some other lesser sanction, which is often used when the accused priest is elderly or infirm. Acknowledging the high number of priests sanctioned with the lesser punishment, Tomasi said it still amounted to disciplinary action and that the abuser is "put in a place where he doesn't have any contact with the children."[258]
>
> Pope Benedict XVI had defrocked 384 priests in the final two years of his pontificate, citing documentation Tomasi's delegation had prepared for another U.N. committee hearing that matched data contained in the Vatican's statistical yearbooks.[259]

These are shocking and alarming statistics. The Catholic Church has spent over $2.5 billion just in the United States confronting the clergy sex-abuse crisis.[260] In March 2013, the Catholic Church announced another settlement in the Archdiocese of Los Angeles, which raised the total settlements for sexual abuse in that archdiocese to almost $700 million to the victims alone; this did not include the costs of therapy, attorneys' fees, and more.[261] In 2007, the Los Angeles Archdiocese, the nation's largest, announced more than $660 million in settlements to 508 victims. That far surpassed the $84 million settlement record then held by the Boston Diocese in 2002.[262]

According to the U.S. Conference of Catholic Bishops' Office of Child and Youth Protection and independent studies commissioned by the bishops, the tallies as of 2012 were that almost 7,000 priest have been accused of sexual abuse since 1950, more than 16,000 victims of sexual abuse have been identified, and over $2.5 billion has been paid out in settlements without

---

[xxx] Defrock comes from frock, an old word for dress. Priests, nuns, monks, and other church officials wear frocks to symbolize their jobs. When they leave or are expelled from the church, they are said to be defrocked.

the costs of attorneys' fees, counseling, and other associated costs related to these particular priests from 2004 to only 2011.[263]

When we look at the abuse that has gone on in the Catholic Church, we may think things are much different for the Protestants, but while comparing the Evangelicals to Catholics on sexual abuse, many think that we are in fact worse, says Boz Tchividjian at the Religion Newswriters Association conference saying too many evangelicals had "sacrificed the souls" of young victims.[264]

Mr. Tchividjian said, "Protestants can be very arrogant when pointing to the Catholics"[265] and "too many Protestant institutions have sacrificed souls in order to protect their institutions."[266] There appears to be "a looming crisis of faith in the Protestant world."[267] We have failed to recognize that for many years, we blamed the sexual abuse in the Catholic Church on the mandatory celibacy of the priests, but now, many believe that sexual abuse in the noncelibate Protestant church is rampant and getting only worse.[268]

We already know data has suggested that victims of sexual abuse are

- three times more likely to suffer from depression,
- six times more likely to suffer from post-traumatic stress disorder,
- thirteen times more likely to abuse alcohol,
- twenty-six times more likely to abuse drugs, and
- four times more likely to contemplate suicide.[269]

Many times, there exists the naïve assumption that because we are Christian or have religious convictions that churches and other religious organizations are safer than secular organizations. Certainly, the Protestant churches over the decades had thought they were a safe haven for children and that children would not be sexually abused in any comparable way to the numbers that had been found in the Catholic Church.[270]

This seems to suggest that having a religious affiliation or a religious background does not deter some from abusing children. A number of studies have documented the impact of abuse that affects victims' spiritual well-being. In one study of 527 victims of child abuse (psychological, sexual, or emotional), it was found that there were significant spiritual injuries such as feelings of guilt, anger, grief, despair, doubt, fear of death, and belief that God was unfair.[271] Sexual abuse in the church has a detrimental effect on the victims' physical and mental well-being but also on their spiritual well-being—the very thing the church was assigned by God to nurture and protect.

Child abusers in the church are very sophisticated and will manipulate their victims and the whole church. One convicted child molester stated,

I consider church people easy to fool ... they have a trust that comes from being Christians ... They tend to be better folks all around. And they seem to want to believe in the good that exists in all people ... I think they want to believe in people. And because of that, you can easily convince, with or without convincing words.[272]

There does not seem to be any evidence to suggest that the "Catholic priests are gangs of sexual predators, as they are portrayed."[273] Though there have been no formal studies comparing the rates of sexual abuse in differing denominations, insurers have been assessing the risks of sexual abuse since they began to offer riders regarding liability policies in the 1980s.[274] "Two of the largest insurers report no higher risks in covering Catholic Churches than Protestant denominations."[275]

There is no hard evidence of an increased risk assessment of sexual abuse in the Catholic Church than in the Protestant denominations—follow the money to the truth. Nationally, these insurance companies are not evaluating the Catholic Church as a higher risk than Protestant churches, which is a significant factual finding. If there were truly a higher amount of sexual abuse in the Catholic Church than in the Protestant denomination, the insurance rates for the Catholic Church would inevitably be higher. However, the rates have not increased.[xxxi]

"It would be incorrect to call (clergy sexual abuse) a Catholic problem," said Church Mutual's risk control manager Rick Schaber. "We do not see one denomination above another. It's equal. It's also equal among large metropolitan churches and small rural churches."[276] Catholic churches are not considered a greater risk or charged higher premiums.

Moreover, the National Center for Missing and Exploited Children notes that the organization has received more than 825,000 reports of child abuse, and there is no statistical evidence that the Catholic Church after accounting for the sizes of churches has a greater likelihood of sexual abuses cases than other denominations or settings.[277] The statistics are saying that the problem with sexual abuse is not limited to the Catholic Church; it affects all churches and denominations.

Boz Tchividjian, director of GRACE, is convinced that the "Protestant world is teetering on the edge of a sex-abuse scandal similar to the one that had rocked the Catholic Church."[278] While Mr. Tchividjian has been careful to note that there is presently insufficient data to compare the prevalence of child sex abuse in the Catholic Church and Protestant church, he

---

[xxxi] As a trial lawyer who handles clergy sexual-abuse cases, I have compiled a list of all clergy sexual-abuse cases I have handled and have found that the Protestant denominations have slightly more lawsuits than the Catholic Church as far as my office is concerned.

notes, "The problem has reached a crisis point."[279] "In 2012, Christian radio host Janet Mefferd declared, 'This is an epidemic going on in churches … When are evangelicals going to wake up and say we have a massive problem in our own churches?'"[280]

While Protestants have assumed their churches were immune to the sexual abuse rampant in the Catholic Church by celibate priests, the Protestant churches may have been worse than the Catholic Church in their response to such abuse.[281]

> Mission fields are "magnets" for would-be molesters; ministries and schools do not understand the dynamics of abuse; and "good ol' boy" networks routinely cover up victims' stories to protect their reputations (just look at the Penn State Sex Abuse Case). It may only be a matter of time before a sexual abuse scandal emerges and "threatens the survival of powerful Protestant institutions."[282]

A sexual-abuse scandal in the Protestant church will be a significant problem for it because it "includes tens of thousands of denominations and nondenominational churches, ministries and boards. Unlike the Catholic Church, there is no Vatican, no central location of authority."[283] Thus, a problem emerges due to the varied and diverse Protestant churches both denominational and nondenominational. Moreover, due to the varied and numerous denominational and nondenominational churches, there is no central mechanism to track sexual-abuse cases and the response in the various churches and denominations.[284] Whereas the Catholic Church has the Vatican—centralized and in control of the Catholic Church as a whole—the Protestant church has no equivalent. The Vatican is at least centralized and could put in a centralized mechanism to stop and track abuse in the church.[285] We must understand as church leaders and builders of the Authentic Church that dealing with these issues is very difficult, problematic, and complex.

> In 1983, Dr. Ronald Summit from UCLA published a pioneering paper that helped professional and laypersons understand the dynamics present in child sexual abuse cases that make it difficult for children to disclose abuse timely, if at all. Although not universally accepted, Summit's work has been widely heralded in the mental health field."[286] Summit's paper emphasized that sexual abuse cases are "engulfed in secrecy, helplessness, entrapment and accommodation, delayed, conflicting and unconvincing disclosure, and retraction. Clergy and laity who take the time to understand these and other dynamics will increase the chance of responding sensitively to the spiritual needs of maltreated children.[287]

There is at least some indication that these "religious" sex offenders may be the most dangerous sex offenders. Studies have shown that sex offenders who have and maintain significant involvement with religious institutions have "more sexual offense convictions, more victims, and younger victims."[288] Moreover, other studies have demonstrated that clergy and nonclergy sex offenders often share the same characteristics except that clergy offenders are more likely to use force in their sexual abuse.[289]

Child molesters, particularly those who meet the criteria of pedophiles, are extremely manipulative of their victims and the church. Offenders report that children can be silenced and the average individual can be fooled and that religious people are even more easily fooled than nonreligious people.[290]

Victims of clergy abuse need all the protections the church can offer. Unfortunately, a large voice of opposition has come from an unlikely source, the Catholic Church. It has taken a very damaging position for victims of sexual abuse as to bills pending in many jurisdictions throughout the country that relate to expanding or dissolving the statute of limitations in sexual-abuse cases. Though in public statements, the Catholic Church says it is "concerned about the prevalence of sin and the crime of sexual abuse" and it claims to "support legislation that protects children," it has come out against these bills and others like it nationwide.[291]

The Catholic Church has said that such laws would have a "detrimental effect and hurt our vital ministries" and that a change in the law would "open private institutions to lawsuits about events that are from 20, 40, or 50 years ago." It says that the existence of ministries would be threatened and parishes and schools might be forced to defend themselves against claims that are many decades old.[292]

It is unfortunate that the incarnational church, a place Christ ordained to be a place of refuge, forgiveness, love, and healing, has turned out to perpetuate additional trauma and pain to victims who have suffered so much. Repeatedly, Catholic Church leaders ask us to "join with them in prayer for those that have experienced the pain of abuse, that they may find their individual paths to healing."[293] But at the same time, the church has put up a legal roadblock against victims finding such paths to healing.

The conditions and effects that victims of sexual abuse go through are potentially devastating when left untreated. The Christian community must take seriously its obligation to care for and treat victims of trauma and abuse with love, care, and understanding.

The Authentic Church must be a voice for those who have been abused, oppressed, or traumatized. It must bring healing through pastoral care and change the environment that further victimizes the victims.

As the apostle Paul said, "We who are strong ought to bear with the failings of the weak and not to please ourselves."[294] This is the rule of pastoral care, the Christian community, and the Authentic Church. We are obligated by the love of Christ and neighbors to help heal the deep wounds of sexual-abuse victims in our congregations and welcome those who ought to be in our congregation for healing.

Practitioners of pastoral care and counseling need to understand the significant effects of abuse and more important bring healing when possible. Victims may keep silent, but the abuse they have suffered still has tremendous physical and psychological effects on their well-being. The churches, the community, the court system, and the legislature must work together to expand the protection afforded victims of sexual abuse to allow healing and closure and seek justice for their harm. The American church will never be the Authentic Church while this terrible conduct continues in its confines.

Let us remember and hold in our prayers so the multitudes of victims of clergy sexual abuse will no longer have to live and continue suffering in silence.

LESSON 8

The Dirty Little Secret of the American Church

Whosoever causes one of these little ones who believe in Me to sin, it would be better for him if a millstone were hung around his neck, and he were drowned in the depth of the sea.

MATTHEW 18:6 (NKJV)

1. What does this scripture say to you?

2. Many people do not realize that the Protestant church, like the Catholic Church, has a widespread problem across all denominational lines. Do you know sexual abuse is a problem not only in Catholic churches but also Protestant churches?

3. Unknown to many in the American church, there have been significant and egregious acts by Protestant clergy of sexual abuse that have failed to generate the same level of outrage in public opinion. Why?

4. A 1990 study by the Freedom from Religion Foundation shows that sexual abuse and pedophilia by clergy is prevalent in Protestant denominations as well as in the Catholic Church. Surprisingly, in America there are more reported cases of sexual abuse among Protestant clergy than among Catholic clergy. During one period, there were approximately two members of the clergy arrested per week for sex crimes against children in North American churches. Almost 60% of those arrested were not Catholics but Protestants. Does this surprise you? If so, why?

5. Why do you think sexual abuse in the American church is not discussed?

6. Have we overlooked Protestant sexual abuse in the churches while publicizing and decrying with outrage the Catholic Church sex-abuse scandal?

7. Why does the Catholic Church get such negative and widespread press with sexual abuse when sexual abuse may be more rampant in the Protestant denominations?

8. Many victims of childhood sexual abuse have so much pain and anger that they have difficulty functioning in everyday life. Because the trauma is so deep and painful, many victims remain silent, suffer in silence, or lash out in hate and rage due to deep and unhealed wounds. Why do you think the church allows this to happen?

9. Neuroscience has taught us, "We can never erase or completely work through a traumatic experience because it remains encoded in our neurophysiology (and) there is no such thing as working something through once and for all." How can the church bring healing to the victim and awareness to the situation?

10. It is important that we understand what the word "trauma" means *wound*. How do you think sexual abuse affects people in everyday life?

11. When we deliberately avoid trying to think about something—often making matters worse—we are employing *suppression*. In contrast, *repression* is an automatic, nonconscious process that inhibits emotionally painful thoughts and memories from being brought forth in consciousness. Many times, victims of sexual abuse do not have the resources to find competent and capable counseling, pastoral care, or medical care to come to a healing place with regard to the abuse they have suffered. What can the church offer victims?

12. A century ago, Freud labored to understand the causes of debilitating symptoms, including anxiety, depression, suicide attempts, painful physical sensations, and eruptions of intense emotions associated with images of hallucinatory vividness. He had worked with 18 patients with such symptoms and concluded that in *every instance*, the symptoms were connected with sexual trauma or abuse in early childhood. What do you think of that?

13. Statistics demonstrate that abusers are usually well known to the victim, as evidenced by the fact that approximately 75–85% of offenders know their victims. How may this relate to the church?

14. Statistically, fewer male victims of sexual abuse will come forward and disclose their abuse to authorities or guardians or engage in any kind of public attention or public reporting: "8% of male victims compared to the 92% who are female." Statistics demonstrate that while approximately 90% of female victims come forward, less than 10% of male victims come forward and report. Moreover, somewhere between "50–80% of all child abuse is considered unreported." What do you think of these statistics?

15. In Matthew 18:6, this scripture that Jesus speaks may relate to sexual abuse: "If anyone causes one of these little ones—those who believe in me—to stumble, it would be better for them to have a large millstone hung around their neck and to be drowned in the depths of the sea." How does this relate to being sexually abused?

16. Do you believe that there is so much at stake when these children are abused at young ages that their futures may be devastated and destroyed? This can and will cause their lives to be disrupted mentally, and for the children to stumble and fall into abuse, addiction, and sin through no fault of their own. Comment on this.

17. Studies have concluded that around "one in four women and one in six men have been victims of sexual violence or abuse at some point in their lives which equates to about 20% of the church." One out of five in the pews of our churches may have been sexually abused. Does this change your opinion on the need to address these issues?

18. The IMA World Health Survey revealed that nearly three quarters of church leaders are not aware of the level of sexual abuse and victimization experienced within their congregations. The same study showed that slightly more than half of the pastors surveyed were not familiar with resources available on how to treat the victims of sexual abuse. Do you have resources available to your congregants?

19. Do you agree that most pastors in the church do not know enough about sexual abuse? Should we start conversations to better understand the issue? If we have a better grasp of the dynamics of sexual abuse, will this help the church develop and transform into a culture that is safer for children and for abuse survivors?

20. When we look at the abuse that has gone on in the Catholic Church, we may think things are much different for the Protestants; but while comparing the evangelicals to Catholics on sexual abuse, many think that Protestants are in fact worse. Boz Tchividjian, at the Religion Newswriters Association conference, said that too many evangelicals had "sacrificed the souls" of young victims. What do you think he means?

21. Mr. Tchividjian said, "Protestants can be very arrogant when pointing to the Catholics" and "too many Protestant institutions have sacrificed souls in order to protect their institutions." There appears to be "a looming crisis of faith in the Protestant world." Do you believe that the issue of sexual abuse goes largely unnoticed in the American church?

22. What do you think about these statistics compiled about sexual-abuse victims? Victims are

- three times more likely to suffer from depression,
- six times more likely to suffer from post-traumatic stress disorder,
- thirteen times more likely to abuse alcohol,
- twenty-six times more likely to abuse drugs, and
- four times more likely to contemplate suicide.

23. In one study of 527 victims of child abuse, it was found that there were significant spiritual injuries inflicted, such as feelings of guilt, anger, grief, despair, doubt, fear of death, and belief that God was unfair. Sexual abuse in the church has a detrimental effect on the victims' physical and mental well-being but also on their spiritual well-being—the very thing the church was assigned by God to nurture and protect. Do you think the experience of sexual abuse can affect the victims' relationship with God?

24. Many of the child abusers in the church are very sophisticated and can manipulate their victims and the whole church. One convicted child molester stated, "I consider church people easy to fool...they have a trust that comes from being Christians...they tend to be better folks all around. And they seem to want to believe in the good that exists in all people...I think they want to believe in people. And because of that, you can easily convince, with or without convincing words."

What do you think about this? What can we do to better protect the children?

25. There does not seem to be any evidence to suggest that the "Catholic priests are gangs of sexual predators, as they are portrayed." Though there have been no formal studies comparing the rates of sexual abuse in differing Protestant denominations, insurers have been assessing the risks of sexual abuse since they began to offer riders regarding liability policies to churches in the 1980s. Two of the largest insurers report no higher risks in covering Catholic Churches than Protestant churches. There is no hard evidence

of a higher risk assessment of sexual abuse in the Catholic Church than in Protestant churches—follow the money to the truth. Nationally, these insurance companies are not evaluating the Catholic Church as a higher risk than Protestant churches, which is a significant factual finding. What do you think about this?

26. "It would be incorrect to call (clergy sexual abuse) a Catholic problem," said Church Mutual's risk control manager. "We do not see one denomination above another. It's equal. It's also equal among large metropolitan churches and small rural churches." Catholic churches are not considered a greater risk or charged higher premiums. What does this say about all churches?

27. The National Center for Missing and Exploited Children notes that the organization has received more than 825,000 reports of child abuse, and there is no statistical evidence that the Catholic Church has a greater likelihood of sexual-abuse cases than other denominations. Boz Tchividjian, director of GRACE, is convinced that the "Protestant world is teetering on the edge of a sex-abuse scandal similar to the one that had rocked the Catholic Church." If this happens, what effect will it have on the American church?

28. A sexual-abuse scandal in the Protestant church would be a significant problem because it "includes tens of thousands of denominations and nondenominational churches, ministries and boards. Unlike the Catholic Church, there is no Vatican, no central location of authority." Why would this be a problem?

29. There is some indication that "religious" sex offenders may be the most dangerous sex offenders. Studies show that sex offenders who have and maintain significant involvement with religious institutions have "more sexual offense convictions, more victims, and younger victims." Moreover, other studies have demonstrated that clergy and nonclergy sex offenders often share the same characteristics except that clergy offenders are more likely to use force in their sexual abuse. What do you think of this?

30. The conditions and effects that victims of sexual abuse go through are potentially devastating when left untreated. The Christian community must take seriously its obligation to care for and treat victims of trauma and abuse with love, care, and understanding. How can we better help victims of sexual abuse?

CHAPTER 9

What Christians (Christian Church) Owe the Jews[xxxii]

And so all Israel will be saved, as it is written: "The Deliverer will come out of Zion, And He will turn away ungodliness from Jacob; For this is My covenant with them, When I take away their sins.

ROMANS 11:26–27 (NKJV)

February 25, 2014 marked the tenth anniversary of the release of Mel Gibson's hugely successful and controversial movie *The Passion of the Christ.* [xxxiii, 295] One of the most contentious issues this movie brought forth was Gibson's widely perceived anti-Semitic portrayal of the Jewish religious leaders as well as the ordinary Jewish people during the time of Christ. Many feared that a distorted and biased portrayal of these aspects of the story would further erode relations between Christians and Jews.

The crux of the issue revolves around several scenes in the movie depicting the so-called trial of Jesus. The Jews' treatment and response to Jesus along with the description of the destruction of the temple when Jesus died were clearly exaggerated and conflated. The movie makes it appear that the death of Jesus caused the temple's destruction. Scripture reports that the temple curtain was torn from top to bottom, the earth shook, the rocks split, tombs broke open, and bodies were raised to life.[296] We must remember this was only a Hollywood

---

[xxxii] This chapter was originally a response paper to Professor George Hunsinger's paper *After Barth: A Christian Appreciation of Jews and Judaism,* which was originally presented at the Karl Barth conference and later published in *Commonweal Magazine*; a longer version appeared in the journal *Pro Ecclesia*.

[xxxiii] My wife is a Ukrainian Jew who fled Ukraine with her family because of anti-Semitic persecution. Many of her family members had been held in Nazi concentration camps decades before and bear the physical and emotional scars of anti-Semitic hatred at the hands of Christians and the Christian Church. Anti-Semitic or anti-Judaic theology therefore cannot be accepted, "For what started out as a tiny mustard seed grows into a large tree" (Matthew 13:31–32).

production. But more important, this raises the question of how the Authentic Church should understand its and God's relationship with Israel and the Jews.

Are the ways these scenes were depicted in the movie justified by anything found in the Gospels, and does that help or hurt Christian and Jewish relations? When Jesus was brought to the Roman governor, he asked Him, "Jesus? Are you the King of the Jews?" Jesus' reply was, "Yes, it is as you say."[297] During this time, it was the governors' custom to release a prisoner to appease the Jewish community under its rule. The Roman governor at that time, as we know, was Pontius Pilate. He asked, "Which of these two do you want me to release," referring to Jesus and Barabbas. They responded by saying to release Barabbas. Pilate asked, "What shall I do then with this Jesus who is called the Christ?" The Jews answered in unison, "Crucify Him! Crucify Him!" Then, as depicted in scripture, they said these very troubling lines that for centuries have been a lightning rod for anti-Semitic beliefs: "Let His blood be on us and on our children."[298] This exchange in the movie has been problematic to Jews and Christians. It has been claimed that Gibson's refusal to bring Jewish scholars onboard as consultants was because many Jews "were afraid of the consequences (of) the impact of this imagery."[299]

In the movie, the tearing of the temple curtain and the subsequent earthquake take place at the time of Jesus' death, but the destruction of the temple did not take place until AD 70.

> According to (Yvonne) Gomez, (a Christian research consultant) this scene points to a "replacement theology" upholding the mistaken medieval idea that Christianity (*Ecclesia*) has replaced Judaism (*Synagoga*). The brokenness visible in the temple evokes the brokenness of *Synagoga*."[300] Both of these two particular scenes in the movie, especially the former, were highly offensive to many. "It positioned the Jewish leaders as a soulless mafia, the apostles and Jesus as outside the Jewish religious life, and the Jewish people as unanimously involved in eagerly seeing Jesus tortured and murdered.[301]

According to the *Catechism of the Council of Trent* (notes iv, 30),

> The question of the theological responsibility for Jesus' death is a long settled one. From a theological perspective, (the Catechism) articulated without hesitancy what should be the major dramatic or moral focus of any dramatization of the event for Christians—a profound self-examination of our own guilt, through sin, for Jesus' death:
> In this guilt are involved all those who fall frequently into sin; for, as our sins consigned Christ the Lord to the death of the cross, most certainly those

who wallow in sin and iniquity crucify to themselves again the Son of God …
This guilt seems more enormous in us than in the Jews since, if they had
known it, they would never have crucified the Lord of glory; while we, on the
contrary, professing to know him, yet denying him by our actions, seem in
some sort to lay violent hands on him.[302]

Anything less than this "overriding preoccupation" to avoid caricaturing
the Jewish people, which history has all too frequently shown us, will result
almost inevitably in a violation of the basic hermeneutic principle of the Council
in this regard: "The Jews should not be presented as rejected or accursed by
God as if this followed from Sacred Scripture (*Nostra Aetate*)."[303]

This movie and the ensuing discussion have brought to light once again the tense relations
between Christians and Jews over the centuries.

In this chapter, I will show why I believe the Christian church must confront many of these
troubling issues in regard to Jewish and Christian relations before we can have an authentic
Christianity.

On September 4, [2014], Pope Francis wrote a letter to Eugenio Scalfari, an
atheist and journalist who writes for the Italian paper *La Repubblica*, replying
to an article Scalfari had written asking, among other things, "What should be
said to the Jewish brethren concerning the promise that God made to them:
Is that an empty promise?" (The Pope answered,) "What I can tell you, with
St. Paul, is that God has never neglected his faithfulness to the covenant with
Israel."[304]

In light of these particular issues, the Authentic Church must have an understanding of
the importance and significance of Israel and the Jews and its relation to Christians and the
Authentic Church. Though we are one people of God demonstrated in two faiths, is not the
Holy Spirit continuing to work through Israel, the Jews, and the Christian church?

When Christians study the Holy Spirit, all too often they minimize, limit, or subordinate
its role and work. The Holy Spirit is part of the Godhead—the Father, Son, and the Holy Spirit
and coequal in power and authority. Some try to relegate the work of the Holy Spirit only to
the New Testament church. In Acts 1:4–5 (NIV), Jesus instructs the apostles, "Do not leave
Jerusalem, but wait for the gift my Father promised, which you have heard me speak about.
For John baptized with water, but in a few days you will be baptized with the Holy Spirit."[305]
This seems to be the launching point for a study of the work of the Holy Spirit. The Holy

Spirit is evident in the Old Testament working through the nation of Israel and in the New Testament church and with all peoples and nations uniting the one people of God in both faiths.

How does the Holy Spirit relate to the radical particular found in Jesus Christ and to Israel, the Gentiles, and all people? We will look at and discuss these issues, and I will demonstrate how the Holy Spirit has been at work for humanity since time primordial and how the Holy Spirit continues to work through Israel and be its consolation in and through the New Testament church and to the world.

The Holy Spirit propagates the work of the Lord and reconciles a fallen humanity with a perfect and righteous God for all time. I will propose that the people of Israel have not been displaced in the plan of God's redemption for humanity but rather that God—through the Holy Spirit—continues to work through Israel and the Jews to bless all nations and see the ultimate fulfillment of God's plan. Last, Israel has not been replaced by Christianity but that Christianity has been grafted into Israel.

The theory that a "strong or soft supersessionism"[xxxiv] of the Christian church has allowed it to extend, fulfill, or replace Israel must be looked at theologically and biblically. The central issue is where Judaism stands in relation to Christianity and the person and work of Jesus Christ. Is Christianity an outgrowth of Judaism? Are they mutually exclusive? Or are they inclusive to one another and what I call dialectically harmonious?[xxxv]

Does any form of supersessionism—be it strong or soft—have anti-Semitic or anti-Judaic elements? What model should be adopted for discussion of the one people and the two faiths of God? Let us see by what process God works through the Jews and Israel.

THE APPEARANCE OF THE HOLY SPIRIT

We see the appearance of the Holy Spirit as early as Genesis 1:2 (NIV): "Now the earth was formless and empty, darkness was over the surface of the deep, and the Spirit of God was hovering over the waters."[306] What is the Spirit of God or the Holy Spirit? Is it God? Is it part of God? Is it fully God? The answer is relevant to Israel and the New Testament church. If the Holy Spirit is God, we must ask what it does. In the Old Testament, the Spirit is the divine

---

[xxxiv] Supersessionism is the traditional Christian belief that Christianity is the fulfillment of Biblical Judaism and therefore that Jews who deny that Jesus is the Jewish Messiah fall short of their calling as God's Chosen people. In its more radical form, supersessionism maintains that the Jews are no longer considered to be God's chosen people. This understanding is generally termed "replacement theology."

[xxxv] I have coined the term *dialectically harmonious* to describe seemingly opposing positions that appear to oppose each other but are compatible with and indispensable to one another.

dynamo that quickens life, empowers people, and inspires prophets. In the synoptic Gospels, the Spirit quickens, empowers, and inspires Jesus and the New Testament church. Luke highlights the intimate connection between the Holy Spirit and Jesus in His birth, baptism, temptations, Nazareth manifesto, healings, prayer life, and passion—to which Paul adds His resurrection.

The role of the Spirit is as the mediator of the Son's relation to the Father in mortal time and eternity, as the source of the otherness and particularity of Jesus, and as the agent of His freedom and obedience. The Spirit radiates the humanity of Jesus. The Holy Spirit forms a body for the Son.[307] God's plan for humanity began in the Godhead when the Father, Son, and Holy Spirit elected humanity to be reconciled to themselves.

> In the beginning, before time and space as we know them, before creation, before there was any reality distinct from God which could be the object of the love of God or the setting for His acts of freedom, God anticipated and determined within Himself (in the power of His love and freedom, of His knowingness and willingness) that the goal and meaning of all His dealings with the as yet non-existent universe should be through His Son. He would be gracious towards humanity, uniting Himself with them. In the beginning, it was the choice of the Father Himself to establish this covenant with man by giving up His Son for them, so that He Himself might become man, representing the fulfillment of His grace. In the beginning it was the Son's choice to be obedient to grace, and therefore to offer Himself up and to become man in order that this covenant might be made a reality.[308]

In his paper on supersessionism, George Hunsinger argues,

> Supersessionism in some form remains unavoidable because there is only one covenant and only one people of God. It is impossible to read Holy Scripture in any other way; there simply is no other covenant than the one established by God with Israel, and thus no other people could possibly be the elect people of God. By virtue of this divine election, Israel's unique status as God's elect is irrevocable and eternal, and nothing Israel can do, whether in obedience or disobedience, can revoke it.[309]

The Holy Spirit has always been working through Israel, then the Gentiles, and all people—God's will.

So what is the status of Israel and its covenant as it relates to the Christian Church?

> [Has] therefore this people ceased to be the chosen, the holy people of God. Into its place there has now stepped the people of Christians from among Jews and Gentiles. (Is) the Church the historical replacement of Israel? Israel as such has become with the foundation and existence of the Church a thing of the past.[310]

> There was for him no doubt that Jesus Christ was a Jew, (CD 2:2:204) … Jesus' "environment" was Jewish. His apostles were Jews. "Whoever has Jesus Christ in faith cannot wish not to have the Jews. He must have them along with Jesus Christ as His ancestors and kinsmen. Otherwise he cannot have even the Jew Jesus. Otherwise with the Jews he rejects Jesus himself. This is what is at stake, and therefore, in fact, the very basis of the Church, when it has to be demanded of Gentile Christians that they should not approach any Israelite without the greatest attention and sympathy" (CD 2:2:289). And even the patriarchs of Israel, Abraham, Isaac and Jacob, Moses, David, and Elijah, "and they alone, ought in strict justice to be called fathers of the church" (CD 2:2:224)[311]

Karl Barth[xxxvi] believed that the standard for theological analysis was the Word.

> It is within the context of the election of Jesus Christ that the election of the Jewish people—and the Church—is situated. According to Barth, "the election of grace, as the election of Jesus Christ, is simultaneously the eternal election of the one community of God by the existence of which Jesus Christ is to be attested to the whole world and the whole world summoned to faith in Jesus Christ. This election of the community of God exists in the twofold form of Israel and the Church. In Barth's words, "to this unity and twofold form of Jesus Christ Himself there corresponds that of the community of God and its election. It exists according to God's eternal decree as the people of Israel (in the whole range of its history in past and future, ante and post Christum

---

[xxxvi] Karl Barth (1886–1968) was the most important Swiss theologian of the twentieth century; his influence extended far beyond Switzerland. He is considered alongside Aquinas, Calvin, and Schleiermacher to be one of the greatest thinkers in the history of the Christian tradition. Barth reshaped Protestant theology into systematic theology with his writing of 9,300 pages of *Church Dogmatics* according to Barbara Zellweger, "Karl Barth Biography." *The Center for Barth Studies*, Princeton Theological Seminary.

natum), and at the same time as the Church of the Jews and Gentiles (from its revelation at Pentecost to its fulfillment by the second coming of Christ)."[312]

For Barth, Israel is representative of those who reject their own election while the church consists of those who live in light of their election. As he states, "Israel is the people of the Jews which resists its election; the Church is the gathering of Jews and Gentiles called on the ground of its election." Summarizing Barth's view, David E. Holwerda observes, "Jesus Christ is the Elect One, but what is elected in Christ is a community with a twofold form, Israel and the Church."[313]

Like Augustine, Barth believed that Israel's existence and unbelief functioned as a sign. Israel's unbelief exemplified the sorry state of humanity in its rebellion against God. In contrast to some theologians such as Kant and Schleiermacher, though, Barth placed a high importance upon Israel's role in the history of redemption. As Michael Wyschogrod states, "Because he reads Scripture obediently, (Barth) becomes aware of the centrality of Israel in God's relation with man and with the very message that Christianity proclaims to the world."[314]

First, he rejected punitive supersessionism in which national Israel is viewed as being permanently rejected because of its disobedience. As John J. Johnson states, "For Barth, the Jews were, are, and will remain the chosen people of God—nothing can alter this divinely ordained fact." In his *Dogmatics in Outline*, for example, Barth asserted that Israel's continuing existence in light of ongoing persecutions is the only "visible and tangible" evidence of God's existence.[315]

Second, Barth affirmed a form of economic supersessionism in which Israel's unique role ended with Christ's death and resurrection.

The new Israel ... is not (like the old Israel) a "nation," a natural society ... but a people gathered solely by the preaching of the Word and the free election and calling of the Spirit. The first Israel, constituted on the basis of physical descent from Abraham, has fulfilled its mission now that the Savior of the world has sprung from it and its Messiah has appeared. Its members can only accept this fact with gratitude and in confirmation of their own deepest election and calling attached themselves to the people of this Savior, their own King, whose members the Gentiles are now called to be as well. Its mission as a natural community has now run its course and cannot be continued or repeated.[316]

Professor George Hunsinger writes, "Loving Christ is inseparable from loving the Jews. Not only when the Jews are not loved Christ himself is dishonored,"[317] but I would go one step further and argue that if the Jews are rejected and despised, so is Jesus Christ, a Jew. Must we reject any form of supersessionism as anti-Semitic and anti-Judaic? One covenant, one people, two faiths expressed in two ways may be an alternative.

Professor Hunsinger has suggested as to the relationship between Jews and Christians that "no one can heal this wound."[318] I propose the wounds could be healed when treated with love, respect, and mutual understanding of both faiths. How do we reconcile these two seemingly dialectical faiths? The only way to love and heal wounds may be found in scripture with acts of mercy and mutual respect through the work and intercession of the Holy Spirit.

Professor Hunsinger has raised this practical point.

> I will suggest that there is only one covenant, and thus only one people of God, and yet there are also two faiths. Which in some ways, though not all, are diametrically opposed—represents a festering wound in the one people of God. No one knows how this wound can be healed. Neither Christians nor Jews know how to heal it. Only God can heal it.[319]

Is there an example that we may look at to discern how these two dialectically opposed or dialectically harmonious faiths may relate? The answer may be found in an unlikely example. The person and work of Jesus Christ may address this particular situation in the exchange between Him and the Samaritan woman at the well. (Whether Jesus is embraced by the Jews as the Messiah or Mediator of God's revelation, or prophet, or great teacher, is not determinative at this point but illustrative.)

THE WOMAN AT THE WELL

Regardless of one's belief or understanding of who Jesus is, He lays out a morally and theologically consistent answer to a most problematic situation: how do we treat others, specifically the Jews, when perceived of different faiths? When Jesus had this great theological exchange with the woman at the well, she was surprised Jesus would engage her in conversation. He asked her for a drink of water knowing she was a Samaritan and Jews did not socialize with or ever acknowledge Samaritans. She replied, "How can you ask me for a drink?" (John 4:9 NIV) She implied that they were of different religious practices but not necessarily of different faiths. Jesus supported that proposition by suggesting, "If you knew the gift of God and who it is that asks you for a drink, you would have asked him and he would have given you living water" (John 4:10 NIV).

Jesus proclaimed to this non-Jew that eternal life was available to all, not just the Jews who worshiped on a special mountain or in Jerusalem. Jesus opened salvation to those who were not Jews but worshiped the one true God Jews and Christians now worship. Jesus said, "A time is coming and has now come when the true worshipers will worship the Father in spirit and truth, for they are the kind of worshipers the Father seeks" (John 4:23 NIV).

This exchange between this great Rabbi, Jesus, and the Samaritan woman stands for the proposition that one should be allowed to continue in his or her cultic worship and faith. Jews and Christian believers do worship the one true God but in different cultural contexts. Worshiping the one God in different ways is theologically acceptable. To worship a different God in the same ways would be heretical as illustrated by this exchange. We do not have a problem in that Jews and Christians ascribe to the one true God of the Old and New Testaments personified in the New Testament as Jesus. This exchange stands for the proposition that all humanity is accepted by God, the great universal hope.

GOD'S PLAN FOR THE JEWS

The core of the conflict between Judaism and Christianity is the acceptance or rejection of the person and work of Jesus Christ. This can be reconciled at this time only by an understanding and appreciation for the special dispensation of the Jews by God. For us as Christians to force or inject our acceptance of the person and work of Jesus Christ as we see it through the theological study of the New Testament onto the Jews may be unbiblical in light of God's directives and dispensations to the Gentiles through the apostle Paul as found in Romans.

> For I could wish that I myself were cursed and cut off from Christ for the sake of my brothers, those of my own race, the people of Israel. Theirs is the adoption as sons; theirs the divine glory, the covenants, the receiving of the law, the temple worship and the promises. Theirs are the patriarchs, and from them is traced the human ancestry of Christ, who is God over all, forever praised! Amen. (Romans 9:3–5 NIV)

> What if God, choosing to show his wrath and make his power known, bore with great patience the objects of his wrath—prepared for destruction? What if he did this to make the riches of his glory known to the objects of his mercy,

whom he prepared in advance for glory—even us, whom he also called, not only from the Jews but also from the Gentiles? (Romans 9:22–24 NIV)

I ask then: Did God reject his people? By no means! I am an Israelite myself, a descendant of Abraham, from the tribe of Benjamin. God did not reject his people, whom he foreknew. Don't you know what the Scripture says in the passage about Elijah—how he appealed to God against Israel? (Romans 11:1–2 NIV)

Again I ask: Did they stumble so as to fall beyond recovery? Not at all! Rather, because of their transgression, salvation has come to the Gentiles to make Israel envious. But if their transgression means riches for the world, and their loss means riches for the Gentiles, how much greater riches will their fullness bring! (Romans 11:11–12 NIV)

In light of these scriptures that relate to Israel, any attempt to make the Jews "believe" through aggressive evangelizing may be attempting to force the hand of God's timeline resulting in a condition of supersessionism, which should not exist. That is why over decades, the issues of supersessionism and anti-Semitism have been a festering wound in Jewish-Christian relations. St. Paul understood the timeline of God as it related to Israel and is consistent in the election of Israel. Even John the apostle wrote of Israel's election: "Then I heard the number of those who were sealed: 144,000 from all the tribes of Israel" (Revelation 7:4 NIV).

It is suggested that soft supersessionism is the view that the new covenant does not replace the old covenant but instead fulfills, extends, and supplements it while also fundamentally confirming it. "One covenant one people and two faiths."[320] This softens the blow though it still regards Judaism as being incomplete or lesser. This proposition may instill a sense of fear and apprehension of Christians among the Jews about the possible coercion and absorption of their distinctiveness by not allowing them to retain their individual identity before God. The Jews feel they have been through enough coercion at the hands of Christians in the past. Look at some Christian history as it relates to Israel and the Jews. Article 24 of the 1920 Nazi Party Platform read,

We demand the freedom of all religious confessions in the state, insofar as they do not jeopardize the state's existence or conflict with the manners and moral sentiments of the Germanic race. The Party as such, upholds the point of view of a positive Christianity without tying itself confessionally to any one confession. It combats the Jewish-materialistic spirit at home and abroad and is convinced that a permanent recovery of our people can only be achieved from within on the basis of the common good before individual good.[321]

Any form of supersessionism does in fact have elements of anti-Judaism and anti-Semitism at its root. The correct analogy or standard in evaluating Christianity is not that it fulfilled, extended, or supplemented Judaism but that Christianity has been grafted into Judaism. Christianity is absorbed and fulfilled by the Jews and Israel through Christ. The foundational basis for this is written by the apostle Paul: "If some of the branches have been broken off (Jew), and you (Gentiles), though a wild olive shoot, have been grafted in among the others and now share in the nourishing sap from the olive root, (Both Jew and Gentile) (Romans 11:17 NIV).

This is made possible by the covenant promised by God through the work of the Holy Spirit and Christ.

Did God reject Israel? By no means. Christians need to understand that God did not reject his people whom He foreknew and had chosen before creation in pretemporal election.[xxxvii] God's plan for humanity is still unfolding and specifically in the nation of Israel and the Jewish people.

What does it mean in Romans 11 when Paul shows the non-repudiation of Israel as a whole belonging to God's covenant by pointing to the remaining "remnant" of Israel? This remnant of the Jews is in the church together with those Gentiles who are called. With their faith in Christ and their subsequent membership in the church they do not lose their membership in Judaism. They stand in continuity with the believers of the first testament.[322] According to Barth, "It would be anti-Judaism if the Gentile Christians were to regard this as irrelevant. They would thereby be ashamed of the Jewish origin of the church. The fact that Jews who believe in Christ do not reject their membership in Israel testifies that reconciliation in Christ is not a repudiation of Israel, not a "new revelation" over against its gracious election but its fulfillment. That means, however, that this remnant stands "for the totality of Israel." It is "the clear proof" that "God's election is not simply transferred to the Gentiles from

---

[xxxvii] Ephesians 1:4 (NIV), "For he chose us in him before the creation of the world to be holy and blameless in his sight", gives support to the doctrine of pretemporal election to demonstrate that every human being was elected for salvation in Christ before the creation of the world.

Israel, departing from Israel as its original object." The remnant confirms the "election of Israel."[323]

Jewish and Christian Dialogue on Faith

The strategy adopted by Christians in the past was "the day is long past when Christians might hope to alleviate this wound by making Israel jealous."[324] This concept should be replaced with a full Christological understanding of the time and eschatological place the Jewish people have inhabited historically and biblically.

The Jews are to be recognized as the complete bearers of God in whom revelation to humanity was exhibited through the prophets, including Jesus Christ, whether accepted or rejected. In light of this knowledge, Karl Barth discouraged all Christian missions from proselytizing Jews in any effort that would target or marginalize them. Although this position of no organized and targeting evangelization to Israel and the Jews runs counter to the Great Commission,[xxxviii] if no one was to preach the message of hope and restoration found in Christ, one could not understand the theological implications it could have on God's redemptive plan for Israel.

The exchange between Jesus and the woman at the well is the model by which all discussions of faith ought to occur—in love, truth, equality, and with a genuine understanding and concern for humanity. This is consistent with both faiths and the Great Commission and properly frames the conduct of Christian interaction with all faiths, including Judaism.

Professor Hunsinger stated, "The covenant of God to Israel is unique, irrevocable and eternal."[325] This basis of theological interpretation is also the basis for the unique nature of God's relationship with Israel. To require Israel to comply with the ordinary requirements and tenets of faith in Christ on the Christian churches' timeline would be like forcing a square block into a circular hole until the time that God has ordained for it to happen.

The Council of Jerusalem

The issues raised at the Council of Jerusalem are relevant to Jewish-Christian relations and practice. Questions were raised such as, Are the new converts that are not Jewish required to follow Jewish customs? The answer was no. The new question in light of the council is,

---

[xxxviii] The Great Commission is Jesus' command to the disciples to go into all the world and preach the gospel and make disciples (Matthew 28:18–20).

do converts from Judaism need to lose their identity and cultural religious practices if they embrace Christ? The answer to this question should also be no.

The Council of Jerusalem as recorded in Acts 15 sheds light on the issue of how Judaism ought to be treated in light of Christianity and supersessionism. The issue of what to do with these new Gentile converts who were not Jewish arose. One question was if they should be circumcised according to the custom of Moses. Many great teachers, including Paul, were in disagreement on this issue. Some believed that according to Jewish Law, to be accepted, they must be circumcised and obey all the requirements of Moses and the law.

Peter said, "God made a choice that the Gentiles might hear the message of the gospel and believe."[326] Might not unbelieving Jews also hear the message in the fullness of time and believe? Peter stated, "God who knows the heart showed that he accepted them by giving the Holy Spirit to them. He made no distinction between us and them; he purified their heart by faith. Why do you try to test God by putting a yoke that they cannot bear?"[327] Then after hearing all the reports of these new converts, James, the pastor at Jerusalem, declared, "We should not make it difficult for the Gentiles turning to God."[328] In sum, they did not have to be circumcised and follow all ritual rules for living.

Though the shoe is on the other foot as it relates now to Christians deciding how to treat the Jews, theologically, ought not the same type of analysis apply? The decision ought to be based on the grace of God to all peoples, customs, and cultures. We should accept that there is a special plan and dispensation for the Jews and that God has promised, "After this I will return and rebuild David's fallen tent. Its ruins I will rebuild and I will restore it that the remnant of men may serve the Lord."[329] They will be purified in their heart by faith too. We need to treat the Jews with the same love, understanding, and equality they treated these new converts back at the Council of Jerusalem who came to be called Christians. This is the model of evangelism, temperance, love, understanding, and mutual respect that theologians and specifically Christians must adopt as it relates to their interactions with Israel and the Jews.

So was it possible to be a Christian without ceasing to be a Jew? This question is as relevant now as it was almost 2,000 years ago. Yes, "it was possible to be a Christian without ceasing to be a Jew."[330] "God is he who [loves his Son Jesus Christ], in his Son Jesus Christ all his children, in his children all human beings, and in human beings the whole creation. (Karl Barth, II/1 315 rev.)

It starts with God the Father, whom all religious Christians and Jews worship. Is not God the starting point for faith, belief, and practice? Israel is not in unbelief toward almighty God; it has not for the most part yet embraced the person and work of Jesus Christ. Support for this proposition can be found in the Chalcedonian Creed (AD 451) which states in part, "Consubstantial [co-essential] with the father ... inconfusedly, unchangeably, indivisibly, inseparably; the distinction of natures being by no means taken away by the union … in one Person and one subsistence."

If Christ is God and the Jews worship the only true God, why is it necessary for Christians to think that only through acknowledgment and acceptance of the person and work of Jesus Christ can the Jews be saved or need to be saved? If God has established a special dispensation to the nation and has further eschatological plans, this position is incomplete and God's plan has not yet been fully unveiled and realized as it relates to Israel and the Jews.

Has the conduct and actions of Christians through the centuries been no better than barbarians forcing a religious belief on those unwilling to accept it or who from a theological standpoint already worship the true God? If they fail to accept it, will we kill, persecute, or exclude them? That is certainly not a picture of the God in Jesus Christ we serve.

We must acknowledge that all supersessionism whether soft or strong has elements of anti-Semitism. If we believe Judaism is missing or incomplete, that goes to the heart of it being a lesser or incomplete religion as compared to Christianity. We must realize that Christianity is an outgrowth of Judaism and if not for Judaism there would be no Christianity. To claim the Christian church replaced, extended, or completed the Judaic promises or covenants is anti-Semitic at its core.

Is a Judaic Christianity possible? The answer is yes as indicated by the Council of Jerusalem along with the story of the woman at the well and other biblical references we have noted. "Christianity cannot have Jesus Christ without also loving the Jews."[331] Christians must embrace this not out of a sense of duty or obligation but to fully understand the significance and relevance of Judaism to Christianity and Christianity to Judaism.

The late Professor Charles R. Erdman, professor of practical theology at Princeton, wrote this as it relates to the issue in his commentary on John 4:21–25.

> Our Lord now makes a revelation appealing to hope. vs. 21–25. He tells the woman that her trouble has not been as to the place of worship, but as to the fact; she has never worshiped at all. "God is a Spirit" and true worship is therefore not a question of place but of faith and love, not a matter of form and ceremony, but of spiritual reality; its essence is found in a true knowledge of God and in fellowship with him as a loving Father. Jerusalem has indeed been the divinely appointed place of worship, related to the revelation of salvation made through the Jews, but the time has come when there are to be no local restrictions to worship. True worshipers will not be concerned with place and symbol, but will worship "in spirit and truth." That there is need of some Mediator to give this fuller knowledge of God, and to bring guilty souls into

fellowship with him, is suggested by the immediate reply of the woman: "I know that Messiah cometh ... he will declare unto us all things." Some hope of such a Savior had been kept alive in her heart, in spite of all her ignorance and sin.

The place and practice of how one worships God is not determinative; God is spirit and must be worshiped in spirit and truth. Do devout Jews worship God in spirit and truth? I believe that like devout Christians, they do. Is there any point in scripture that shows many of these elements operating at the same time? The work of the Holy Spirit through Israel and its future recognition of the Messiah prove that both faiths are dialectically harmonious.

THE CONSOLATION OF ISRAEL

I believe that representative Israel has already received the Messiah found in Christ. Let us turn to scriptures for support of this proposition.

> Now, there was a man in Jerusalem called Simeon, who was righteous and devout. He was waiting for the consolation of Israel, and the Holy Spirit was on him. It had been revealed to him by the Holy Spirit that he would not die before he had seen the Lord's Messiah. Moved by the Spirit, he went into the temple courts. When the parents brought in the child Jesus to do for him what the custom of the Law required, Simeon took him in his arms and praised God, saying: "Sovereign Lord, as you have promised, you may now dismiss your servant in peace. For my eyes have seen your salvation, which you have prepared in the sight of all nations: a light for revelation to the Gentiles, and the glory of your people Israel.[332]

At the same time to confirm the prophecy as spoken by Simeon that this baby was in fact the Messiah, Anna, a prophetess from the tribe of Asher who was at the temple daily in prayer and fasting, said, "Gave thanks to God and spoke about the child to all who were looking forward to the redemption of Jerusalem."[333]

Here we have two old Jewish saints representing as it were the very best of the old covenant that was giving way to the new.[334] This takes place via the coming and recognition of the true Messiah and Lord of the world. This person in Jesus was recognized and acknowledged as the consolation of Israel by the Jews. This was the first of gifts that were to come by the power of the Holy Spirit. Israel as represented by Simeon and Anna received the Messiah.

The Consolation of Israel and the First Palm Sunday

We have celebrated Palm Sunday for the last twenty centuries. This seemingly Christian holiday may offer insight as to how the Holy Spirit works in and through Israel. It will also shed more light on the issue of supersessionism. The gospel accounts record that the first Palm Sunday coincided with Passover; this was the day of Jesus' triumphant entry into Jerusalem and the beginning of His last week of human life. He fulfilled Old Testament prophecy when He entered Jerusalem with those in attendance laying out their robes and waving palm branches in reverence and celebration of Him. These were Jews welcoming and praising Him saying, "Hosanna in the Highest! Blessed is He who comes in the name of the Lord! Hosanna in the Highest!"[335] So for a moment, Israel had received its Savior. This also confirms the acceptance of Israel to God and God to Israel through Christ.

The theological problem we discussed as to whether Israel/Jews worship the same God as Christians and whether the Christian church has replaced Israel was addressed by Thomas Torrance on the issue of how we are to relate our Trinitarian (Father, Son and Holy Spirit) understanding of God to the unitary understanding of God that occurs in traditional Judaism. He sheds light on how God related with and through Israel, then to Christians, and ultimately to all humanity.[336]

> The historical dialogue with Israel's God chose to reveal himself and actualize that self revelation to mankind in such a way that Israel the immediate receiver would be molded and shaped into an appropriate vessel for its connection to all peoples. Throughout all the vicissitude of Israel's national, social and religious existence the Word of God came to Israel mediated through servants of the Lord like Moses, Elijah, Jeremiah … but always in such a way that the holy presence of God himself in his Word imprinted his truth upon the innermost being of this people with the result that all its relations with God … so that it could be the bearer of divine revelation for all mankind.
>
> We should avoid compromising the truth on the one hand and being narrow-minded on the other. And we should always welcome and accept those others in a way that honors and reflects the Lord's welcome.[337]
>
> Jews and Christians together are one in Christ for the time being, and apparently until the end of history.[338]

Let's begin to treat each other with love, humility, respect, and understanding as brothers and sisters in one faith in God. Israel is not in disobedience to Christ but rather in a special relationship with Christ until the time is fulfilled when God's covenant working through Christ to Israel is fulfilled.

> This is the formulation which we have adopted and this or a similar formulation is necessary if the unity of the election of the community (grounded in the election of the one Jesus Christ) is to remain visible. We cannot, therefore, call the Jews the "rejected" and the Church the "elected" community. The object of election is neither Israel for itself or the Church for itself, but both together in their unity.[339]

God's plan for Israel started with the mediation of God's presence to Israel and the Jews and then to the Gentiles and the world; it will end where it all began with God's people's hearts being purified by faith in the Messiah. Jews and Christians, the Old and New Testament church, are dialectically harmonious until the fulfillment of all things. This should and ought to be reflected in the Authentic Church.

LESSON 9

What Christians (Christian Church) Owe the Jews

And so all Israel will be saved, as it is written: "The Deliverer will come out of Zion, And He will turn away ungodliness from Jacob; For this is My covenant with them, When I take away their sins."

ROMANS 11:26–27 (NKJV)

1. What does this scripture say to you?

2. February 25, 2014, marked the tenth anniversary of the release of Mel Gibson's hugely successful and controversial movie *The Passion of the Christ*. One of the most contentious issues this movie brought forth was Gibson's widely perceived anti-Semitic portrayal of the Jewish religious leaders as well as the ordinary Jewish people during the time of Christ. What do you think of the movie overall?

3. How can the Authentic Church understand God's relationship with Israel and the Jews?

4. A popular theological concept related to Israel and the New Testament church is called "Replacement Theology," upholding the mistaken medieval idea that Christianity (*Ecclesia*) has replaced Judaism (*Synagoga*). What do you think of that concept?

5. Much anti-Semitic theology has come from the displaced understanding regarding the execution of Jesus Christ. The *Catechism of the Council of Trent* states:

    > In this guilt are involved all those who fall frequently into sin; for, as our sins consigned Christ the Lord to the death of the cross, most certainly those who wallow in sin and iniquity crucify to themselves again the Son of God…This guilt seems more enormous in us than in the Jews since, if they had known it, they would never have crucified the Lord of glory; while we, on the contrary, professing to know him, yet denying him by our actions, seem in some sort to lay violent hands on him.

    The question of the theological responsibility for Jesus' death is a long-settled one. Who was responsible for the death of Jesus?

6. The Pope was recently questioned, "What should be said to the Jewish brethren concerning the promise that God made to them: Is that an empty promise?" (The Pope answered,) "What I can tell you, with St. Paul, is that God has never neglected his faithfulness to the covenant with Israel." Do you agree with this statement?

7. Has this movie and the ensuing discussion brought to light once again the tense relations between Christians and Jews over the centuries?

8. The Authentic Church must have an understanding of the importance and significance of Israel and the Jews and their relation to Christians and the Authentic Church. Though we are one people of God demonstrated in two faiths, is not the Holy Spirit continuing to work through Israel, the Jews, and the Christian church?

9. In Acts 1:4–5, Jesus instructs the apostles, "Do not leave Jerusalem, but wait for the gift my Father promised, which you have heard me speak about. For John baptized with water, but in a few days you will be baptized with the Holy Spirit." This seems to be a good launching point for a study of the work of the Holy Spirit. Is the Holy Spirit also evident in the Old Testament working through the nation of Israel and in the New Testament church and with all peoples and nations uniting the one people of God in both faiths?

10. Do you agree with what I proposed, that the people of Israel have not been displaced in the plan of God's redemption for humanity but rather that God—through the Holy Spirit—continues to work through Israel and the Jews in order to bless all nations and see the ultimate fulfillment of God's plan? Has Israel been replaced by Christianity or has Christianity been grafted into Israel?

11. Are you familiar with the term "Supersessionism"? Supersessionism is the traditional Christian belief that Christianity is the fulfillment of biblical Judaism and therefore that Jews who deny that Jesus is the Jewish Messiah fall short of their calling as God's Chosen people. In its more radical form, supersessionism maintains that the Jews are no longer considered to be God's chosen people. This understanding is generally termed "Replacement Theology."

12. Do you believe the Christian church has been allowed to extend, fulfill, or complete Israel and Judaism?

13. Where does Judaism stand in relation to Christianity and the person and work of Jesus Christ?

14. Is Christianity an outgrowth of Judaism? Are they mutually exclusive? Or are they inclusive to one another in what I call "dialectically harmonious"? (I have coined the term "dialectically harmonious" to describe seemingly opposing positions that appear to oppose each other but rather are compatible and indispensable to one another.) What do you think of this concept?

15. Does any form of supersessionism have anti-Semitic or anti-Judaic elements? If so, why?

16. Do we see the appearance of the Holy Spirit as early as Genesis 1:2?

17. What is the Spirit of God or the Holy Spirit? Is it God? Is it part of God? Is it fully God?

18. Did the Holy Spirit form a body for the Son?

19. So what is the status of Israel and its covenant as it relates to the Christian Church?

    [Has] therefore this people ceased to be the chosen, the holy people of God. Into its place there has now stepped the people of Christians from among Jews and Gentiles. (Is) the Church the historical replacement of Israel? Has Israel as such become one with the foundation and existence of the Christian church a thing of the past?

20. Are the patriarchs of Israel Abraham, Isaac and Jacob, Moses, David, and Elijah, and they alone, ought in strict justice to be called the forefathers of the church?

21. Do you believe "Israel is the people of the Jews which resists its election; the Church is the gathering of Jews and Gentiles called on the ground of its election"?

22. Must we reject any form of supersessionism as anti-Semitic and anti-Judaic? One covenant, one people, two faiths expressed in two ways may be an alternative. Do you accept this?

23. It has been stated that regarding relations between Jews and Christians, "no one can heal this wound." I propose the wounds could be healed when treated with love, respect, and mutual understanding of both faiths. How do we reconcile these two seemingly dialectical faiths?

24. Do you agree that there is only one covenant, and thus only one people of God, and yet there are also two faiths?

25. Is there a biblical example we may look at to discern how these two dialectically opposed or dialectically harmonious faiths may relate?

26. How ought we treat others, specifically the Jews, when they are perceived to be of different faiths? Alternatively, is it possible to have one faith expressed in two ways?

27. Is worshiping the one God in two different ways theologically acceptable?

28. Is the core of conflict between Judaism and Christianity the acceptance or rejection of the person and work of Jesus Christ?

29. What do these scriptures say about Israel and its relation to the Christian church?

    Romans 9:3–5

    Romans 9:22–24

    Romans 11:1–2

    Romans 11:11–12

30. Some believe Christians ought to make the Jews "believe" through aggressive evangelizing. That may be attempting to force the hand of God's timeline, resulting in a condition of supersessionism, which should not exist. Do you understand how that would happen?

31. John the Apostle wrote of Israel's election, "Then I heard the number of those who were sealed: 144,000 from all the tribes of Israel." See Revelation 7:4. What do you believe this represents?

32. What about the novel proposition that Christianity has been grafted into Judaism? Rather, is Christianity absorbed and fulfilled by the Jews and Israel through Christ?

33. See Romans 11:17. Explain this application.

34. Jews who believe in Christ do not reject their membership in Israel. Does this fact testify that reconciliation in Christ is not a repudiation of Ancient Israel but a confirmation?"

35. What do you think about the strategy adopted by Christians in the past that "the day is long past when Christians might hope to alleviate this wound by making Israel jealous"?

36. Should the exchange between Jesus and the woman at the well be the model by which all discussions of faith ought to occur?

37. Are the issues raised at the Council of Jerusalem relevant to Jewish-Christian relations and practice today? Questions were raised such as, "Are the new converts that are not Jewish required to follow Jewish customs?" How could this apply to the Christian church? See Acts 15)

38. Do converts from Judaism to Christianity need to lose their identity and cultural religious practices if they embrace Christ?

39. Does the Council of Jerusalem as recorded in Acts 15 shed light on the issue of how Judaism ought to be treated in light of Christianity?

40. Is it possible to be a Christian without ceasing to be a Jew?

41. What do you think of this theological analysis: If Christ is God and the Jews worship the only true God, why is it necessary for Christians to think that only through acknowledgment and acceptance of the person and work of Jesus Christ can the Jews be saved or need to be saved? If God has established a special dispensation to the nation of Israel and has further eschatological plans, this position is incomplete, and God's plan has not yet been fully unveiled and realized as it relates to Israel and the Jews.

42. Is a Judaic Christianity possible?

43. Do you believe that representative Israel has already received the Messiah found in Christ? The first Palm Sunday coincided with Passover; this was the day of Jesus' triumphant entry into Jerusalem and the beginning of his last week of human life. He fulfilled Old Testament prophecy when he entered Jerusalem with those in attendance laying out their robes and waving palm branches in reverence and celebration of him. These were Jews welcoming and praising him, saying, "Hosanna in the Highest! Blessed is He who comes in the name of the Lord! Hosanna in the Highest!" So for a moment, Israel had received its Savior. This also confirms the acceptance of Israel to God and God to Israel through Christ. What do you think of this?

44. Will all of Israel be saved?

CHAPTER 10

Between a Rock and a Hard Place:
The Mediation of Moses (Old) and Christ (New)[xxxix]

Why, then, was the law given? It was given alongside the promise to show people their sins. But the law was designated to last only until the coming of the child (Jesus) who was promised. God gave his law through angels to Moses, who was the mediator between God and the people.

GALATIANS 3:19 (NLT)

One of the most important concepts the Authentic Church must understand and translate into theology and practice is the systematic narrative of the Old Testament and its relation to the mediation and priestly office of Christ. These concepts are indispensable to the creation and building of new churches and ministries. No church attempting to have an authentic theology can afford not to acquire a working knowledge and understanding of the priestly foundation and mediation of Christ that has its roots in ancient Israel.

In this chapter, we will discuss those roles and how they relate to the foundational theological principles of the Authentic Church. We will look to Moses for a picture of the mediator between humanity and God and discern those principles that lay the groundwork for the role Christ would have as priest and mediator in the Authentic Church.

Who was Moses? What did he teach? What was his role? Was he a mediator between God and Israel? What if any is his theological or spiritual relation to the mediation of Jesus Christ? We will address these important issues in this chapter.

[xxxix] This chapter was originally adopted from a paper submitted for the class "The Many Faces of Moses" for Dr. Stephen Garfinkel at Princeton Theological Seminary; he was visiting professor from the Jewish Theological Seminary in New York and associate provost of the Bible Department Faculty.

Moses is highly regarded by the adherents of three religions: Christianity, Judaism, and Islam. Yet each of these understands his role quite differently. All agree that he was a great man, led Israel out of Egyptian bondage, and received the law from God. To this day he is a singular figure in the Jewish faith and consciousness.[340]

Moses had a unique role as mediator between God and the people of Israel. We shall explore that role and the relationship between Moses and Jesus and the types of mediation that took place. It has been said that Moses prepared the ground for a unique form of mediation later found in Jesus Christ.

Modern Judaism teaches that the need for a mediator is "unbearable" and "an intrusion" because they are taught to relate to God in terms of how we see ourselves. According to many rabbis, we are given a soul at birth which is pure and holy, and though we possess an inclination towards both good and evil, the inclination to do good is stronger than the tendency towards evil. The modern Jewish view emphasizes that we are made in God's image, and therefore essentially good. Judaism is an optimistic and positive religion. We are led to believe that the drama of everyday life is played out against this backdrop of hope. And if that is so, we have the potential to make noble and lofty ideals a reality.[341]

So why is there a need for Moses or any other person as mediator or priest between God and man?

Between God and man stands no one—not God-man, not angel, not advocate. Nor is intercession or intervention required. As nothing comes between soul and body, father and child, potter and vessel, so nothing separates man from God, soul of his soul, his Father and Fashioner.[342]

Was Moses God, God man, angel, prophet, mediator, something more or something less? Some Jewish theologians believe,

Man occupies a position in the Jewish view which makes mediation not only superfluous but unbearable. It is an intrusion which violates man's rights and injures his dignity. Righteousness, to Judaism, cannot be imputed, it must be attained ... Man is able to stand by himself; herein lies his dignity.[343]

According to the scriptures, God has made us in His image, but part of this image includes the ability to choose: "I have set before you life and death, blessings and curses. Now choose life, so that you and your children may live."[344]

Dr. J. H. Hertz, chief rabbi of Britain in the early part of this century, comments on this text: "Jewish ethics is rooted in the doctrine of human responsibility, that is, freedom of will." Hertz said, "In the moral universe, man ever remains his own master. The giving of the Commandments presupposes that we have the ability to choose to follow them."[345]

> The ability to choose places the yoke of moral and ethical responsibility upon us. We are accountable to God and to each other for our decisions. We are not programmed robots designed by an impersonal Creator to helplessly act out a destiny that is not of our choosing. Sometimes our choices are wrong, but according to contemporary Jewish thought, evil is not inevitable, but merely an obstacle which we have the power to overcome.[346]

So why then the need or necessity for this role of mediator?

Though mediation implies failure or inadequacy of the human effort to reach out to God, Judaism was founded on the premise that man is capable by virtue of his moral effort to approach and understand God. Hence, God's coming to man's aid becomes unnecessary and interferes with human development.[347]

The Hebrew scriptures reveal how mediators were central to the Jewish religion from the beginning. God established His covenant with Israel at Mount Sinai, calling the new nation a "kingdom of priests."[348] This was an honor as well as a responsibility. By their faithfulness in keeping the commandments, the Jewish people were to mediate between God and the Gentile nations. They were to reflect the reality of a living God to the rest of the world so all its people might know Him.[349] But would that faithfulness or unfaithfulness require a mediator?

Exodus seems to be the point at which the people of Israel ask for a mediator.

> When the people saw the thunder and lightning and heard the trumpet and saw the mountain in smoke, they trembled with fear. They stayed at a distance and said to Moses, "Speak to us yourself and we will listen. But do not have God speak to us or we will die." (Exodus 20:18, 19 NIV)

So the request went out from the people of Israel that they indeed needed a mediator between them and God to receive the messages of God and talk to God on their behalf. They needed a mediator, and that mediator was Moses. Even Moses, who interceded for the nation when God thought to destroy them, was not allowed to experience God's unbounded splendor.[350]

> And the Lord said, "I will cause all my goodness to pass in front of you, and I will proclaim my name, the Lord, in your presence … But," he said, "you cannot see my face, for no one may see me and live." (Exodus 33:19, 20 NIV)

Moses was between a rock and a hard place, and that situation would continue until his death.

Mediation in the Bible

> On the human plane, mediation takes place in the Bible, as it has in many cultures throughout history, both in innocent circumstances, when people are at odds with one another. People use interpreters to mediate the metaphorical distance between them created by a foreign language (Gen. 42:23) and envoys to mediate the real distance created by the geography of the region (2 Chron. 32:31). They also use mediators to argue a case or to negotiate terms of peace with a hostile party, as Moses did with Pharaoh on behalf of Israel (Exod. 6:28–30). Both kinds of mediation are sometimes intertwined in the Bible, as when Moses used Aaron to mediate between himself and Pharaoh (Exod. 7:1–2) and Joab used the wise woman of Tekoa to mediate his message about Absalom to David (2 Sam 14:2–20).[351]
>
> God's dealings with (humanity) throughout Scripture also incorporates these two kinds of mediation. Some kind of mediation between God and humanity is necessary simply because God is separate from all He has created and, yet, graciously extends His fellowship to His creatures. Mediation takes on a particularly important role, however, in light of humanity's rebellion against the Creator. The situation of hostility that resulted from Adam's fall could only be remedied through the mediation of a third party.[352]

The greatest of all mediators in the Old Testament is Moses. He served as a mediator and foreshadowed things to come when at God's initiative he communicated the terms of the

Sinaitic covenant with Israel (Exodus 19:9, 20:19, 24:1–2, 34:27–28; Leviticus 26:46; Deuteronomy 5:5). He also served as the Israelites' intercessor after they broke the covenant and stood in danger of God's righteous wrath according to the covenant's terms (Exodus. 32:7–14, 33:12–23; Numbers 14:13–19).

After Moses' death and in the face of continued violations of the covenant, other figures arose to urge Israel's compliance with the law and intercede for Israel during times of disobedience. Samuel pled with God for the people generally and for the king in particular (1 Samuel 12:16–18, 13:13–14, 15:10–11); the true prophets attempted to stand between God and a disobedient people to avert disaster, and the priests, when they were faithful to their appointed tasks, offered sacrifices to atone for the people's sins (Leviticus 4:1–5:19).[353]

What effect or role can a mediator have as it relates to a person's relationship with God? Can a mediator such as Moses change God's mind? It can be argued biblically that at times yes. A mediator can plead the case of the accused, defend them, and ask for mercy to change God's mind. When the Israelites disobeyed God and cast the idol made from gold into a calf, worshiped it, and lied about how it was made, Moses interceded on their behalf for their sin and reminded God of all the wonderful promises He had made to their forefathers and how they would be numerous and prosperous. After this defense by Moses, the Lord withheld punishment and judgment: "And the Lord repented of the evil which he thought to do unto his people" (Exodus 32:14).

Look at what the great Charles Spurgeon[xl] said about Moses' necessity in the mediation as it relates to God and Israel: "Speaking after the manner of men, the mediation of Moses wrought this change in the mind of God. God in Moses seemed to overcome God out of Moses. God in the Mediator … appears to be stronger for mercy than God apart from the Mediator.[354]

Moses was intricately involved in his relationship with God maybe even more so than he was with Israel.

> Moses is the most highly regarded figure in Jewish history. He was the man to whom God spoke face to face (Ex. 33:11). Moses saw the glory of God (Ex. 33:18–23), and the glow on his face reflected that fact (Ex. 34:30). He was the man God chose to lead Israel out of Egypt to the Promised Land. But most significant of all to the Jewish people was that through Moses came the law. In

---

[xl] Charles Spurgeon was a famous British Baptist preacher, pastor, and theologian who was called to the pastorate at London's famed New Park Street Chapel when he was only nineteen. He wrote theologically significant books and preached around the world. His sermons have been translated and reproduced for reading and instruction for many.

fact, the law became so identified with Moses that it was commonly referred to as the Law of Moses. The law was the heart of Jewish life; the Old Testament commandments and rituals were their highest priority. Paul mentions in Romans 2 that the Jews boasted in the law. Moses had not only given them the Ten Commandments but he had penned the entire Pentateuch.[xli] Some Jews believed that Moses was greater than the angels.[355]

Moses had a remarkable life. The hand of God preserved him as a baby and even preserved his body after his death. God cared and esteemed Moses so much that after his death, the Archangel Michael was disputing with the devil about the body of Moses (Jude 1:9). The devil thought it was of the utmost importance to obtain the body of Moses because Moses was that significant to the people as mediator and even may have been seen as a god. Maybe that is why God personally buried the body of Moses. He the Lord "buried him in Moab ... but to this day, no one knows where his grave is."[356]

There were too numerous miracles to list during Moses' life. During the most memorable times of Israel's history, God worked through Moses. He led the children of Israel out of Egypt and through the wilderness. He instructed them from the mouth of God. The Levitical system came through Moses. Moses gave the plans for the tabernacle, the ark of the covenant, and everything that went with it. As great as Moses was, however, the Holy Spirit in this section calls on us to gaze on Jesus, who is far greater than Moses.[357]

MOSES—THE SHADOW OF THINGS TO COME

In the New Testament, we learn that Moses' faithfulness was a testimony of greater things that were yet to come in Christ. Hebrews 10:1 (NIV) says, "The law, having a shadow of good things to come and not the very image of the things, can never with those sacrifices which they offered year by year continually make those who come to it perfect." The law was the shadow of good things yet to come in Christ. Jesus said, "Had ye believed Moses, ye would have believed me; for he wrote of me" (John 5:46 NIV). It is difficult based on the teachings of Christ to believe what Moses wrote yet reject Jesus.[358] "The Lord your God will raise up for you a prophet like me from among you, from your brothers—it is to him you shall listen" (Deuteronomy 18:15 NIV).

[xli] The Torah is the central religious teaching in Judaism. Christian scholars usually refer to the first five books of the Hebrew Bible as the Pentateuch, meaning five books, or as the Law, or Law of Moses. It also contains the oral translation of ancient teachings.

This verse is the only place in the entire Torah where Moses explicitly identifies himself as a prophet of the Lord. Moreover, this is also the only passage where Moses identifies the coming of the Messiah as "a Prophet like me" (Deuteronomy 18:15; John 6:14).[359]

It appears that there was a significant spiritual relationship between Moses and Jesus.

Moses' mediatory role not only involved communicating the terms of the covenant from God to Israel but also serving a priestly function in light of Israel's sinfulness. Moses both gave directions for building the earthly tabernacle (Hebrews 8:5) and sprinkled the people, the scroll, the tent, and the vessels with blood since "without the shedding of blood there is no forgiveness (Hebrews 9:22)."[360]

Jesus too performed all these functions; but His work and what it affected were superior to the mediatorial role of Moses, for He was the mediator of a new covenant. First, He says, the prophecy in Jeremiah 31:31–34 of a new covenant proves that the first one was not blameless (Hebrews 8:7)—the use of the word *new* in that passage implies the obsolescence of the old (Hebrews 8:13). Second, Christ's service as high priest involved the shedding of His blood rather than animal blood (Hebrews 9:11–15). As a result of this sacrifice, all the transgressions condemned by the old covenant were forgiven (Hebrews 9:15) and blood sacrifice of any type need never be offered again (Hebrews 9:18–26; cf. 7:27). This does not mean, however, that Christ's work as Mediator in other capacities had ended. Just as Moses, the priests, and the prophets continued to mediate between God and Israel after the covenant was established, so Jesus "always lives to intercede" on our behalf and therefore to bring complete salvation to us (Hebrews 7:25; cf. John 15:26–16:11, 17:1–25; Romans 8:26–34).[361]

This extensive and complex argument is to call the Authentic Church to obedience.

This is most clearly articulated in Hebrews 12:18–29, where the author reminds his readers of the magnificent display of God's power and holiness that accompanied Moses' mediation of the first covenant. In a way similar to Paul (2 Cor. 3:9), the author argues that Moses' mediation of the old covenant was a magnificent event, accompanied by splendid displays of God's power which, appropriately, struck terror into the hearts of God's people (vv. 18–21). Since Jesus is the mediator of a new covenant of forgiveness (v. 24), our fear of the future judgment should be even more intense than that of ancient Israel if we turn our backs on Him (vv. 25–29).[362]

For Paul and the author of Hebrews, Christ's role as Mediator received a covenantal interpretation that echoes the Old Testament at every step. Whereas Moses mediated a temporary covenant whose primary purpose was to pronounce the just penalty of death over those who sinned, Jesus mediated the new covenant predicted by the prophets. Since this covenant was accompanied by Christ's superior, high-priestly role with its superior sacrifice "once and for all," it is the answer to the plight of sin that the first covenant made so clear and was unable to fully resolve.[363]

> Paul echoes the new covenant language of the Old Testament when he tells us that believers have peace with God (Rom 5:1), have experienced the outpouring of God's love in their hearts through the Holy Spirit (Rom 5:5), and have been reconciled to God (Rom 5:10–11; cf. 2 Cor. 5:11–20). All of this, he says, has happened through faith in Christ, whose death served as the ultimate atoning sacrifice for sin (Rom 3:21–26; 5:1, 6–9). The covenant mediated through Moses was glorious, he says, but the new covenant is far more so, for unlike the old covenant that punished sin and therefore brought death, the new covenant brings life (2 Cor. 3:4–18; John 1:17; cf. Gal 3:19–22). Paul ties these concepts neatly together in 1 Timothy 2:4–6 when he declares that God's desire to save all people is expressed in the "one mediator," Christ Jesus, who gave himself as a ransom for all.[364]
>
> As mediator of the Law Covenant we believe he typified a "greater than Moses" who would accomplish blessings through the new covenant that Moses could never have achieved in his time.[365]

JESUS AND HIS SIMILARITY TO MOSES AS MEDIATOR

Since Moses was so highly esteemed by the Jewish people, the writer of Hebrews doesn't just bluntly state that Jesus is greater than Moses. He handles the matter more delicately. Before taking up Jesus' superiority to Moses, he points out the resemblance between the two.[366]

Jesus was faithful to God. Jesus did the work that the Father appointed Him to do. In John 6:38–39 He says, "I came down from heaven, not to do mine own will but the will of Him that sent me. And this is the Father's will who hath sent me, that of all that He hath given me I should lose nothing, but should raise it up again at the last day." Jesus says in John 7:18, "He that speaketh of himself seeketh his own glory; but he that seeketh His glory that sent him, the same is true, and no unrighteousness is in Him." In John 8:29 He says, "He that sent me is with me. The Father hath not left me alone; for I do always those things that please Him," while in John 17:4–5 we read, "I have finished the work which thou gavest me to do. And now, O Father, glorify thou me with thine ownself with the glory which I had with thee before the world was." Jesus always did the Father's will. He was ever faithful.[367]

Though Moses and Jesus were chosen by God and faithful, there was a difference; Jesus was counted worthy of more glory than Moses inasmuch as He who had built the house had more honor than the house itself. Moses was but a member of the spiritual household God through Christ had built. God through Christ created Israel and the church. That is evidence of His deity: "For every house is built by some man, but he that built all things is God."[368] Since Jesus created all things (John 1:3), He therefore is God.[369]

SIMILARITIES OF MOSES AND JESUS

The Old and New Testaments contain many similarities between the person and work of Moses and Jesus as Mediator and priest. Let us compare and contrast these similarities.

- Both were sent from God (Exodus 3:1–10; John 8:42).
- Both were Jews (Exodus 2:1–2; Matthew 1:1–16; Luke 1–2; Hebrews 7:14).
- Both had faithful Jewish parents (Exodus 2:2; Hebrews 11:23; Matthew 2:13–14).
- Both were born under foreign rule (Exodus 1:8–14; Luke 2:1).
- Both were threatened by wicked kings (Exodus 1:15–16; Matthew 2:16).
- Both spent their early years in Egypt miraculously protected from those who sought their lives (Exodus 2:10; Matthew 2:14–15).
- Both rejected the possibility of becoming rulers in this age (Hebrews 11:24; Matthew 4:8–9).
- Both were initially rejected by the Jews (Exodus 32:1; Isaiah 53:3; Matthew 27:21–22; Romans 11:25).
- Both were accepted by Gentiles (Exodus 2:14–22; Acts 10:45; 1 Timothy 3:16).
- Both were criticized by their families (Numbers 12:1; Mark 3:20–21).
- God spoke directly to both (Exodus 3:1–10; Deuteronomy 34:10; Matthew 3:16–17).

- Both were teachers (Deuteronomy 4:1–5; Matthew 22:16; John 3:2).
- Both gave the people bread from heaven (Exodus 16:14–15; Matthew 14:19–20).
- Both were appointed as saviors of Israel (Moses as Israel's deliverer from the bondage of Pharaoh; Jesus as Israel's deliverer from the bondage of Satan).
- Both were shepherds of Israel (John 10:10–11; Matthew 9:36; Exodus 12:50).
- Both fasted for forty days in the wilderness (Exodus 34:28; Matthew 4:2).
- Both were mediators of a covenant of blood (Exodus 24:7–8; Matthew 26:26–28; Mark 14:24; Luke 22:20; Hebrews 9:11–15)[370]

The word *mediator* occurs only in the New Testament, and its references always come in connection with the covenants either of the Law of Moses or the Gospel of Christ.

Interestingly, one of the key uses of the word is used by Paul in Galatians with a decidedly negative tone: "Wherefore then serveth the law? It was added because of transgressions … and it was ordained by angels in the hand of a mediator. Now a mediator is not a mediator of one, but God is one" (Galatians 3:19–20 KJV).

> The most sustained theological treatment of the concept of the mediator in the Bible, however, comes from the author of the letter to the Hebrews. The author writes to a church that has endured persecution (10:32–34) for its faith and, becoming weary in its trial, is tempted to convert to Judaism (13:9–13), a widely known and well-respected religion within the Roman Empire at the time. The response to this church is a carefully argued reminder of Christ's superiority to every aspect of Israel's Old Covenant, and a crucial step in this argument is that Christ is the mediator of a new covenant (8:6; 9:15; 12:24).[371]

This is what the author writes encouraging the people to continue to follow the mediation of Christ over Moses.

> Therefore, holy brethren, who share in a heavenly call, consider Jesus, the apostle and high priest of our confession. He was faithful to Him who appointed Him, just as Moses also was faithful in God's house. Yet Jesus has been counted worthy of much more glory than Moses as builder of a house has more honor than the house. (For every house is built by someone, but the builder of all things is God.) Now Moses was faithful in all God's house as a servant, to testify to the things that were to be spoken later, but Christ was faithful over God's house as a son. And we are His house if we hold fast our confidence and pride in our hope.[372]

This scripture passage the author of Hebrews writes to Israel was for them to learn from their rejection and mistakes in the past and properly understand the role of the mediator in Moses and Jesus to obey God.

> Today, when you hear his voice, do not harden your hearts as in the rebellion. Who were they that heard and yet were rebellious? Was it not all those who left Egypt under the leadership of Moses? And with whom was he provoked forty years? Was it not with those who sinned, whose bodies fell in the wilderness? And to whom did he swear that they should never enter his rest, but to those who were disobedient? So we see that they were unable to enter because of unbelief. (Hebrews 3:8–19 NIV)

> The author to the Hebrews contrasts Jesus with Moses. He spoke with God face to face as a man speaks with his friend. The book of Numbers says that Moses differed from all the prophets. Moses was faithful in all God's house (Numbers 12:6–7). The Jews could not conceive of anyone being closer to God than Moses.[373]

What about this Jesus, who is like Moses a new mediator of a new covenant?

THE LAW OF MOSES THE MEDIATION OF CHRIST

What is the relationship between the law given to Israel and the role of mediator? "Why then, was the law given at all? It was added because of transgressions until the Seed to whom the promise referred had come. The law was given through angels and entrusted to a mediator" (Galatians 3:19 NIV).

If that promise was enough for salvation, why serve the law? Though the Israelites were God's particular people, they were sinners as were others. The law was not intended to discover a way of justification different from that made known by the promise but to lead people to see their need of the promise by showing the sinfulness of sin and pointing to Christ through whom alone they could be pardoned and justified. Hence, the law could not be designed to set aside the promise. A mediator comes between two parties but is not to act for one of them. The great design of the law was that the promise by faith of Jesus Christ might be given to those who believe so being convinced of their guilt and the insufficiency of the law to affect righteousness for them they might be persuaded to believe on Christ and thus obtain the benefit of the promise.[374] Many in ancient Israel and those today continue rejecting God's law and the mediation of His covenant. "But our ancestors refused to obey him. Instead, they rejected him and in their hearts turned back to Egypt" (Acts 7:38 NIV).

Moses and Jesus were rejected by many, but the significant roles they played in the life of Israel and the New Testament church have far-reaching implications for all humanity and its relationship with God. The mediator has and continues to be a central figure in the Old and New Testaments and continues the work of reconciliation between God and humanity.

Moses was and is a significant figure for Jews and Christians. For the Jews, he personifies the meditational role of bridging the gap between God and humanity, and Jesus in the type of Moses as mediator dispenses a new and different mediation that had not been accomplished before. Moses and his mediation are indispensable to a full understanding of the type of role Christ would be as humanity's mediator.

Comparison of the Mediation of Moses and Jesus, the New Mediator of a New Covenant

Hebrews (written between AD 60 and 90) is the central New Testament text on the priesthood of Christ and his sacrificial and meditorial role. Hebrews presents the person and work of Christ's priesthood and mediation against the background and support of the Jewish system from Moses on through the prophets culminating in the finished work of Christ.[375] "Hebrews 3:1–6 compares Jesus with Moses in order to lay a foundation for the exhortation that follows in 3:7–4:11. The comparison points up three important truths."[376] First, the old covenant is indispensable to the new covenant. Second, the limited access to God through a human mediator (only Moses was given face-to-face access to God) has been opened to all by the provision of direct access to God for all His people through Jesus Christ. Third, though both Moses and Jesus were faithful in their positions, the access secured by Moses as a faithful servant of God has been far expanded by the access to God enjoyed by Jesus, God's Son. The contrast between Jesus and Moses serves as a device to persuade the readers to accept and enjoy their direct access to God, and to recognize Jesus Christ as the faithful Mediator between God and humans.[377]

Why would the author of Hebrews[xlii] compare Jesus to Moses? This may seem anticlimactic after the author of Hebrews established Jesus' superiority to angels. It would seem He was greater than Moses. However, in first-century Jewish thought, Moses was held in almost

---

[xlii] The book of Hebrews could be found in the collection of New Testament writings after Timothy and Philemon and before the book of James. Though the author is not identified, many believe it was written by the apostle Paul between 60 and 70. The purpose of the book was to show Jesus Christ as the perfect fulfillment of Judaism.

godlike esteem, even higher than angels. So contrasting Jesus to Moses is a step beyond Hebrews 1:5–13, not a step back. The comparison was not simply a literary exercise that enabled the writer to speak of the excellence of Jesus or exhibit his exegetical skill. The writer chose to acknowledge the faithfulness of Moses because this appears to have been a significant consideration to the men and women he addressed.[378] Maybe the author of Hebrews was building a powerful argument for its readers to believe that Jesus should be embraced as Moses was for He is the full personification of Moses and is greater.

> The comparison was also bound to arise in the minds of first-century Christians, for the name of Moses appears more times in the Old Testament and in fact in all of the Bible (847 total times: 762 in the Old Testament and 85 in the New Testament) than any other proper name except for Jesus and David.[379]

This suggests the importance of Moses and signifies that the essence of his mediation is relevant for Old Testament Jews, New Testament Christians, and the Authentic Church alike.

The Great Universal Hope of the Mediator

The Authentic Church must be familiar with the experiences of the past to better understand the future. History will remind the church of its failures to live up to God's standards. Human history is full of wrong thinking, wrong decisions, and wrong turns. Humankind will need to recall its past so it can fully benefit from the gracious provisions of the old and new covenants. Christ will provide the needed lessons to remind the world how much has been done for them and how much there is for them to do. Undoubtedly, Moses will rejoice when he sees the fulfillment of the promises to Israel fulfilled in Christ.[380]

It could be argued that Moses disobeyed God and wasn't permitted to take Israel into the Promised Land or that he failed in his role as mediator, but the case can be made that Moses was special and obtained favor in the sight of God and did all God had commanded. The issue of Moses not being able to go into the Promised Land may have been one of two possibilities. As a biblical figure, it was a spiritual example to show that his failure and prohibition to enter the Promised Land was the result of his imperfection as a mediator. Or he did not follow the exact instructions of God and was thereby punished, which would be an example to all humanity to obey and listen to precisely what the Word has required of us and that even the mediator, Moses, was not outside God's punishment.

Moses' willingness to risk his life for the sake of a sinful people foreshadows the final and ultimate mediator, Jesus (Hebrews 12:24). In both cases, they found favor with God and stood in the gap to bring reconciliation between humanity and God. God's promise to dwell with His people is ultimately fulfilled through the gift of His Spirit (John 14:26). Moses' intimate relationship with God in which he experienced the presence of God illustrates God's redemptive plan to have an eternal relationship with all people.[381]

The prophet Jeremiah wrote that God has not forgotten about Israel but rather God had promised, "I will be the God of all the clans of Israel."[382] That God will make a new covenant with Israel, but it would not be like the old one with the forefathers—Noah, Moses, Abraham, Isaac, and Jacob—but a new one where God "puts (the) law in their minds and writes it on the hearts."[383] He would be their God, they would be his people, and He would "forgive their wickedness and remember their sins no more."[384]

The only mediation capable of taking away sins was found and personified in the person and work of Jesus Christ.

The life of Moses as a biblical figure, prophet, and mediator had its highs and lows though one thing was constant: the teachings and writings about Moses have had a significant theological and religious impact on the major religions of the world. Therefore, the question of whether Moses was the mediator between God and Israel pales in comparison to the teachings we glean from the story of his life, his friendship with God, and his intercession for the people of God.

The significance of the life of Moses gives us a foundation for better understanding the person and work of Jesus Christ.

> Therefore, when Christ came into the world, he said: "Sacrifice and offering you did not desire, but a body you prepared for me; with burnt offerings and sin offerings you were not pleased. Then I said, "Here I am it is written about me in the scroll—I have come to do your will, O God." (Hebrews 10:5–7 NIV)

The full mediation of Moses is realized and personified by a Jesus—a new, more-effective mediator who is able to save the whole world.

LESSON 10

Between a Rock and a Hard Place: The Mediation of Moses (Old) and Christ (New)

Why, then, was the law given? It was given alongside the promise to show people their sins. But the law was designated to last only until the coming of the child (Jesus) who was promised. God gave his law through angels to Moses, who was the mediator between God and the people.

GALATIANS 3:19 (NLT)

1. What does this scripture say to you?

2. In your own words, who was Moses?

3. What was his role?

4. Explain what a mediator between God and Israel is.

5. Is there a need for Moses or any other person to act as a mediator or priest between God and man?

6. Did Moses have any theological or spiritual implications to the mediation of Jesus Christ?

7. Judaism was founded on the premise that man is capable by virtue of his moral effort to approach and understand God. Hence, God's coming to man's aid becomes unnecessary and interferes with human development. Is this consistent with both the Old and New Testaments?

8. Does the Old Testament reveal how mediators were central to the Jewish religion from the beginning?

9. Did the role of Israel, through its faithfulness in keeping the commandments and example between God and Israel, reflect the reality of a living God to the rest of the world so all people may know him?

10. When the Israelites saw thunder and lightning and heard the trumpet and saw the mountain in smoke, they trembled with fear. They stayed at a distance and said to Moses, "Speak to us yourself and we will listen. But do not have God speak to us or we will die" (Exodus 20:18, 19). Why did they say this?

11. God's dealings with humanity throughout scripture incorporates these two kinds of mediation, between God and humanity and between people who are at odds with one another. Are mediators necessary, biblically and practically?

12. What effect or role can a mediator have as it relates to a person's relationship with God?

13. Can a mediator such as Moses change God's mind?

14. In the New Testament, we learn that Moses' faithfulness was a testimony of greater things that were yet to come in Christ. Hebrews 10:1 says, "The law, having a shadow of good things to come and not the very image of the things, can never with those sacrifices which they offered year by year continually make those who come to it perfect." The law was the shadow of good things yet to come in Christ. Jesus said, "Had ye believed Moses, ye would have believed me; for he wrote of me" (John 5:46). It is difficult based on the teachings of Moses to reject Jesus. He wrote, "The Lord your God will raise up for you a prophet like me from among you, from your brothers—it is to him you shall listen" (Deuteronomy 18:15). In light of those scriptures, how are Moses and Jesus similar?

15. Do you agree that Moses mediated a temporary covenant whose primary purpose was to pronounce the just penalty of judgment over those who sinned? And that Jesus mediated a New Covenant predicted by the prophets, a covenant that was accompanied by Christ's superior, high-priestly role with its superior sacrifice "once for all." Is it the answer to the plight of sin that the first covenant was made so clear and was unable to be fully resolved?

16. The New Covenant is unlike the Old Covenant that punished sin and therefore brought death; the New Covenant brings _____ and _____.

17. 1 Timothy 2:4–6 declares that God's desire to save all people is expressed in the "one mediator," Christ Jesus, who gave himself as a ransom for all. Is it possible that all people would be saved?

18. What do you think of the similarities of Moses and Jesus?

- Both were sent from God (Exodus 3:1–10; John 8:42).
- Both were Jews (Exodus 2:1–2; Matthew 1:1–16; Luke 1–2; Hebrews 7:14).
- Both had faithful Jewish parents (Exodus 2:2; Hebrews 11:23; Matthew 2:13–14).
- Both were born under foreign rule (Exodus 1:8–14; Luke 2:1).
- Both were threatened by wicked kings (Exodus 1:15–16; Matthew 2:16).
- Both spent their early years in Egypt miraculously protected from those who sought their lives (Exodus 2:10; Matthew 2:14–15).
- Both rejected the possibility of becoming rulers in their age (Hebrews 11:24; Matthew 4:8–9).
- Both were initially rejected by the Jews (Exodus 32:1; Isaiah 53:3; Matthew 27:21–22; Romans 11:25).
- Both were accepted by Gentiles (Exodus 2:14–22; Acts 10:45; 1 Timothy 3:16).
- Both were criticized by their families (Numbers 12:1; Mark 3:20–21).
- God spoke directly to both (Exodus 3:1–10; Deuteronomy 34:10; Matthew 3:16–17).
- Both were teachers (Deuteronomy 4:1–5; Matthew 22:16; John 3:2).
- Both gave the people bread from heaven (Exodus 16:14–15; Matthew 14:19–20).
- Both were appointed as saviors of Israel (Moses as Israel's deliverer from the bondage of Pharaoh; Jesus as Israel's deliverer from the bondage of Satan).
- Both were shepherds of Israel (John 10:10–11; Matthew 9:36; Exodus 12:50).
- Both fasted for forty days in the wilderness (Exodus 34:28; Matthew 4:2).
- Both were mediators of a covenant of blood (Exodus 24:7–8; Matthew 26:26–28; Mark 14:24; Luke 22:20; Hebrews 9:11–15)

What does this suggest to you?

19. Moses was faithful, as a servant in God's house, to testify to the things that were to be spoken, but Christ was faithful as the son in God's house. What is the difference in the two mediators?

20. Is Moses' mediation indispensable to a full understanding of the type of role Christ would be as humanity's Mediator?

21. Is the Old Covenant indispensable to the New Covenant? If so, why?

22. Has the limited access to God through a human mediator (only Moses was given face-to-face access to God) been opened to all by the provision of direct access to God for all his people through Jesus Christ?

23. Both Moses and Jesus were faithful in their positions, though the access secured by Moses as a faithful servant of God was expanded by the access to God enjoyed by Jesus, God's Son. Is Jesus the mediator of a better, different covenant?

24. Will Moses rejoice when he sees the fulfillment of the promises to Israel fulfilled in Christ?

25. The question of whether Moses failed as mediator between God and Israel pales in comparison to the teachings we glean from the story of his life, his friendship with God, and his intercession for the people of God. The significance of the life of Moses gives us a foundation for better understanding the person and work of Jesus Christ.

    Is the full mediation of Moses realized and personified by Jesus—a new, more-effective mediator who is able to save the whole world? How does Hebrews 10:5–7 relate to Jesus as a better mediator than Moses?

26. One of the most important concepts the Authentic Church must understand and translate into theology and practice is the systematic narrative of the Old Testament and its relation to the mediation and priestly office of Christ. Is the Old Testament relevant for a better understanding of Jesus Christ?

CHAPTER 11

If Christ Had Not Come

If I had not come and spoken to them, they would not be guilty of sin. Now however, they have no excuse for their sin.

JOHN 15:22 (NIV)

In Luke 2:11, we have the angel's pronouncement, the wonderful words that celebrate the birth of our Lord: "For unto you is born this day in the city of David a Savior, which is Christ the Lord." What if that pronouncement had never been made? What if Christ had never been born? What would our world be like today without the influence of Christ and His people?[385]

Many people live lives devoid of God dependent on themselves alone and make decisions on their own. They do not need nor want spiritual direction or comfort. Whether we accept Jesus Christ as Lord and Savior, we must confront and dialogue the issues of why Christ came to earth and the profound implications it would have if He had not come.

We all know the Christmas story of a baby being born in a small, dingy manger, but do we understand the theological implications of that first Christmas—what it means for us all? This discussion ought to garner interest in the believer as well as the nonbeliever as it has implications far reaching as is eternity.

We will discuss its implications and explain what the Incarnation is and why God chose to come to earth in human form, and we will look at how the world would have been changed had Christ not come. Let us take this journey together to examine the reasons why He came, His objective found in His person and work, and what it would mean if He had not come.

Jesus hinted at the hopelessness of man had He not been born in a manger. He said in John 15:22 (NIV), "If I had not come and spoken to them, they would not be guilty of sin. Now, however, they have no excuse for their sin."[386] Why is it so important that Jesus said if He did not come, we would not be aware of our sin? Is that the most important reason He came? Not to heal the sick, free the oppressed, bring comfort to those who mourned, bring hope to the hopeless, bring peace and not strife, and bring forgiveness and love? Jesus said, "If I had not come." Suppose He had not come. How spiritually and morally destitute would the world be? Even with the influence of God's people, this world is wicked, violent, and oppressive, but if Christ had not been born, how much worse would it be? Life without Christ is unthinkable.[387]

Christ leaving His heavenly Father and coming to a helpless world brought hope, recognition, salvation, reconciliation, and the understanding of sin and death and the possibility of eternal life.[388] Throughout biblical history, God has been present in the affairs of humanity. Only by understanding humanity's sinfulness would they recognize the need for a Savior and how lost without God they were.

God was great at Sinai when He appeared on the mountaintop in the pillar of cloud and fire and wrote with His finger the Ten Commandments on tablets of stone. God was wonderful in the Incarnation; He left His throne in glory, came to earth, wrapped Himself in a baby's skin, and was born of a virgin. John leads up to this by saying,

> In the beginning was the Word, and the Word was with God, and the Word was God. He was with God in the beginning. Through him all things were made; without him nothing was made that has been made … The Word became flesh and made his dwelling among us. We have seen his glory, the glory of the One and Only, who came from the Father, full of grace and truth.[389]

This is the mystery revealed of the Incarnation.

No wonder angels sang, "Glory to God in the highest, and on earth peace to men on who his favor rests."[390] No wonder stars went on parade! No wonder shepherds left their flocks and wise men came from afar to worship! On that first Christmas night, because of that, the world will never cease to sing,

Silent Night! Holy Night!
All is calm, all is bright
'Round yon Virgin, Mother and Child!
Holy Infant, so tender and mild,
Sleep in heavenly peace.[391]

That night, God came to earth. That night, the Redeemer was born. That was the Incarnation. Why did God come to us?

Some time ago Henry Rogers, a (famed) lawyer, wrote a book entitled *The Eclipse of Faith*, in which he imagined that some powerful hand had wiped the influence of Christ completely out of our civilization. He imagined himself going into the library and finding all of the writings of Christ's life and work had disappeared. He opened his law books and found that all the legal safeguards protecting children, the poor, and the innocent had been removed. He turned to his histories of art and there found many of the world's greatest masterpieces such as Leonardo da Vinci's "The Last Supper," and Rembrandt's "The Prodigal Son" had perished. In like manner, he turned to his books of literature. There he found blank pages where formerly there had been great writings of Browning, Longfellow and many others. Next, he turned to the world of music and found that most of the great hymns of the church had vanished. Among them were "Fairest Lord Jesus," and "The Old Rugged Cross." Then Rogers realized that without Christ the vast majority of churches, hospitals, schools, orphanages and benevolent institutions would perish. The lawyer cried out and said that he did not want to live in a world without Christ. Christ taught the equality of man. He taught that we are to love all (people) and treat them as we would like to be treated.[392]

Cynthia Pearl Maus, in her anthology *Christ and the Fine Arts*, includes this vivid assessment of this proclaimed Savior of the world, not what the world would accept or want.

Here is a man who was born in an obscure village, the child of a peasant woman. He grew up in another village, and that a despised one. He worked in a carpenter's shop for thirty years, and then for three years he was an itinerant preacher. He never wrote a book. He never held an office. He never owned a home. He never had a family. He never went to college … He never traveled, except in His infancy, more than two hundred miles from the place where He was born. He had no credentials but Himself. While still a young man, the tide of popular opinion turned against Him. His friends ran away. One of them betrayed Him. He was turned over to His enemies. He went through the mockery of a trial. He was nailed on a cross between two thieves. His executors gambled for the only piece of property He had on earth, His seamless robe. When He was dead, He was taken down from the cross and laid in a borrowed grave through the courtesy of a friend. Twenty wide centuries have come and gone, and today Jesus is the centerpiece of the human race, and the leader of all progress.

In one of the most famous daily devotional books, Mrs. Charles E. Cowman shows in her book, *Streams in the Desert,* a Christmas card that depicted a clergyman who fell asleep on Christmas Eve and dreamed of a world without Jesus. There were no stockings waiting to be filled, no churches anywhere, and nothing could be found that related to the birth of the Savior. During his dream, the pastor was asked to visit a dying woman, but when he opened the Bible he was horrified to discover it ended with the book of Malachi, there was no New Testament. Suddenly, he awakened to hear the choir singing in the church and realized the awful things seen in his sleep were illusions, but he was left to consider what the world would be like if the Son of God had not come to Bethlehem.[393]

Christmas carols would not be heard, Sunday schools would be nonexistent, and for the most part, people would be lost without hope when they died.

If Christ had not come … we would not know the Father. It is sometimes easy to forget that without Christ, God would be, for many people, an inscrutable, faraway, mysterious Being. Even today in some countries, countless thousands and even millions of people worship images of wood or stone, hoping to appease a detached deity. For them, the idols represent gods who are harsh, condemning, and difficult to please.[394]

If Christ had not come … prayer would be impossible. Within the ancient world, only special people had access to God. Moses went into the mountain to meet the Almighty; Elijah prayed and God responded by preventing rain from falling over a period of three and a half years; Isaiah, Daniel, and others prayed and received responses from heaven, but such experiences were unknown among ordinary citizens. The priest alone interceded because no one else had access to the Holy of Holies. … When Jesus preached, He introduced ideas never before expressed. His words were astonishing; His thoughts electrifying. He said to His disciples that "men ought always to pray." The workman could pray at his plow, the mother in her kitchen, a child at a bedside, the nurse walking through a hospital ward, the doctor with a patient, the scholar among the books, the professor with the students. Prayer might be likened to a long distance telephone call to heaven; a call necessitating the assistance of an operator. Jesus claimed He would always be on duty to put callers through to the otherwise unreachable palace in heaven.[395]

If Christ had not come, we would not have a priesthood that is better than the old for the remission of our sins. The apostle Paul discussed in Hebrews 7:18–29 what the Incarnation meant to us and the process by which Jesus in his person and work was our high priest and how that can and did affect our relationship with God in heaven. He discusses and distinguishes the role of the Old Testament priest to that of the new, better priest in Christ.

> The former regulation is set aside because it was weak and useless (for the law made nothing perfect), and a better hope is introduced, by which we draw near to God. And it was not without an oath! Others became priest without any oath, but he became a priest with an oath when God said to him: "The Lord has sworn and will not change his mind: "You are a priest forever." Because of this oath, Jesus has become the guarantee of a better covenant. Now there have been many of those priests, since death prevented them from continuing in office; but because Jesus lives forever, he has a permanent priesthood. Therefore he is able to save completely those who come to God through him, because he always lives to intercede for them. Such a high priest meets our need--one who is holy, blameless, pure, set apart from sinners, exalted above the heavens. Unlike the other high priests, he does not need to offer sacrifices day after day, first for his own sins and then for the sins of his people. He sacrificed for their sins once for all when he offered himself. For the law appoints as high priests men who are weak; but the oath, which came after the law, appointed the Son, who has been made perfect forever.[396]

The apostle Paul lays out to the Hebrews a great Christological analysis of the person and work of Jesus Christ and that Jesus is the only high priest, that there could be no other high priest, and no one could satisfy or substitute for Jesus as our high priest. He is the decisive factor in reconciling all of humanity with God in heaven "once for all." That's why He had to come! That is not to say that others cannot do priestly duties for we have had human priests for centuries, but that would be different from the person and the work Jesus did as our high priest "once for all". This theme is echoed in Isaiah 53, which discusses the person and work of this high priest. It is of course important for the Authentic Church to have a solid scriptural and hermeneutical baseline to evaluate the Christologies of theologians to see its consistency or inconsistency with the actual person and work of Jesus Christ delineated in scripture.

Isaiah 53:1–3 (NIV) gives us a unique description of the person and work of the Redeemer who is found in Jesus Christ.

Who has believed our message and to whom has the arm of the Lord been revealed? He grew up before him like a tender shoot, and like a root out of dry ground. He had no beauty or majesty to attract us to him, nothing in his appearance that we should desire him. He was despised and rejected by men, a man of sorrows, and familiar with suffering. Like one from whom men hide their faces he was despised, and we esteemed him not (person). Surely, he took up our infirmities and carried our sorrows, yet we considered him stricken by God, smitten by him, and afflicted. But he was pierced for our transgressions, he was crushed for our iniquities; the punishment that brought us peace was upon him, and by his wounds we are healed (work).

As no other description does, this personifies the person and the work of Jesus Christ and what He did for humanity. Professor Hunsinger of Princeton Theological Seminary has suggested throughout lectures on this topic that the person of Jesus Christ equals the work and the work equals the person of Jesus Christ. One cannot be separated from the other; both are indispensable to His mission. A very interesting and sometimes overlooked portion of the Nicene Creed (AD 325) supports this proposition: "Who, for us men for our salvation, came down from heaven, and was incarnate by the Holy Spirit of the Virgin Mary, and was made man; and was crucified also for us … suffered and was buried; and the third day He rose again."

We find further support for the person and work of Christ in the Chalcedon Creed (AD 451).

The distinction of natures being by no means taken away by the union, but rather the property of each nature being preserved, and concurring in one Person and one Subsistence, not parted or divided into two persons, but one and the same Son, and only begotten, God the Word, the Lord Jesus Christ.

THE INCARNATION

The Authentic Church needs to look back at church history to recover and rediscover the great tenets of our faith; they lay out the great Christological view of all of Orthodox Christianities worldwide. The work of Christ was to mediate and reconcile human kind with an omnipotent, omnipresent, and omniscient God.

It was a vicarious work that Jesus became that substitute; He became that exchange that satisfied this all-powerful, sinless God. This person and work could not be satisfied based upon God's holiness by any entity other than Christ. Jesus was indispensable in both person and work. Former professor of practical theology at Princeton Theological Seminary Prof. Charles R. Erdman wrote in his commentary to Mark (in 1917),

> We have however, four accounts of this announcement of glad tidings and we calmly call each of the books contained in these accounts a gospel. Each was written with a slightly different purpose, and each has given us an original portrait of Christ. In Matthew we see the predicted King of the Jews, in Mark the Royal Servant, in Luke the Divine man, in John the Incarnate God. It is natural, therefore, that Matthew should open his narrative by tracing the genealogy of Jesus to David the King, that Mark should begin with a public ministry of Jesus, that Luke should give us the narrative of his birth and infancy and boyhood, and that John should give us a glimpse of his divine pre-existence and eternal glory. All, of course, wrote of the same Savior and all agreed as to the essential facts of his person and work.

What are we then to think of the person and work of Jesus Christ? He is a mediator in such a way that His incarnate person embraces both sides of the mediating relationship. He is God, of the nature of God, and man, of the nature of man, in one and the same person. He is not two realities, a divine and a human joined but one reality who confronts us as God and man. We are not to think of Jesus Christ, St. Athanasius[xliii] used to argue, as God in man, for that could be said of a prophet or a saint and stops short of what the Incarnation of the Son of God really was. Rather, we must think of Jesus Christ as God coming to us as man. Nor must he be interpreted just as the appearance of God in a human form or in the mode[xliv] of a human life, for that also would fall short of what the Incarnation was. The Incarnation means that in Jesus Christ is wholly God and wholly man but very God though he is the Son of God comes to us as a man.[397] That is a succinct statement about a high view or high Christology of Jesus Christ. Jesus Christ is the mediator of divine revelation; Professor George Hunsinger of Princeton Theological Seminary taught, "That would be from the high vector to the low vector (from God to us) and reconciliation in virtue of what he is in his own personal identity and reality the reconciliation would be (from) the low vector (to high) (from us to God)."[398] He

---

[xliii] St. Athanasius was the bishop of Alexandria, confessor, and doctor of the church born c. 296 and died 2 May 373. He was the greatest champion of Catholic belief on the Incarnation and earned the title of Father of Orthodoxy.

[xliv] Modalism is the most common theological error in understanding the Trinity. It is an unorthodox belief that God is one person who has revealed Himself in three forms or modes in contrast to the Trinitarian doctrine in which God is one being eternally existing in three persons rather than Jesus in the Incarnation acting as Son.

does not mediate a revelation or a reconciliation that is other than what He is as though He were only the agent or instrument of that mediation to humanity. Jesus is the *only* mediating agent who could satisfy the necessity of penal substitution for a sinful humanity. But no other person could take part or help in that mediation process.

> Let us take the forgiveness of sins that lies at the very heart of the evangelical message. Where we are told in the gospel that Jesus said to someone, "My son, my daughter your sins are forgiven." How are we to understand that? Are the words spoken by Jesus and forgiveness merely the words of a creature even the best and greatest of creatures? But how can a creature forgive sins? The Old Testament makes clear to forgive sin is to undo it, to blot it out as though it had not taken place but to undo an event like that, to undo the time with which it was bound up is an utterly stupendous thing which only God himself can do.[399]

This is the work of the high priest only. As suggested by the apostle Paul, the high priest could be found only in the person and work of Jesus Christ.

The Person and Work

There is no middleman between this mediation of Christ and God; it is a work done exclusively and only by Jesus Christ. It is not done by those who have been baptized, ordained, or appointed priests but only through Christ. This rings true to the issues and themes of the Reformation.

In his commentary on Galatians, Luther writes,

> Now he is not the Son as it relates to this particular issue that he became a curse for us. Paul guarded his words carefully and spoke precisely and here again a distinction must be made. Paul's words clearly show this, for he does not say that Christ became a curse on his own account but that he became a curse for us. That now he is not the Son of God born of a virgin. But he is a sinner who has and bears the sin of Paul the former blasphemer, persecutor and assaulter of Peter who denied Christ. Of David who was an adulterer and a murderer and who caused the Gentiles to blaspheme the name of the Lord. Romans 2:24. In short, he has and bears all the sins of all men in his body. Not in the sense that he has committed them but in the sense that he took these sins committed by us upon his own body in order to make satisfaction for them in his own blood. (Luther, 227)

He is and was our sacrifice and penal substitute.

Knowing now what Christ has done, if Christ had not come, how would things be different for humanity? The reason Christ came was to lift the cloak of sin and death that consumed humanity and release it in our lives. If Christ had not come, the world would be lost in sin—we would be powerless to be free from its cause and effect.

We would never experience the grace of God to fully understand its implications that separate us from God and how we are forgiven and free. Our purpose is to love God with all our heart, soul, mind, and strength and to love our neighbors as ourselves; we cannot do that without the recognition of sin and its propitiation.

Because Christ came, it opens a new field of thought that gives us a greater and deeper appreciation for the wonderful works of Christ and His glorious gospel and how that has altered the course of human history.

If Christ had not come, the Bible would close with the last verse of Malachi, a depressing and hopeless scripture that offers nothing to humanity: "I will come and strike the land with a curse" (Malachi 4:6 NIV). Its messages would be as difficult for us to grasp as it was for those who lived in the days when it was written and has little application to the modern world. Isaiah 53 would be as hard for us to fathom as it was for the Ethiopian eunuch who asked, "How can I understand unless someone explains it to me? … Tell me, please, who is the prophet talking about, himself or someone else?" (Acts 8:31, 34 NIV).

If Christ had not come, we would have no New Testament with its four Gospels portraying wonderful stories and miracles in the life of Christ and narratives that present Him as Servant and King, Son of Man and Son of God, a bright light of hope for all humanity.[400]

If Christ had not come, the beautiful story of the first Christmas, the baby in Bethlehem, which for more than two thousand years has captivated the world with peace, love, and joy, would never have been told. The star in the East would have failed to shine; the angels singing would be silenced; the shepherds on the hills would have heard and seen nothing; there would be no "peace on earth" and no "good will toward men."[401]

If Christ had not come, there would have been no miracles. The paralyzed man of Capernaum would have spent his days never moving from the mattress for there would have been no "Great Physician" to whom his friends could carry him. The invalid man at the pool of Bethesda, who had suffered thirty-eight years, who had no one to help him was told, "pick up your mat and walk" and was healed. The ten lepers, displaced and ostracized from their homes, would have grown more desperate, angry, and hateful until at last, their bodies decaying while alive, finally would have succumbed to the grave. The woman with the issue of blood who suffered for 18 years would not be free of that torment. And not to mention the countless lives that have never seen nor touched Jesus yet have received Him in their lives and who have been transformed by His love and forgiveness. Those that were hungry, poor, forgotten with no hope would never receive hope. And we would be lost in sin for eternity, totally separated from God forever.[402]

The world would be a world devoid of kindness, hope, and love. This is a picture of a world without Christ. The world would be lost in its unknown sin and rebellion toward God. But since we have seen a picture of what the world would be if Christ had not come, we see a world of which Christ had come for all humanity, including you and me.

LESSON 11
If Christ Had Not Come

If I had not come and spoken to them, they would not be guilty of sin. Now however, they have no excuse for their sin.

JOHN 15:22 (NIV)

1. What does this scripture say to you?

2. In Luke 2:11, we have the angel's pronouncement, the wonderful words that celebrate the birth of our Lord: "For unto you is born this day in the city of David a Savior, which is Christ the Lord." What does that mean to you?

3. Many people live lives devoid of God, dependent on themselves alone to make decisions. They do not need nor want spiritual direction or comfort. Whether we accept Jesus Christ as Lord and Savior, we must confront and dialogue the issues of why Christ came to earth and the profound implications it would have if he had not come. What do you think?

4. We all know the Christmas story of a baby being born in a small, dingy manger, but do we understand the theological implications of that first Christmas—what it means for us today?

5. Jesus hinted at the hopelessness man would experience had He not been born in a manger. Jesus said in John 15:22, "If I had not come and spoken to them, they would not be guilty of sin. Now, however, they have no excuse for their sin." Why is it so important that Jesus said if he did not come, we would not be aware of our sin?

6. Is that the most important reason he came?

7. Suppose Jesus had not come. How spiritually and morally destitute would the world be?

8. Explain in your own words what the Incarnation is.

9. The Incarnation meant Christ leaving his heavenly Father and coming to a helpless world to bring hope, recognition, salvation, reconciliation, and the understanding of sin and death and the possibility of eternal life. Throughout biblical history, God has been present in the affairs of humanity. Only by understanding humanity's sinfulness could people recognize the need for a Savior and understand how lost they were without God. What does the Incarnation mean to you?

10. What if some powerful hand had wiped the influence of Christ completely out of our civilization? How would the world be different?

11. God was wonderful in the Incarnation; he left his throne in glory, came to earth, wrapped himself in a baby's skin, and was born of a virgin. John leads up to this by saying,

> "In the beginning was the Word, and the Word was with God, and the Word was God. He was with God in the beginning. Through him all things were made; without him nothing was made that has been made…The Word became flesh and made his dwelling among us. We have seen his glory, the glory of the One and Only, who came from the Father, full of grace and truth."

What does this verse mean to you?

12. That night, God came to earth. That night, the Redeemer was born. That was the Incarnation. Why did God come to us?

13. Cynthia Pearl Maus, in her anthology *Christ and the Fine Arts*, includes this vivid assessment of the proclaimed Savior of the world, not what the world would accept or want.

> Here is a man who was born in an obscure village, the child of a peasant woman. He grew up in another village, and that a despised one. He worked in a carpenter's shop for thirty years, and then for three years he was an itinerant preacher. He never wrote a book. He never held an office. He never owned a home. He never had a family. He never went to college…He never traveled, except in His infancy, more than two hundred miles from the place where He was born. He had no credentials but Himself. While still a young man, the tide of popular opinion turned against Him. His friends ran away. One of them betrayed Him. He was turned over to His enemies. He went through the mockery of a trial. He was nailed on a cross between two thieves.

His executors gambled for the only piece of property He had on earth, His seamless robe. When He was dead, He was taken down from the cross and laid in a borrowed grave through the courtesy of a friend. Twenty wide centuries have come and gone, and today Jesus is the centerpiece of the human race, and the leader of all Progress.

What do you think of this statement?

14. If Christ had not come...we would not know the Father. It is sometimes easy to forget that without Christ, God would be, for many people, an inscrutable, faraway, mysterious being. Even today, in some countries, countless thousands and even millions of people worship images of wood or stone, hoping to appease a detached deity. For them, the idols represent gods who are harsh, condemning, and difficult to please. Is this a picture of what the entire world would be like if Christ had not come?

15. If Christ had not come...prayer would be impossible. Within the ancient world, only special people had access to God; such experiences were unknown among ordinary citizens. The priest alone interceded because no one else had access to the Holy of Holies. How would that be different for us today? Or is it?

16. If Christ had not come, we would not have a priesthood that is better than the old one for the remission of our sins. The Apostle Paul discussed in Hebrews 7:18–29 what the Incarnation meant to us and the process by which Jesus in his person and work was our high priest. What does that mean to us today?

17. The Apostle Paul lays out to the Hebrews a great Christological analysis of the person and work of Jesus Christ and expresses that Jesus is the only high priest, that there could be no other high priest, and that no one could satisfy or substitute for Jesus as our high priest. He is the decisive factor in reconciling all of humanity with God in heaven "once for all." Explain the "once for all" concept.

18. Isaiah 53:1–3 gives us a unique description of the person and work of the Redeemer who is found in Jesus Christ.

    Who has believed our message and to whom has the arm of the Lord been revealed? He grew up before him like a tender shoot, and like a root out of dry ground. He had no beauty or majesty to attract us to him, nothing in his appearance that we should desire him. He was despised and rejected by men, a man of sorrows, and familiar with suffering. Like one from whom men hide their faces he was despised, and we esteemed him not (person). Surely, he took up our infirmities and carried our sorrows, yet we considered him stricken by God, smitten by him, and afflicted. But he was pierced for our transgressions, he was crushed for our iniquities; the punishment that brought us peace was upon him, and by his wounds we are healed (work).

    Explain in your own words the person and work of Jesus Christ.

19. A very interesting and sometimes overlooked portion of the Nicene Creed (AD 325) supports this proposition: "Who, for us men for our salvation, came down from heaven, and was incarnate by the Holy Spirit of the Virgin Mary, and was made man; and was crucified also for us…suffered and was buried; and the third day He rose again." Is this old creed relevant for today?

20. We find further support for the person and work of Christ in the Chalcedon Creed (AD 451):

> "The distinction of natures being by no means taken away by the union, but rather the property of each nature being preserved, and concurring in one Person and one Subsistence, not parted or divided into two persons, but one and the same Son, and only begotten, God the Word, the Lord Jesus Christ."

What does this mean?

21. Do you believe the person and work of Christ was to mediate and reconcile human kind with an omnipotent, omnipresent, and omniscient God?

22. It was a vicarious work that Jesus became that substitute; he became that exchange that satisfied this all-powerful, sinless God. This person and work could not be satisfied based upon God's holiness by any entity other than Christ. Jesus was indispensable in both person and work. Do you understand what a vicarious work is?

23. What do you think of the person and work of Jesus Christ? Is he a mediator in such a way that his incarnate person embraces both sides of the mediating relationship? He is God, of the nature of God, and man, of the nature of man, in one and the same person. He is two realities, a divine and a human joined, but one reality who confronts us as God and man. Are we to think of Jesus Christ, as St. Athanasius used to argue, as God in man? For that could be said of a prophet or a saint and stops short of what the Incarnation of the Son of God really was. Rather, we must think of Jesus Christ as God coming to us as man.

24. Jesus is the *only* mediating agent who could satisfy the necessity of penal substitution for a sinful humanity. Could any other person take part in or help with that mediation process?

25. Do you agree in this Reformed theology? There is no middleman between man and Christ; it is a work done exclusively and only by Jesus Christ for humanity. It is not done by those who have been baptized, ordained, or appointed priests.

26. Modalism is a most common theological error in understanding the Trinity. It is an unorthodox belief that God is one person who has revealed himself in three forms, or modes, in contrast to the Trinitarian doctrine in which God is one being eternally existing in three persons rather than Jesus in the Incarnation acting as Son. Do you understand the difference? Explain.

27. Knowing now what Christ has done, if Christ had not come, how would things be different for humanity?

28. If Christ had not come, the Bible would close with the last verse of _____, a depressing and hopeless scripture that offers nothing to humanity.

29. If Christ had not come, we would have no New Testament with its four Gospels portraying wonderful stories and miracles in the life of Christ and narratives that present Christ in his 3 offices _____, _____, and _____ Son of Man and Son of God, a bright light of hope for all humanity.

30. If Christ had not come, _____ _____ _____ of _____,
the baby born in Bethlehem, which for more than two thousand years has captivated the
world with peace, love, and joy, would never have been told.

31. If Christ had not come, the world would have no _____. The
_____ of Capernaum would have spent his days never moving
from the mattress, for there would have been no "Great Physician" to whom his friends
could carry him. The _____ at the pool of Bethesda, who had
suffered thirty-eight years, who had no one to help him was told, "pick up your mat and
walk" and was healed. The _____, displaced and ostracized
from their homes, would have grown more desperate, angry, and hateful until at last, their
bodies decaying while alive, they finally would have succumbed to the grave.

———•— CHAPTER 12 —•———

Missional Objectives of the Authentic Church:
The Poor, Homeless, Displaced and Aliens[xlv], [403]

For the administration of this service not only supplies the needs of the saints, but also is abounding through many thanksgivings to God, while, through the proof of this ministry, they glorify God for the obedience of your confession to the gospel of Christ, and for your liberal sharing with them and all men, and by their prayer for you, who long for you because of the exceeding grace of God in you. Thanks be to God for His indescribable gift!
2 CORINTHIANS 9:12–15 (NKJV)

Jürgen Moltmann, a German Reformed theologian wrote, "Fellowship with Christ always leads us deeper into suffering with humanity."[404] The Authentic Church must partake of that suffering. One of the most difficult ministries to begin in a new or start-up church is the directive of ministry to the poor. How can a start-up ministry have any effective ministry to the poor with little or no financing, that being balanced with the Lord's directive to take care of the poor and displaced? It's not only possible but also necessary. A ministry such as this could start very small with collecting coats from friends and family and giving them to those without, making sandwiches for those in our community who don't get enough to eat, or collecting socks and gloves from those who have and donating them to those in need.

Our mission field is the community in which the church is planted. The Authentic Church

---

[xlv] This chapter was originally adopted from a paper submitted for missional hermeneutics taught by Darrell Guder, professor of missional and ecumenical theology emeritus at Princeton Theological Seminary, where he served as Henry Winters Luce Professor of Missional and Ecumenicals Theology. It was a privilege to be in the last class Dr. Guder taught at Princeton Theological Seminary and to encounter missional hermeneutics for the first time.

believes that our missional objectives must be meeting the community and the congregation's needs where they are today.

One of the most important aspects of any ministry is consistency. You have to be at a specific place and time to allow those in need to realize it is the time and place of ministry and you are always there for them. This is a key component to having a successful ministry to the poor, homeless, and displaced. The overriding principle in the mission of the church should be to meet the needs of the poor, displaced, and undocumented aliens. Who knows if one of us will ever be in need of a meal, clothing, toothbrush, or socks?

The outreach to the poor that started at our local community church didn't start at a budget or staff meeting, but organically. I received a phone call. "Is this Pastor Rob?" I said yes. "Do you recognize my voice?" I said it sounded familiar but no. The caller identified herself as my fifth-grade teacher. She said that she operated a ministry to the poor she had started from the trunk of her car and that the church sponsoring her work no longer wanted to. I told her sight unseen to bring her ministry to our church though it was just forming and very small. I gave her what little resources we had: a storage area, space in the sanctuary to do the outreach on Saturdays, and money to support the ministry in our town.

From this very simple beginning, our mission to the poor has grown into one of the largest outreach programs in the county. We currently have numerous volunteers who set up and minister to those in need. We give blankets, coats, clothing, food, propane gas, tents, medical treatment, haircuts, and other necessities we store in a facility adjacent to the premises.

Most important, unlike any others I know of, our outreach provides a sense of community for those going through difficult personal or financial crises. Although many of the homeless do not attend our church services, we bring our services to them. After years of trying unsuccessfully to get those who were receiving support from the ministry into our regular Sunday church services, we decided to bring a chapel service to them on the day of the outreach. We have people who will offer spiritual guidance, prayers, support, and spiritual counseling to those who come. The chapel service begins before the outreach. This ministry has helped address the physical and spiritual needs of thousands over the years. The small financial burden it places on the church (most all resources are donated) is dwarfed by the tremendous spiritual blessings people in the community receive through this ministry as well as for the volunteers who help.

When a church looks at its financial bottom line, if it has a ministry to the poor, it may quickly realize it is a drain on the church's few resources. If one is objective about the benefits from the ministry to the poor, the church may not be able to justify it. In many cases, the resources go to those who may never attend a Sunday service or support the ministry they benefit from. But is the financial bottom line of the church more important than the opportunity to touch the souls of those in need in one's community? At times, it can be frustrating to use social and financial resources for what often seems like a bottomless pit, but we must remember the words of Christ, "Whatever you did for one of the least of these brothers of mine, you did for me."[405]

What does the Bible dictate to us about the treatment of the displaced, homeless, strangers, and aliens? Ephesians 2:19 (ESV) says, "So then you are no longer strangers and aliens, but you are fellow citizens with the saints and members of the household of God." Though we may travel far and wide, there is nothing like returning home after a trip. Having a place where we always belong is a great blessing whether it is a castle or a tent. John Howard Payne captured well the love people have for their home in the song "Home Sweet Home" from his operetta *Clari, Maid of Milan*: "Be it ever so humble, there's no place like home!"[406] Many of the people we minister to don't have homes, and the items they received from this outreach are indispensable for their daily living. For many, the church and the community of believers is the only place they could call home. Many call it their safe house.

Ought not the Christian church and the mission of the church, which is to be inclusive of all humanity, help address such local concerns? Do not those verses and the verse from Ephesians incorporate the universal hope and mission of the church? In our church, we serve immigrants and refugees who do not speak English and have little or nothing and at the same time partake in and benefit from our outreach. Yes, we have the poor, homeless, displaced, and even illegal aliens in our Authentic Church, but isn't that what church is supposed to be?

Given the longing we all have for a place to call home, it follows that one of the worst fates that can ever befall us is homelessness. This is the plight of countless people locally and all around the world who due to politics, finances, mental and physical conditions, and other reasons have been displaced. We are in this together. Moreover, all people who do not know the Lord and Savior Jesus Christ suffer this condition spiritually speaking. Without personal faith in His person and work, we have no home in the one kingdom that will last forever—the kingdom of God. But many have dire spiritual and physical needs the church must address regardless of the expense.

The experience of being an outsider or stranger is not restricted to people living far from their countries. You can feel like a stranger in your own country and even in your own town, home, or family. For personal, political, or religious reasons, someone can feel distanced from and even rejected by his or her family or people. The author of Psalm 69 gives voice to this when persecuted for his faithfulness to God: "I am a stranger to my brothers, an alien to my own mother's sons."[407] Even at Nazareth, right at the start of his ministry, Jesus probably felt like an outsider when He declared, "No prophet is accepted in his home town."[408] Condemned to death and rejected by the Jewish authorities, unjustly prosecuted like the psalmist, he was the outsider par excellence.[409] Many who are displaced, down on their luck, or homeless feel disconnected from society. The Authentic Church is the hope for these people materially and spiritually.

I am sure many of us have interacted with strangers, foreigners, the homeless, and aliens. Maybe those people are of a different background, race, ethnic group or come from a different country. How is the church to treat these people in light of the directives of the Bible? How are we to act to others and to the world at large? How are we to act and react in a Christian context to these issues that are relevant to Christianity today? We may look to ancient Israel for clarity on the proper role and conduct for the treatment of those in need.

Almost as soon as they had settled in the Promised Land, the people of Israel found themselves faced with the question of what to do about foreigners. Among the foreigners in Israel were those who had accompanied them on their flight from Egypt (Exodus 12:38); there were also Canaanites like Rahab and those who came later to Israel such as Ruth the Moabite and Uriah the Hittite. At the time of King Solomon, there were about 150,000 such aliens in Israel (2 Chronicles 2:17) or about a tenth of the country's population. As is usual today, most of these were unskilled laborers and workers (1 Chronicles 22:2; 2 Chronicles 8:7–8).[410]

The Israelites were neither better nor worse than other peoples, but because they believed they were God's chosen people and here for a specific purpose, they too often looked down on the foreigners in their midst. Is this what the Christian church is doing today? This is why the Mosaic Law contains detailed teachings concerning aliens and strangers. This teaching is reiterated by the prophets who continually reminded the Israelites of how they should behave toward strangers. Unlike the Old Testament, the New Testament says less about foreigners because Jesus destroyed the dividing wall between Jews and non-Jews. By His death on the cross, He made a new covenant from which no people on earth were excluded (Ephesians 2:11–19).[411] All are equal and valuable in heaven's economy.

Mosaic Law frequently associates aliens[xlvi] and strangers with widows, orphans, the poor, and Levites. This emphasizes that a foreigner's life is not an easy one. Their work is often hard and poorly paid, and they may not be able to afford good housing. In addition to any material difficulties they face are emotional challenges, they are an uprooted people deprived of the comfort of their native culture, language, family, and friends; they are alone. This loneliness is all the more painful because it is seldom a personal choice; hence, the tendency for foreigners to stick together. They attempt thereby to recreate their home environments.[412]

Let us explore an overview of this theme of strangers, aliens, and the displaced throughout

---

[xlvi] *Alien* used in a biblical context is not different from its English usage term, one belonging to a foreign country or nation; a foreigner is not a naturalized citizen of the country in which he or she is living.

the Bible for guidance. Israel's self-identity was tied to the knowledge that the nation's ancestors starting with Abraham and Sarah and continuing through to the exodus from Egypt were sojourners, immigrants, and aliens, explains Charles Van Engen.[413] Israel's history was used by the Lord to "participate in God's mission to the nations."[414] For example, Abraham's missionary call required him to become a pilgrim in another land; there, he became a great nation and indeed a blessing to every nation (Genesis 12:1–3).[415] The great father of Israel and the one who would bless humanity in the future was a stranger and alien, homeless in his sojourns.

Another agent of God's mission for the world is Joseph. Forced to live as a stranger, immigrant, and even as a slave in Egypt, he endured false accusations, prison, and loneliness. Yet the Lord used him to save his family, the Egyptians, and the surrounding nations from the effects of a great famine (Genesis 50:20).[416] He too was an alien and stranger.

Additionally, Daniel (Daniel 1:3–7), an exiled prisoner, was sent by God to provide counsel to the kings of Babylon and Persia.[417] Unfortunately, during times when Israel refused to fulfill its role to be a missionary of God to the world, God used foreign nations to judge His people, hoping they would return to Him.[418] He too was an alien and stranger.

Finally, the story of Ruth represents how the Lord used a Moabite widow to heal a daughter of Israel, Naomi, of her bitterness (Ruth 1:20). Boaz, the righteous Israelite, follows the commands of God by welcoming Ruth to the community, protecting her from abuse, and allowing her to glean from his vineyard (Ruth 2:8–9).[419] The Bible directs that aliens, strangers, and the displaced be treated with love, compassion, equality, and dignity.

Charles Van Engen states, "It is precisely because Ruth is a stranger, a widow, and an alien, that God was able to use her in the environment of the faithfulness, compassion, and love of Boaz to bring about the healing of Naomi's bitterness."[420]

God commanded the Israelites to love strangers who entered their land more than thirty times in the Hebrew Bible.[421] God tells them not to oppress or exploit aliens in their midst but to embrace them as their family members. This is because the Israelites were once strangers in the land of Egypt: "You shall also love the stranger, for you were strangers in the land of Egypt" (Exodus 23:9).[422] This ministry to the poor must be integrated into *A New Model of the Authentic Church*. R. K. Harrison suggests that the Israelites' love for strangers in their land demonstrates their gratitude to God for liberating them from slavery and restoring their right to be free individuals.[423]

> The Spirit of the Lord is upon me, because he has anointed me to bring good news to the poor He has sent me to proclaim release to the captives and recovery of sight to the blind to let the oppressed go free, to proclaim the year of the Lord's favor. (Luke 4:18; cf. Isaiah 61:1–2a)

This Old Testament verse is of interest because the Israelites used it to rejoice in their freedom and Jesus quoted this scripture when He spoke of His person, work, and relation to humanity.

Elliot Wright wrote, "The modern church should pay close attention to the way Jesus identified himself with the poor, the oppressed and those of no social status. He brought dignity, hope and a feeling of worth to those most dejected and unacceptable."[424]

The Authentic Church needs to be missionally minded. It is imperative that the Authentic Church be integrated into society and meet the needs of society while still keeping its Christian perspective. Let us briefly explore the components of the missional church and its relation to meeting the needs of the poor, homeless, displaced, and aliens.

> The church growth and church health movements as well as the emerging church movements are driven by changes in our cultural environments and seek to respond to these changes by focusing on strategies, methods and programs or by attempting to return to early church practices. The missional discussion, while also recognizing these changes, calls us first to go back to the biblical narrative, to theologically and missiologically define the nature and essence of the church. A key point in missional theology is that understanding the nature of the church is foundational to clarifying the purpose for which the church exists. How does our understanding of the church's nature impact our thinking in regard to the church's purpose, structures and strategies for participating in God's mission in the midst of ever-changing social environments? While valuing structure, programs and new methods of reaching the culture, those must follow the theological and missiological work by first understanding the church's nature and essence as depicted in the biblical text. It is for this reason that certain authors and church ministries sometimes call themselves both emergent and missional—they incorporate concepts and practices from more than one stream of the conversation about the church and its calling.[425]

The Authentic Church incorporates and balances these elements.

Missional theology has been attempting to address two primary concerns: the Western church's struggle to forge ahead in mission in a postcolonial world, and the need for a missionary ecclesiology (theology of the church) in a post-Christendom[xlvii] world (where the

---

[xlvii] In missional theology, the term *Christendom* refers to the European system of state-church partnership and cultural power and authority in which the church was the protected, privileged, established, and an institutional form of religion in society. In North America, although we have not had a state-church, the legacy of European Christendom has exercised itself more in functional terms rather than through legally established status.

church no longer has power and privilege).[426] The church successfully took the gospel to the ends of the earth during the colonial era. The nineteenth century was indeed the golden age of missions. The movement was shaped by Western expansion and often included the extension of Western cultures to the developing and undeveloped sectors of the world. Western churches saw themselves as supporting missions work to largely non-Christians.[427]

Missional theologians believe that two major problems have developed in the Western church largely because of its once self-perceived privileged status in society and because of its Western individualism and the success it had in colonizing other cultures. These problems have made it difficult for the church to be true to its missionary nature. To address this crisis, missional theologians call for the church to take a double posture in society as an alternative community in the culture that is shaped by the scriptures and the redemptive reign of God and as an agent that is critical of the status quo. Missional theologians see such a double posture as an antidote to a church that has largely accommodated to North American culture and in doing so has "lost its saltiness," where its missionary nature has been eclipsed by its past established position in society.[428]

Over the past century, a number of theologians have recognized that mission is not simply a peripheral theme in the biblical story. Rather, it is a central thread in the biblical writings and central to the identity of the church. Thus, a missional hermeneutic is a way of reading scripture in which mission is a central interpretive key that unlocks the whole narrative of Scripture. It does not simply study the theme of mission but reads the whole of the biblical canon with mission as one of its central themes. This will explore what it might mean to read both the Old Testament and the New Testament with a missional hermeneutic, and what that might mean for the missional praxis of the church, specifically preaching, theological education, and the life of the local congregation.[429]

Deuteronomy mobilizes the church to live with gratitude and generosity for the sake of the world. Reading the Bible missionally includes attending to biblical ethics and seeing how they are embedded in theology to shape and as a display to people before the world. Deuteronomy gives a pattern for a community in which every person, especially the most vulnerable, can thrive.[430]

These missional theologians see the individualism of the Western church as a major contributing factor to the individualist notion of mission resulting in missions being defined in terms of the activities of individual Christians. They believe that a more communal church would be more effective in connecting society to the gospel and would aid the church in being a prophetic voice (critical factor) that pointed out the destructive evils of society. At the risk of oversimplifying, one could summarize by saying that a strengthening of the communal and critical dimensions of the church (missional influence) are the missional theologians' antidote to the established individualism and conformity of the church to culture (Christendom influence) that have hindered our effectiveness for the gospel as God's missionary people.[431]

They affirm that God's mission includes our societies and communities as well as distant peoples and cultures. They deny that the urgency of mission to nominally Christian cultures is equal to that of distant cultures and people groups that have never heard the gospel.[432] This is a full and complete understanding of the Great Commission. It encapsulates both aspects of world evangelization—those close and those far.

In his well-known prophetic description of the Last Judgment in Matthew 25:35, Jesus, by associating with the foreigner, the hungry and thirsty, the naked, the sick, and the prisoners, draws our attention to the precarious living conditions of many. Jesus is not preaching salvation by works in this text, but He clearly shows us that true belief in Him necessarily manifests itself in acts of solidarity with those most in need, including the displaced: "I was a stranger and you invited me in."[433]

The homeless, the poor, the displaced, and foreigners have been created in the image of God and therefore have great dignity and are worthy of respect and love. The Israelites had even more reason to show respect to foreigners since because of their history, they were well qualified to identify with them: "Do not oppress an alien; you yourselves know how it feels to be aliens, because you were aliens in Egypt" (Exodus 23:9, 22–31). Respect for foreigners begins with respecting their basic rights. Mosaic Law cites the following: Sabbath rest (Exodus 20:10, 23:12; Leviticus 25:6; Deuteronomy 5:14), a fair wage (Deuteronomy 24:14–15), and access to unbiased justice (Leviticus 24:22; Deuteronomy 1:16, 24:17–27:19).[434]

As a nation, Israel had to respect the rights of those living in its midst. The Israelites had to go further. The command to love your neighbor (Leviticus 19:18) was extended to the foreigner: "When an alien lives with you in your land, do not ill-treat him. The alien living with you must be treated as one of your native-born. Love him as yourself, for you were aliens in Egypt" (Leviticus 19:33–34; Deuteronomy 10:19). Love your neighbor as yourself; love the alien as yourself. From this commandment, we can draw two conclusions: aliens are our neighbors though they may not share our background, culture, or religion. Second, if the Israelites had to take special care of aliens because of their particular circumstances, we should show greater understanding and concern for the aliens in our midst. Jesus affirms this teaching of the law and brings out its full meaning in the parable of the good Samaritan.

> "And who is my neighbor?" In reply, Jesus said: "A man was going down from Jerusalem to Jericho, when he fell into the hands of robbers. They stripped him of his clothes, beat him and went away, leaving him half dead. A priest happened to be going down the same road, and when he saw the man, he

passed by on the other side. So too, a Levite, when he came to the place and saw him, passed by on the other side. But a Samaritan, as he traveled, came where the man was; and when he saw him, he took pity on him. He went to him and bandaged his wounds, pouring on oil and wine. Then he put the man on his own donkey, took him to an inn and took care of him. The next day he took out two silver coins and gave them to the innkeeper. "Look after him," he said, "and when I return, I will reimburse you for any extra expense you may have." "Which of these three do you think was a neighbor to the man who fell into the hands of robbers?" The expert in the law replied, "The one who had mercy on him." Jesus told him, "Go and do likewise." (Luke 10:29–37 NIV)

Jesus clearly link commandments of love your neighbor and to love the alien.[435]

The story about a man robbed and beaten on the road from Jerusalem to Jericho is one of the best known of Jesus' parables. If we follow the clues left by Luke in his crafting of the narrative, we read the parable as a story illustrating that love of one's neighbor emphasized in the preceding conversation.

On one occasion an expert in the law stood up to test Jesus. "Teacher," he asked, "what must I do to inherit eternal life?" "What is written in the Law?" he replied. "How do you read it?" He answered: "'Love the Lord your God with all your heart and with all your soul and with all your strength and with all your mind; and Love your neighbor as yourself.'" "You have answered correctly," Jesus replied. "Do this and you will live." But he wanted to justify himself, so he asked Jesus "And who is my neighbor?" (Luke 10:25–29 NIV)

By turning the question of who my neighbor is into a question about which one was a neighbor to the man who fell into the hands of the robbers, the parable refuses to set any limits on the command to love. The Samaritan functions as a model of Christian love. If a despised Samaritan can show love of neighbor in this way, certainly a Christian reader can do that same (v. 37: "Go and do likewise") and more so the Authentic Church. This interpretation of the parable has considerable force; after all, it appears to be the way Luke read the parable and wished his first readers to hear it; it can inspire concrete acts of compassion toward those in need no matter their race, class, or nationality.[436] The Authentic Church must be missionally minded in its areas of influence.

In 1 Peter, Christians are called to live in contrast to society and the world around them. The world has always been a challenge for Christians to not take part in idolatry, materialism, debauchery, and other forms of evil.

Dear friends, I urge you, as aliens and strangers in the world, to abstain from sinful desires, which war against your soul. Live such good lives among the pagans that, though they accuse you of doing wrong, they may see your good deeds and glorify God on the day he visits us. (1 Peter 2:11–12 NIV)

Framing our relationship to the world as "aliens and strangers," the writer reminds us that we are "only passing through" this world; since Jesus' kingdom does not belong to this world, neither do we. If we are indeed aliens and strangers to this world, we should not overinvest in it but give much more attention to the spiritual kingdom that will never end.

Therefore, we should "abstain from sinful desires." However, there is the second and larger concern here: our lives (now at peace because of Jesus) might announce the kingdom of God to those who might even accuse us falsely. The result of our lives, according to this text, is that others might be prepared to worship God when He comes again because of the way we treated them in this world.

Peter's point is that as saints, we are no longer citizens of this present evil age but are destined for another world in which we will live eternally as heavenly citizens, children in the family of God.[437] But this does not excuse us to live rightly in the here and now.

A pilgrim in a hurried world and flurried,
Where hearts are aching and where hopes are buried;
Where bowers of ease and pleasures are enticing,
Where heedless lives the good are sacrificing;
A world of turmoil and of strife and danger—
Yes, I'm a pilgrim here, and I'm a stranger.
   —Wm. M. Runyon

Peter reminds his readers that they are "God's elect, strangers in the world ... who have been chosen" (1 Peter 1:1–2 NIV). Being God's chosen people does not keep us from life's storms but is our security in life's storms. The psalmist reminds us, "God is our refuge and strength, an ever-present help in trouble." When we are in the midst of a "storm, we usually ask God to calm it. Until he does, we may pray: 'Lord, keep me afloat during this storm.' The sea around us might be raging but in our hearts, there can be the peace of God."[438]

Though we travel as strangers or temporary residents in this world, the Lord wants us to do good along the way and promote the well-being of church and society. The pilgrim Abraham was a great man of faith who interceded for Sodom and rescued Lot. Like Abraham, Peter urges believers to make a difference in this world for God and do good by loving their neighbors whoever they may be. We are called to take part of God's love and practice and throw out lifelines and thus fulfill our part of the Great Commission to those in need. Many of us have been strangers at some time in our lives.[439] Jesus has looked at all peoples whether stranger, alien, foreigner, homeless, or displaced persons as one.

Ephesians 2:11–21 supports this proposition. After the advent of Jesus Christ, the distinction between native and foreigner, Jew and Gentile, has been transcended: "So then you are no longer strangers and sojourners but you are fellow citizens with the saints and members of the household of God."[440]

The Authentic Church needs to realign itself with the missional purpose of the gospel. A ministry to the poor, displaced, and aliens is spiritual food for the church and an indispensable ministry every church must have. It should not matter what size your budget is, your church can minister to the poor. Along with the teachings and preaching of God's Word, those in need can receive material necessities to survive and spiritual food to encourage them. How could you hear a sermon or sit in church if you haven't eaten in two days? The church must be socially active and missionally minded and not relegate the ministry of the poor as an afterthought or to government programs. Whether there is enough room in the church's budget should not be dispositive. Jesus fed the multitudes in Word and in deed; the Authentic Church ought to do the same.

Lesson 12

Missional Objectives of the Authentic Church: The Poor, Homeless, Displaced and Aliens

For the administration of this service not only supplies the needs of the saints, but also is abounding through many thanksgivings to God, while, through the proof of this ministry, they glorify God for the obedience of your confession to the gospel of Christ, and for your liberal sharing with them and all men, and by their prayer for you, who long for you because of the exceeding grace of God in you. Thanks be to God for His indescribable gift!

2 Corinthians 9:12–15 (NKJV)

1. What does this scripture say to you?

2. Jürgen Moltmann, a German Reformed theologian wrote, "Fellowship with Christ always leads us deeper into suffering with humanity." How does that apply to the Authentic Church?

3. Should an overriding principle in the mission of the church be to meet the needs of the poor, homeless, displaced, and undocumented aliens?

4. One of the most difficult ministries to begin in a new or start-up church is a ministry to the poor. How can a start-up ministry have an effective ministry to the poor with little or no financing while at the same time balancing that with the Lord's directive to take care of the poor and displaced?

5. The Authentic Church believes that our missional objectives must be meeting the community and the congregation's needs where they are today. Missions begin at home. What do you think of that concept?

6. When a church looks at its financial bottom line, if it has a ministry to the poor, it will quickly realize that it may drain the church's few resources. In light of that, should the church still pursue the ministry?

7. What about the issue of resources going to those who may never attend a Sunday service or support financially the ministry they benefit from?

8. What does the Bible dictate to us about the treatment of the displaced, homeless, strangers, and aliens? Look at the directives the Lord gave Israel: "You shall also love the stranger, for you were strangers in the land of Egypt" (Exodus 23:9). Is that relevant to the church today?

9. The Bible says, "So then you are no longer strangers and aliens, but you are fellow citizens with the saints and members of the household of God." Does that apply to today's immigrants?

10. Should the Christian church and the mission of the church, which is to be inclusive of all humanity, help address such local concerns such as homelessness, displaced individuals, and aliens?

11. Many who are displaced or homeless feel disconnected from society. The Authentic Church may be the only hope for these people, materially and spiritually. Is that a ministry for the local church, government agencies, or both?

12. In light of biblical directives, how is the Authentic Church to treat people of different backgrounds, races, and ethnicities who come from different countries?

13. How are we to act and react in a Christian context to these issues that are relevant to Christianity today? Should we look to ancient Israel for direction on the proper role and treatment of those in need?

    Review these scriptures in light of the subject matter and comment on them.

    What does Exodus 12:38 say on this matter?

    What does 2 Chronicles 2:17 say on this matter?

    What does 1 Chronicles 22:2 say on this matter?

What does 2 Chronicles 8:7–8 say on this matter?

14. How is Israel's history used by the Lord to "participate in God's mission to the nations"?

15. Abraham's missionary call required him to become a pilgrim in another land; there, he became a great nation and indeed a blessing to every nation (Genesis 12:1–3). Were Abraham and his people homeless, displaced, and aliens in a foreign land?

16. Joseph was forced to live as a stranger, an immigrant, and even as a slave in Egypt; he endured false accusations, prison, and loneliness. Yet the Lord used him to save his family, the Egyptians, and the surrounding nations from the effects of a great famine (Genesis 50:20). Daniel (Daniel 1:3–7) an exiled prisoner, was sent by God to provide counsel to the kings of Babylon and Persia. The story of Ruth represents how the Lord used a Moabite widow to heal a daughter of Israel, Naomi, of her bitterness (Ruth 1:20). What do these examples tell us about the standard of how the church needs to help those in need?

17. Jesus said, "The Spirit of the Lord is upon me, because he has anointed me to bring good news to the poor He has sent me to proclaim release to the captives and recovery of sight to the blind to let the oppressed go free, to proclaim the year of the Lord's favor" (Luke 4:18; cf. Isaiah 61:1–2a). Has the church embraced this directive?

18. Should the American church pay close attention to the way Jesus identified himself with the poor, the oppressed, and those of no social status? He brought dignity, hope, and a feeling of worth to those most dejected and unacceptable.

19. Missional theology has been attempting to address two primary concerns: the Western church's struggle to forge ahead in mission in a postcolonial world, and the need for a missionary ecclesiology (theology of the church) in a post-Christendom world (where the church no longer has power and privilege). Is Missional Theology relevant in today's world?

20. Missional hermeneutics is a way of reading scripture in which mission is a central interpretive key that unlocks the whole narrative of scripture. Reading the Bible missionally includes attending to biblical ethics and seeing how they are embedded in theology to shape and act as a display to people before the world. Do you believe the church should be more conscious of this?

21. Missional theologians call for the church to take a double posture in society. One as an alternative community in the culture that is shaped by the scriptures and the redemptive reign of God and the other as an agent that is critical of the status quo. Is there a scriptural basis for that?

22. Is Matthew 25:35 relevant to the discussion?

23. "Do not oppress an alien; you yourselves know how it feels to be aliens, because you were aliens in Egypt" Exodus 23:9. How are we to understand this and apply it?

24. The story about a man robbed and beaten on the road from Jerusalem to Jericho is one of the best known of Jesus' parables. "A man was going down from Jerusalem to Jericho, when he fell into the hands of robbers. They stripped him of his clothes, beat him and went away, leaving him half dead. A priest happened to be going down the same road, and when he saw the man, he passed by on the other side. So too, a Levite, when he came to the place and saw him, passed by on the other side. But a Samaritan, as he traveled, came where the man was; and when he saw him, he took pity on him. He went to him and bandaged his wounds, pouring on oil and wine. Then he put the man on his own donkey, took him to an inn and took care of him. The next day he took out two silver coins and gave them to the innkeeper. 'Look after him,' he said, 'and when I return, I will reimburse you for any extra expense you may have.' Which of these three do you think was a neighbor to the man who fell into the hands of robbers?" The expert in the law replied, "The one who had mercy on him." Jesus told him, "Go and do likewise." (Luke 10:29–37)

   Has the modern church done the same?

25. Christians are called to live in contrast to society and the world around them. Is that what the American church is doing? See 1 Peter 2:11–12. What does this tell us?

26. Peter reminds his readers that they are "God's elect, strangers in the world…who have been chosen". See 1 Peter 1:1–2. What does this mean?

27. Ephesians 2:11–21 supports the proposition. After the advent of Jesus Christ, the distinction between native and foreigner, Jew and Gentile, has been transcended: "So then you are no longer strangers and sojourners but you are fellow citizens with the saints and members of the household of God." Is this how the church is acting?

28. The Authentic Church needs to realign itself with the missional purpose of the gospel. A ministry to the poor, the displaced, and aliens is spiritual food for the church and an indispensable ministry every church must have. It should not matter what size your budget is, your church can minister to the poor. Do you believe that should be part of the missional objectives of the church?

——— CHAPTER 13 ———

The Mustard-Seed Principle of Building a Ministry

Another parable put he forth unto them, saying, The kingdom of heaven is like to a grain of mustard seed, which a man took, and sowed in his field: Which indeed is the least of all seeds: but when it is grown, it is the greatest among herbs, and becometh a tree, so that the birds of the air come and lodge in the branches thereof.

MATTHEW 13:31–32 (KJV)

If you want to start a ministry, understand the principle of the mustard seed. It will encourage you to start a ministry regardless of your resources of time, money, or talents. It does not require you to invest in elaborate items or spend resources unnecessarily; it requires you to optimize your resources so the ministry can grow.

The mustard-seed principle says that you can start a ministry even if it is small and insignificant in the beginning. It is ultimately not how you start a ministry but how you allow it to unfold as you learn how to make your ministry effective. The principles of the mustard-seed ministry mirror the principles of the kingdom of God and like it work in a natural progression. This principle celebrates the beginning as well as the successes in ministry while protecting you against unreasonable expectations and unrealistic goals that can lead to failure and the destruction of the work and the workers alike. Mustard-seed ministries start where you are planted and grow at the same speed as you develop your ministry skills. In this model, you can start small without all the unneeded pressures and resources that accompany overreaching.

What are mustard seeds, and what can we discern from them that will encourage and help us step out of our comfort zones and begin a new work?

Mustard seeds are the small round seeds of various mustard plants. The seeds are usually about 1 or 2 mm in diameter. Mustard seeds may be colored from yellowish white to black. They are important herbs in many regional foods. The seeds can come from three different plants: black mustard (Brassica nigra), brown Indian mustard (B. juncea), and white mustard (B. hirta/Sinapis alba) … Mustard seeds generally take three to ten days to germinate if placed under the proper conditions, which include a cold atmosphere and relatively moist soil. Mature mustard plants grow into shrubs.[441]

In the New Testament of the Judeo-Christian Bible, the mustard seed is used by Jesus in the parable of the mustard seed as a model for the Kingdom of God which initially starts small, but grows to be the biggest of all garden plants. Faith is also spoken about in the context of a mustard seed.[442]

The earliest reference to a mustard seed is in India from a story of Gautama Buddha in the fifth century BC. Gautama Buddha told the story of the grieving mother and the mustard seed. When the mother loses her only son, she takes his body to the Buddha to find a cure. The Buddha asks her to bring a handful of mustard seeds from a family that has never lost a child, husband, parent, or friend. When the mother is unable to find such a house in her village, she realizes death is common to all, and she cannot be selfish in her grief.[443]

The parable of the mustard seed is one of the shorter parables; it is in three of the canonical Gospels. The differences between its depiction in the Gospels of Matthew (13:31–32), Mark (4:30–32), and Luke (13:18–19) are minor. In the Gospels of Matthew and Luke, it is immediately followed by the parable of the leaven, which shares this parable's theme of the kingdom of heaven growing from small beginnings.[444] In Matthew, the parable is as follows.

He told them another parable: "The kingdom of heaven is like a mustard seed, which a man took and planted in his field. Though it is the smallest of all your seeds, yet when it grows, it is the largest of garden plants and becomes a tree, so that the birds of the air come and perch in its branches."[445]

Mark's Gospel has it,

"Again," he said, "What shall we say the kingdom of God is like, or what parable shall we use to describe it? It is like a mustard seed, which is the smallest seed you plant in the ground. Yet when planted, it grows and becomes the largest of all garden plants, with such big branches that the birds of the air can perch in its shade."[446]

In the Gospel of Luke, we read,

> Then Jesus asked, "What is the kingdom of God like? What shall I compare it to? It is like a mustard seed, which a man took and planted in his garden. It grew and became a tree, and the birds of the air perched in its branches."[447]

The plant referred to here is generally considered to be black mustard, a large annual plant up to 9 feet (2.7 m) tall, but growing from a proverbially small seed (this smallness is also used to refer to faith in Matthew 17:20 and Luke 17:6). According to rabbinical sources, Jews did not grow the plant in gardens, and this is consistent with Matthew's description of it growing in a field. Luke tells the parable with the plant in a garden instead; this is presumably recasting the story for an audience outside Judea/Palestine.[448]

I. Howard Marshall writes that the parable "suggests the growth of the kingdom of God from tiny beginnings to worldwide size." The Parable of the Leaven (which in the Gospels of Matthew and Luke immediately follows) shares this theme of large growth from small beginnings. As with the Parable of the Sower, which in Matthew and Mark occurs earlier in the same chapter, the man sowing the seed represents Jesus, and the plant is the Kingdom of God.[449]

The nesting birds may refer to Old Testament texts which emphasize that the universal reach of God's empire, such as Daniel 4:12. However, a real mustard plant is unlikely to attract nesting birds, so that "Jesus seems deliberately to emphasize the notion of astonishing extravagance in his analogy." Other commentators have suggested that the birds represent Gentiles seeking refuge with Israel or the "sinners" and tax collectors with whom Jesus was criticized for associating. A few commentators view the birds negatively, as representing false teachers invading the church. Some have identified a "subversive and scandalous" element to this parable, in that the fast-growing nature of the mustard plant makes it a "malignant weed" with "dangerous takeover properties." Pliny the Elder, in his Natural History (published around AD 78) writes that "mustard … is extremely beneficial for the health. It grows entirely wild, though it is improved by being transplanted: but on the other hand when it has once been sown it is scarcely possible to get the place free of it, as the seed when it falls germinates at once."[450]

This principle of growth and duplication is important in that the gospel, like the mustard seed, must germinate in all regions of the world.

Ben Witherington, (an American New Testament scholar), notes that Jesus could have chosen a genuine tree for the parable, and that the mustard plant demonstrates that "Though the dominion appeared small like a seed during Jesus' ministry, it would inexorably grow into something large and firmly rooted, which some would find shelter in and others would find obnoxious and try to root out."[451]

What a beautiful way and process to start a ministry. So what relevance or encouragement can this story of the mustard seed give to *A New Model of the Authentic Church*? It is advised that when you begin your ministry, you should not be deterred because the beginning may be small and insignificant. The most important aspect is that you start. Even if you start alone with yourself, God, and prayer, you will be able to accomplish what God has planned for you. There are several benefits to starting small like a mustard seed and growing in time over time.

First, when you start small, you can develop proportionally with the ministry. Many times when we begin a ministry, we are ill equipped and not fully developed in many areas. With the mustard-seed principle, we can learn and develop as the ministry grows. We can see the ministry reach goals and see positive development in ourselves as we learn and develop at the same time.

Second, as time goes on and the mustard seed (ministry) grows, we will see progress, evaluate the progress, make adjustments, and navigate the ministry in a more natural progression.

Third, this principle protects us from having too large of a ministry we may not be prepared for. This guards against being overrun and overwhelmed by things happening too quickly. The process of the mustard seed shows consistent, solid growth that will be beneficial to all the ministers and ministry and have a solid foundation.

Last, the principle of the mustard seed uses existing resources rather than spending money we may not have when we begin the ministry. An example would be that you use your house and start a home fellowship. Invite friends and family over for coffee and the reading and sharing of scripture. This is a mustard-seed principle of building an Authentic Church. It all begins small. As time goes on and more people want to take part and contribute, you find a more suitable place to gather. But starting small and developing and growing together is an important principle to beginning any ministry. "The 'mustard seed' is a symbol of the small beginnings and wide extension of the message of the Kingdom and its effects; and to regard the leaven as typifying its silent work and permeating power."[452] This is a biblical model for beginning any ministry—whether a church, outreach, fellowship, or Bible study.

The mustard-seed principle is very helpful and encouraging for those who want to start a ministry. It encourages because it allows the ministry to begin immediately and start the ministry using the resources one already has. It is encouraging because it belies the presumption that starting a ministry is costly and difficult. Beginning is halfway done. Sometimes, the most difficult thing is to start the ministry. Many find all kinds of reasons not to start a ministry, but the mustard-seed principle encourages you to start with what you have now and let it grow.

It is a wonderful process and experience to watch something that you have planted and watered grow. We must remember that "so neither the one who plants nor the one who waters is anything but only God, who makes things grow" (1 Corinthians 3:7 NIV) Knowing that to be true, God still needs someone to dig the hole, plant the seed, water the garden, and let God bring the harvest. Build your ministry today!

LESSON 13

The Mustard-Seed Principle of Building a Ministry

Another parable put he forth unto them, saying, The kingdom of heaven is like to a grain of mustard seed, which a man took, and sowed in his field: Which indeed is the least of all seeds: but when it is grown, it is the greatest among herbs, and becometh a tree, so that the birds of the air come and lodge in the branches thereof.

MATTHEW 13:31–32 (KJV)

1. What does this scripture say to you?

2. What are mustard seeds, and what can we discern from them that will encourage and help us to step out of our comfort zones and begin a new work?

3. The parable of the mustard seed suggests the growth of the kingdom of God from tiny beginnings to worldwide size. Is this relevant to church planting and growth?

4. Why would it be helpful for you to understand the principle of the mustard seed as it relates to ministry?

5. The strength of mustard-seed ministries is that you start where you are planted and grow at the same speed as you develop your ministry skills. Comment on this.

6. What relevance or encouragement can the story of the mustard seed give to *A New Model of the Authentic Church*?

7. The most important aspect is that you _____ the ministry.

8. The mustard-seed principle does not require you to invest in elaborate items or spend resources unnecessarily; it requires you to optimize your resources so the ministry can grow, while protecting you against unreasonable expectations and unrealistic goals that can lead to failure. What are the benefits of the mustard-seed principle? List 4.

    1. _____
    2. _____
    3. _____
    4. _____

9. Is the mustard-seed principle a biblical model for beginning any ministry—whether a church, outreach, fellowship, or Bible study?

10. We must remember that "so neither the one who plants nor the one who waters is anything but only God, who makes things grow". See 1 Corinthians 3:7. How is this relevant to any ministry?

11. If you were asked to begin a "mustard-seed ministry" today, what would it be, and what would you do?

12. What resources do you have now to begin a ministry? List at least 4:

    1. _____
    2. _____
    3. _____
    4. _____

── CHAPTER 14 ──
How to Start Your Ministry and Obtain Tax-Exempt Status

When Peter came into the house, Jesus was the first to speak. "What do you think, Simon?" he asked. "From whom do the kings of the earth collect duty and taxes—from their own sons or from others?" "From others," Peter answered. "Then the sons are exempt," Jesus said to him. "But so that we may not offend them, go to the lake and throw out your line. Take the first fish you catch; open its mouth and you will find a four-drachma coin. Take it and give it to them for my tax and yours."

MATTHEW 17:25–27 (NIV)

The purpose of this chapter is to provide potential ministries with an overview of IRS (Internal Revenue Service) regulations and instructions regarding obtaining tax-exempt status for those who feel called to begin a ministry at the grassroots. Some who are called to ministry may find the need to begin their ministry part-time while holding onto full- or part-time jobs. Some may even choose to work full- or part-time (tentmaking) for the life of their ministry but desire to have a tax-exempt status for their ministry.

The most significant and effective theologian, pastor, and evangelist the apostle Paul, who we have used as a model in this book, said, "I am a tent maker and support this ministry." Like Paul, some may be called to begin a new work or add your work of ministry while still "making tents."

If that is the case, this instructional overview will help demystify the process of successfully incorporating a ministry and obtaining tax-exempt status with the IRS. There are hundreds of pages that relate to tax-exempt guidelines in order to receive tax-exempt status. I have identified and extracted the basic, relevant materials and forms that will help you receive tax-exempt status for your ministry based on my experience of doing this for my ministry and others.

Congress has enacted special tax laws that apply to churches, religious organizations, and ministers in recognition of their unique status in American society and of their rights guaranteed by the First Amendment. Churches and religious organizations are generally exempt from income tax and receive other favorable treatment under the tax law; however, certain income of a church or religious organization may be subject to tax such as income from an unrelated business.[453]

It is important to note that there must be comprehensive documentation to support the application. Over the years, the IRS has become more stringent in appraising tax-exempt status because of the tremendous financial benefits it allows. So in applying to the IRS for tax exemption, one must have a fully functional and developed plan of ministry. If supporting documentation is incomplete, you will be rejected immediately.

If you follow this general outline and answer fully all the requirements that demonstrate this organization is a real charitable organization under 501(c)(3), it will entitle you to tax benefits and provide the public credibility you will need to allow people to financially support your ministry and receive tax benefits for doing so.

One of the most important issues the IRS will scrutinize is the section dedicated to paid salaries of employees and gross receipts. It is wise and expeditious to not speculate or overestimate wages or income the ministry will handle. More often than not, ministries don't generate enough revenue for salaries for several years. If for the first year, compensation is over $50,000 total to employees or gross receipts more than $10,000, the IRS will scrutinize the applications more carefully. On the other hand, if compensation to employees and receipts will be less than $10,000 for a four-year period, that will enable the exemption to be approved more easily. Because of concerns about the separation of church and state, the federal government provides lawful tax benefits to nonprofit organizations recognized as exempt from federal income tax under Section 501(c)(3) of the Internal Revenue Code.

THE BENEFITS OF RECEIVING 501(c)(3) STATUS

Aside from added credibility, the benefits of receiving 501(c)(3) status include an exemption from federal income tax along with eligibility to receive tax-deductible charitable contributions. In addition, some organizations may be exempt from certain employment taxes. Recognition of exemption under section 501(c)(3) of the IRC[xlviii] assures foundations and other grant-making institutions that they can issue grants or sponsorships to permitted beneficiaries. Moreover, state and local officials may additionally grant exemption from income, sales, or property taxes. Last, the US Postal Service offers reduced postal rates to certain 501(c)(3) organizations.

[xlviii] The IRC is the Internal Revenue Code that governs tax-exempt organizations.

The first step to take is to determine if your organization qualifies for tax-exempt status. The types of organizations that qualify are "charitable organizations." The three most significant types of organizations that are considered are religious, charitable, and educational organizations. Others include social welfare organizations, agricultural/horticultural organizations, labor organizations, business leagues (trade associations), social clubs, fraternal societies, employee benefit associations or funds, veterans' organizations, political organizations, and other miscellaneous organizations.

There are three key components for an organization to qualify for federal income tax exempt status under section 501(c)(3) of the IRC. One is that a nonprofit organization must be organized and operated exclusively for one or more exempt purposes. *Organized* as defined under 501(c)(3) is a corporation, trust, or unincorporated association. An organization's organizing documents (article of incorporation, trust documents, articles of association) must[xlix]

- limit its purposes to those described in section 501(c)(3) of the IRC,
- not expressly permit activities that do not further its exempt purposes, i.e., unrelated activities, and
- permanently dedicate its assets to exempt purposes.

Because a substantial portion of an organization's activities must further its exempt purposes, certain other activities are prohibited or restricted including but not limited to the following.

- It must refrain from participating in the political campaigns of candidates for local, state, or federal office.
- It must restrict its lobbying activities to an insubstantial part of its total activities.

These areas cause many organizations to lose their tax exemption status.

[xlix] Depending on what state you live in, you must register for incorporation with the secretary of state and register the name of the organization and receive a federal ID number. It would be wise to review the IRS regulations above regarding exempt purposes and have the corporation's organizing documents consistent with IRS guidelines. For example, a church needs an EIN when it opens a bank account, to be listed as a subordinate in a group ruling, or if it files returns with the IRS (for example, Forms W-2, 1099, 990-T). An organization may obtain an EIN by filing Form SS-4, Application for Employer Identification Number, according to its instructions. If the organization is submitting IRS Form 1023, Application for Recognition of Exemption Under Section 501(c)(3) of the Internal Revenue Code, Form SS-4 should be included with the application.

Tax information for charitable, religious, scientific, literary, and other organizations are exempt under IRC section 501(c)(3). An organization may obtain many of the benefits of 501(c)(3) status by affiliating itself with an existing charity that acts as its agent. The existing charity must be given full control and authority over the joining program to qualify.

PROCESS TO OBTAIN TAX-EXEMPT STATUS

To be tax exempt, an organization must have one or more exempt purposes stated in its organizing document. Section 501(c)(3) of the IRC lists the following exempt purposes: charitable, educational, religious, scientific, literary, fostering national or international sports competition, preventing cruelty to children or animals, and testing for public safety.

Once you determine your organization/church qualifies for tax-exempt status, you must complete Form SS-4 to obtain an Employer Identification Number.

After you complete the SS-4, the next form to be completed is the 1023 Form[1]/[li] (Application for Exemption.) See the chart below as to religious organizations and the 1023 Form.

The most common types of 501(c)(3) organizations are charitable, educational, and religious. Here are examples.

---

[1] A filing fee of $400 is associated with this form if your entity has gross receipts that do not exceed $10,000 for a four-year period. If the entity's gross receipts exceed $10,000, the filing fee is $850.

[li] Form 1023 must be completed by the twenty-seventh after the entity was legally formed. If the annual gross receipts are less than $5,000, this form is not required until ninety days after the end of the tax year in which the organization exceeds gross receipts of $5,000.

Charitable

Charitable organizations conduct activities that promote:

relief of the poor, the distressed, or the underprivileged;

advancement of religion;

advancement of education or science;

erection or maintenance of public buildings, monuments, or works;

lessening the burdens of government;

lessening neighborhood tensions;

eliminating prejudice and discrimination;

defending human and civil rights secured by law; and

combating community deterioration and juvenile delinquency.

The entity must also submit information showing how the organization supports education, for example, contributes to an existing educational institution, endows a professional chair, contributes to paying teachers' salaries, or contributes to an educational institution to enable it to carry on research.

Educational

Schools such as primary or secondary school, a college, or a professional or trade school.

Organizations that conduct public discussion groups, forums, panels, lectures, or similar programs.

Organizations that present a course of instruction by means of correspondence or through the use of television or radio.

Museums, zoos, planetariums, symphony orchestras, or similar organizations.

Nonprofit day-care centers.

Youth sports organization.

Religious

The term *church* includes synagogues, temples, mosques, and similar types of organizations.

Although the IRC excludes these organizations from the requirement to file an application for exemption, many churches voluntarily file applications for exemption.

Such recognition of the IRS assures church leaders, members, and contributors that the church is tax exempt under section 501(c)(3) of the IRC and qualifies for related tax benefits.

Other religious organizations that do not carry out the functions of a church such as mission organizations, speakers' organizations, nondenominational ministries, ecumenical organizations, or faith-based social agencies may qualify for exemption. These organizations must apply for exemption from the IRS.

The application for exemption must be very detailed and supported by comprehensive documentation. It must include a full description of the proposed activities of your organization, by-laws, documents of incorporation, bulletins, websites, informational material, list of officers, mission statement, and/or vision statement. It should include each of the fundraising activities of a Section 501(c)(3) organization and a narrative description of anticipated receipts and expected expenditures.

When describing the activities your organization expects to engage in, you must include the standards, criteria, procedures, or other means by which your organization adopted or planned for to carry out those activities.

Often, your organization's articles of organization contain descriptions of your organization's purposes and activities. Your application should describe completely and in detail your past, present, and future planned activities.

You must also include financial statements in your application showing your receipts and expenditures and a balance sheet for the current year and the three preceding years (even if they are future estimates). For each accounting period, you must describe the sources of your receipts and the nature of your expenditures if you have any.

Religious Organizations and Tax Exemption

To determine whether an organization meets the religious purposes test of Section 501(c)(3), the IRS maintains two basic guidelines.

1. The particular religious beliefs of the organization must be truly and sincerely held. (They actually evaluate the content and doctrine to see if it is a legitimate content and not something fabricated to receive tax-exempt status.)
2. The practice and rituals associated with the organization's religious beliefs or creeds must not be illegal or contrary to clearly defined public policy.

Your entity will not qualify for treatment as an exempt religious organization for tax purposes if its actions as contrasted with its beliefs (even if they are sincerely held religious beliefs) are contrary to well-established and clearly defined public policy.

A church, its integrated auxiliaries, or a convention or association of churches *is not required* to file Form 1023 to be exempt from federal income tax or to receive tax-deductible contributions, doing so may be advantageous. You can submit information showing that your organization is a church, synagogue, association, or convention of churches, religious order, or religious organization that is an integral part of a church and is engaged in carrying out the function of a church. Many churches seek recognition of tax-exempt status from the IRS because this recognition assures church leaders, members and contributors that the church is recognized as exempt and qualifies for related tax benefits; contributors would know their contributions are generally tax deductible.

In determining whether a religious organization is also a church, the IRS does not accept at face value every assertion that the organization is indeed a church. Because beliefs and practices vary so widely, there is no single definition of the word *church* for tax purposes. The IRS considers the facts and circumstances of each organization applying for church status. That is why it is important to submit articles of incorporation, a mission and vision statement, and a statement of faith along with bulletins and orders of service to establish that you have ongoing meetings as a church.

To learn more about the rules, regulations, and criteria, obtain 501(c)(3) IRS Publication 557—Tax Exempt Status For Your Organization. This publication is a good resource that is provided free by the IRS. Once your application is reviewed by the department in the IRS that handles 501(c)(3) tax exemptions, you will be assigned an advisor to help and guide you through the process.

This process, if done properly, will take between 60 and 120 days to finalize.

Obtaining tax-exempt status is something that should be considered prayerfully. If you choose to go that route, it will give the ministry legal status and credibility and donors some tax benefits.

God bless you in your endeavor to build the Authentic Church.

LESSON 14
How to Start Your Ministry and Obtain Tax-Exempt Status

When Peter came into the house, Jesus was the first to speak. "What do you think, Simon?" he asked. "From whom do the kings of the earth collect duty and taxes—from their own sons or from others?" "From others," Peter answered. "Then the sons are exempt," Jesus said to him. "But so that we may not offend them, go to the lake and throw out your line. Take the first fish you catch; open its mouth and you will find a four-drachma coin. Take it and give it to them for my tax and yours."

MATTHEW 17:25–27 (NIV)

1. What does this scripture say to you?

2. Congress has enacted special tax laws that apply to churches, religious organizations, and ministers in recognition of their unique status in American society and of their rights guaranteed by the First Amendment. Churches and religious organizations are generally exempt from income tax. Would you want your organization to have the benefits of being tax exempt?

3. In applying to the IRS for tax exemption, one must have a fully functional and developed plan of ministry. It is important to note that there must be comprehensive documentation to support the application. Do you have a functional plan prepared? Briefly explain.

4. Do you know that the benefits of receiving 501(c)(3) status include an exemption from federal income tax along with eligibility to receive tax-deductible charitable contributions? This means contributions are tax deductible to persons who donate. Do you believe this will help build your ministry?

5. If you apply for and receive tax exempt status for your organization, do you know that activities are prohibited or restricted, including but not limited to the following:

   • It must refrain from participating in the political campaigns of candidates for local, state, or federal office.
   • It must restrict its lobbying activities to an insubstantial part of its total activities.

   Would this affect your ministry?

6. To be tax exempt, an organization must have one or more exempt purposes. What would yours be?

7. To determine whether an organization meets the religious purposes test of Section 501(c)(3), the IRS maintains two basic guidelines. 1. The particular religious beliefs of the organization must be truly and sincerely held. (They actually evaluate the content and doctrine to see if it is a legitimate contact and not something fabricated to receive tax-exempt status) and 2. The practice and rituals associated with the organization's religious beliefs or creeds must not be illegal or contrary to clearly defined public policy. Do you satisfy those guidelines?

8. The most common types of 501(c)(3) organizations are charitable, educational, and religious.

Charitable	Educational	Religious
Charitable organizations conduct activities that promote:	Schools such as primary or secondary school, a college, or a professional or trade school.	The term *church* includes synagogues, temples, mosques, and similar types of organizations.
relief of the poor, the distressed, or the underprivileged;	Organizations that conduct public discussion groups, forums, panels, lectures, or similar programs.	Such recognition of the IRS assures church leaders, members, and contributors that the church is tax exempt under section 501(c)(3) of the IRC and qualifies for related tax benefits.
advancement of religion;		
advancement of education or science;		

Does your organization have at least one of these purposes?

9. You must include a full description of the proposed activities of your organization, bylaws, documents of incorporation, bulletins, websites, informational material, list of officers, mission statement, and/or vision statement. Have you prepared those?

10. In determining whether a religious organization is also a church, the IRS does not accept at face value every assertion that the organization is indeed a church. Can you provide documentation and proof that you are a church?

11. Obtaining tax-exempt status is something that should be considered prayerfully. Have you done so?

ABOUT THE AUTHOR

Robert Fuggi received his Juris Doctor from Regent University School of Law and his Master of Divinity and Master of Theology from Princeton Theological Seminary. He is currently a candidate for PhD at Regent University School of Divinity. A trial lawyer certified by the Supreme Court of New Jersey, he's successfully litigated hundreds of trials from wrongful death to institutional abuse.

His high-profile cases have been featured in the *Daily News, The Washington Post, The Press of Atlantic City, The Trentonian, The Asbury Park Press, The Observer*, among others. Robert Fuggi has been honored as one of the National Trial Lawyers Top 100.

As the founding pastor of Toms River Community Church, Robert Fuggi proactively models the change he desires to see in the American church.

He started the School of Biblical Studies and Theological Inquiry for pastoral and lay students. He also founded a highly active community outreach program for the homeless, which is one of the largest in his community.

Robert Fuggi and his wife, Lana, live in New Jersey. They have three children: Robby, Danny, and Christian.

EPILOGUE

I believe what we have proposed theologically is not a new way to do church but rather the old and intended way Christ wanted the church to be.

This new paradigm of *A New Model of the Authentic Church* is attainable in society and culture. It is as relevant as it was when the church started with a group of ordinary people, fishermen, tax-collectors, living and working 2,000 years ago.

I hope this model can be developed and applied to existing churches—institutional and independent—and to new, start-up churches I hope this book encourages.

I would be willing to speak, lecture, and conduct seminars to further explain and apply the concepts of *A New Model of the Authentic Church*.

If you would like to contact me or have me speak or lead an Authentic Church seminar at your church or meeting, please email requests to anewmodeloftheauthenticchurch@gmail.com.

In communion,
Robert Fuggi

ENDNOTES

CHAPTER 1—THE DECLINE OF THE AMERICAN CHURCH

1   Haggai 2:9 NIV.

2   Matthew 13:32 NIV.

3   Matthew 9:37–38 NIV.

4   Dietrich Bonhoeffer and John W. Doberstein, *Life Together: The Classic Exploration of Christian Community*. (New York: HarperOne, 1954.)

5   Matthew 13:15 NIV.

6   Jack Wellman, "Why We Are Losing So Many Churches In The United States?" *Christian Crier,* October 26, 2013, accessed June 12, 2015. http://www.patheos.com/blogs/christiancrier/2013/10/26/why-we-are-losing-so-many-churches-in-the-united-states/

7   Ibid.

8   Ibid.

9   Molly Worthen, "One Nation Under God?" *The New York Times*, December 22, 2012, accessed July 7, 2014.

10   Ibid.

11   Ibid.

12   Ibid.

13   Ibid.

14   Albert Mohler, "The Scandal of Biblical Illiteracy: It's Our Problem," *Christian Headlines*, accessed September 20, 2016, http://www.christianheadlines.com/columnists/al-mohler/the-scandal-of-biblical-illiteracy-its-our-problem-1270946.html.

15   CiaoBella, "Barna Research: 'Christian' Closer to 8%, Not 40% in the USA," blog post, *Armageddon Alert*, 1 December 2012, accessed 20 September 2016, http://armageddonalert.blogspot.com/2012/12/barna-research-christian-closer-to-8.html

16   Ibid.

17   Staff, by reporter, "Research Explores What Millennials Think of Church," 27 March 2015, accessed 20 September 2016, http://www.thereporter.com/article/NG/20150327/NEWS/150329875

18   Barry A. Kosmin and Ariela Keysar, *American Religious Identification Survey [ARIS 2008]*, n.d.

19   Ibid.

20   Michael Snyder, "How Will The Shocking Decline Of Christianity In America Affect The Future Of This Nation?" *End Of The American Dream*, 18 January 2012, accessed 7 July 2014, http://endoftheamericandream.org/archives/how-will-the-shocking-decline-of-christianity-in-america-affect-the-future-of-this-nation

21 Ibid.

22 Ibid.

23 Ibid.

24 Ibid.

25 Cathy Lynn Grossman, "Most Religious Groups in USA Have Lost Ground, Survey Finds." *USATODAY. com*. USA Today, 17 March 2009, accessed 18 June 2015.

26 Ibid.

27 Melton, J. Gordon, "American Religion's Mega-Trends: Gleanings from Forty Years of Research," the ARDA Association of Religion Data Archives; accessed 27 September. 2016. http://www.thearda.com/rrh/papers/guidingpapers/Melton.pdf

28 Ibid.

29 Ibid.

30 Grossman, "Most Religious Groups."

31 David Briggs, "Is Religion In America in Decline?" TheHuffingtonPost.com, 2 April 2011, accessed 7 July 2014. http://www.huffingtonpost.com/david-briggs/is-religion-in-america-in_b_843801.html

32 Dean R. Hoge, Donald A. Luidebs, and Benton Johnson, "Mainline Churches: The Real Reason for Decline," *First Things*, http://www.leaderu.com/ftissues/ft9303/articles/johnson.html.

33 Michael Dowd, "Evidence: The Decline of Christianity in America," *The Evolutionary Evangelist*. Thank God for Evolution, 2009; accessed 7 July 2014. http://thankgodforevolution.com/node/2049

34 Ibid.

35 Ibid.

36 Katherine Bindley, "Religion Among Americans Hits Low Point, As More People Say They Have No Religious Affiliation: Report," TheHuffingtonPost.com, 13 March 2013, accessed 7 July 2014. http://www.huffingtonpost.com/2013/03/13/religion-america-decline-low-no-affiliation-report_n_2867626.html

37 Ibid.

38 Ibid. (internal citations omitted).

39 Christopher Hadaway and Penny Marler Long, "How Many Americans Attend Worship Each Week? An Alternative Approach to Measurement," *Journal for the Scientific Study of Religion*, September 2005; accessed 27 September 2016.

40 Kelly Shattuck, "7 Startling Facts: An Up Close Look at Church Attendance in America." *Church Leaders: Lead Better Every Day*. Churchleaders.com, 18 Feb. 2013; accessed 7 July 2014. http://churchleaders.com/pastors/pastor-articles/139575-7-startling-facts-an-up-close-look-at-church-attendance-in-america.html

41 Ibid.

42 Ibid.

43 Ibid.

44 Naftali Bendavid, "Europe's Empty Churches Go on Sale," *Wall Street Journal*, 2 January 2015; accessed 28 July 2015, https://www.wsj.com/articles/europes-empty-churches-go-on-sale-1420245359

45 Ibid.

46 Ibid.

47 Ibid.

48 Kelly Shattuck, "7 Startling Facts."

49 Ibid.

50 Ibid.

51   Matthew 9:37–38 NIV.

52   Jeff Brumley, "Survey Finds Christians Using Jesus to Pursue 'way of Self'" *Baptist News Global*, 8 June 2016, accessed 20 September 2016, https://baptistnews.com/article/survey-finds-christians-using-jesus-to-pursue-way-of-self/#.WKcJOPL0TIg

53   Kosmin, *American Religious Identification Survey.*

54   Ibid.

Chapter 2—The Plague of the American Church

55   M. G. Easton, "plague," *Easton's Bible Dictionary*, 7 July 2015.

56   Catherine Bowler, "Blessed: A History of the American Prosperity Gospel," dissertation, Duke U, 2010; graduate program in religion; accessed 27 January 2016. http://dukespace.lib.duke.edu/dspace/bitstream/handle/10161/2297/D_Bowler_Catherine_a_201005.pdf?sequence=1

57   "Prosperity Theology," Wikipedia.

58   Ibid.

59   Ibid.

60   Ibid.

61   Hannah Rosin, "Did Christianity Cause the Crash?" *The Atlantic*, December 2009; accessed 6 November 2015. https://www.theatlantic.com/magazine/archive/2009/12/did-christianity-cause-the-crash/307764/

62   Bowler, "Blessed."

63   Ibid.

64   Ibid.

65   Eric Demeter, "The Prosperity Gospel Creates Poor Christians," *RELEVANT Magazine.* 20 August 2015; accessed 6 November 2015. http://www.relevantmagazine.com/god/worldview/prosperity-gospel-creates-poor-christians

66   Leonardo Blair, "Creflo Dollar Will Get $70 Million Gulfstream G650 Jet Says Church; World Changers Board Says It Is 'Necessary' for Ministry," *CP Church and Ministry, The Christian Post*, 2 June 2015; accessed 6 November 2015. http://www.christianpost.com/news/creflo-dollar-will-get-70-million-gulfstream-g650-jet-says-church-world-changers-board-says-it-is-necessary-for-ministry-139858/

67   Rosin, Hannah. "Did Christianity Cause the Crash?"

68   Ibid.

69   Bowler, "Blessed."

70   Hannah, "Did Christianity Cause the Crash?"

71   Ibid.

72   R. Albert Mohler, "Does God Want Us to Be Rich? TIME Looks at Prosperity Theology." AlbertMohler.com, 13 September 2006; accesssed 6 November 2015. http://www.albertmohler.com/2006/09/13/does-god-want-us-to-be-rich-time-looks-at-prosperity-theology/

73   Ibid.

74   Ibid.

75   Ibid.

76   Jack Zavada, "Prosperity Gospel: Christ Centered or Self Centered?" *Religion & Spirituality.* About.com, 14 January 2016; accessed 10 February 2016. http://christianity.about.com/od/Word-Of-Faith/a/Prosperity-Gospel.htm

77 "How the Health and Wealth Gospel Twists Scripture," *Watchman.org*, 6 March 2015; accessed 30 March 2016 http://www.watchman.org/articles/other-religious-topics/how-the-health-and-wealth-gospel-twists-scripture/(internal citations omitted).

78 Scott McKnight, "The Problem for the Prosperity Gospel," Beliefnet, March 2009; accessed 6 March 2015. http://www.beliefnet.com/faiths/christianity/2009/03/the-problem-for-the-prosperity-gospel.aspx

79 Ibid.

80 Bowler, "Blessed."

81 Ibid.

82 David Jones, "The Bankruptcy of the Prosperity Gospel: An Exercise in Biblical and Theological Ethics," Bible.Org, 6 October 2006; accessed 5 March 2015. https://bible.org/article/bankruptcy-prosperity-gospel-exercise-biblical-and-theological-ethics

83 Ibid.

84 1 Timothy 6:10 NIV.

85 Eric Demeter, "Prosperity Gospel Creates Poor Christians."

86 Romans 5:3–5 NIV.

87 Jones, "Bankruptcy."

CHAPTER 3—A NEW REFORMATION

88 Justin Holcomb, "The Connection between Halloween & Reformation Day," *Christianity.com*, 28 October 2013; accessed 1 November 2015. http://www.christianity.com/christian-life/art-and-culture/the-connection-between-halloween-reformation-day.html

89 Ibid.

90 Ibid.

91 "Martin Luther and the 95 Theses," *History.com*, 1 January 2009; accessed 5 November 2015. http://www.history.com/topics/martin-luther-and-the-95-theses

92 Holcomb, "Halloween & Reformation Day."

93 Ibid.

94 Max Pfingsten, "Martin Luther, the 95 Theses and the Birth of the Protestant Reformation," *History 101: Western Civilization*, Study.com; accessed 1 November 2015. http://study.com/academy/lesson/martin-luther-the-95-theses-and-the-birth-of-the-protestant-reformation.html

95 Ibid.

96 "Martin Luther and the 95 Theses," *History.com*.

97 Ibid.

98 Pfingsten, "Martin Luther."

99 "Martin Luther and the 95 Theses," *History.com*.

100 Ibid.

101 Ibid.

102 Ibid.

103 James Kittleson, "The accidental revolutionary," *Christian History*, 115, 17.

104 Pfingsten, "Martin Luther."

105 Martin Luther, "95 Theses," accessed 5 November 2015 http://www.luther.de/en/95thesen.html.

106 John Bruce, "The Verse of the Reformation," *Christian Blogs*, accessed 29 October 2015. http://www.deliveredbygrace.com/the-verse-of-the-reformation

107 "Cleansing of the Temple," Wikipedia; accessed 18 January 2016. https://en.wikipedia.org/wiki/Cleansing_of_the_Temple

108 Ibid.

109 Matthew 21:12–13.

110 Mark Manolopoulos, "Jesus's Provocative Political Protest," Consortiumnews.com, 11 January 2013; accessed 30 March. 2016. https://consortiumnews.com/2013/01/11/jesuss-provocative-political-protest/

111 Ibid.

112 "Cleansing of the Temple," Wikipedia.

113 Jack Zavada, "Jesus Clears the Temple of Money Changers," *Religion & Spirituality*, About.com, 6 August 2015; accessed 15 January 2016. http://christianity.about.com/od/New-Testament/a/JZ-Money-Changers.htm

114 Charles Erdman, *The Gospel of Matthew* (Philadelphia: Westminster, 1919), 168.

115 Ibid., 31.

116 Wilfred J. Hahn, "Money Changers in the Temple—Then and Now," *Mulberry Ministry*, www.eternalvalue.com; accessed 1 November 2015. http://www.eternalvalue.com/adownload/EVR-12-2005.pdf

117 Ibid.

118 Brandan Robertson, "We Need Reformation (A Sermon for Reformation Day)," *Nomad*, Patheos, 26 October 2015; accessed 1 November 2015. http://www.patheos.com/blogs/revangelical/2015/10/26/we-need-reformation-a-sermon-for-reformation-day.html

119 Timothy George, "Contemplate Christ," *Christian History* 115, 22–24.

120 Ibid.

121 Ibid.

122 Ibid.

123 Josh Bruce, "Reformation Day 2011," *Delivered By Grace*, 30 October 2011; accessed 1 November. 2015. http://www.deliveredbygrace.com/reformation-day-2011/

124 Ibid.

125 Ibid.

Chapter 4—Tentmaking: The Model of St. Paul

126 Ellen White, "The Apostle Paul and Manual Labor Part 1," *Bible Prophecy*, World's Last Chance, n.d.; accessed 29 September 2016. https://www.worldslastchance.com/updates/the-apostle-paul-and-manual-labor-part-1.html

127 Ruth Siemens, "The Vital Role of Tentmaking in Paul's Mission Strategy," *International Journal of Frontier Missions* 14.3 (1997), *IJFM.org*; accessed 7 July 2014.

128 Ibid.

129 Ibid.

130 White, "The Apostle Paul."

131 Siemens, "Tentmaking."

132 Ibid.

133 Ibid.

134 Kurt T. Kruger, "Why Study Tentmaking? Part 2," *Peace in Frankfort*, Blogspot.com, 18 September 2014; accessed 12 December 2014, http://peaceinfrankfort.blogspot.com/2014/09/one-of-obstacles-that-tentmaking-has-to.html.

135 Adelle Banks, "Big Churches, Big Bucks: Southern Senior Pastors Take Top Salaries," Religion News Service, 9 September 2014; accessed 12 December 2014. http://religionnews.com/2014/09/09/big-churches-big-bucks-southern-senior-pastors-take-top-salaries/

136 Audrey Barrick, "Church Pastors' Pay Rises to More than $80,000," *CP Church and Ministry*, Christian Post, 19 August 2008; accessed 12 December 2014. http://www.christianpost.com/news/church-pastors-pay-rises-to-more-than-80-000-33898/

137 "Welcome to the National Congregations Study Site"; accessed 12 December 2014, http://www.soc.duke.edu/natcong/.

138 "Characteristics of U.S. Congregations, by Faith Group—Part 1," *The US Congregational Life Survey*. UScongregations.org, 17 February 2014; accesssed 12 December 2014, http://www.uscongregations.org/charact-cong.htm.

139 Ibid.

140 "Fast Facts about American Religion," *Hartford Institute for Religion Research*; accessed 12 December 2014. http://hirr.hartsem.edu/research/fastfacts/fast_facts.html

141 "Pastors Paid Better, But Attendance Unchanged," The Barna Group, 29 May 2001; accessed 12 December 2014. https://www.barna.com/research/pastors-paid-better-but-attendance-unchanged/

142 Jack Wellman, "Should Pastors Be Paid? A Bible Study," *What Christians Want To Know*, 20 July 2013; accessed 12 December 2014. http://www.whatchristianswanttoknow.com/should-pastors-be-paid-a-bible-study/

143 Ibid.

144 "Characteristics of U.S. Congregations, by Faith Group—Part 1," *The US Congregational Life Survey*. UScongregations.org, 17 February 2014; accessed 12 December 2014, http://www.uscongregations.org/charact-cong.htm.

145 Ibid.

146 1 Corinthians 9:15–16, 18 NIV.

147 "Have Americans lost their faith … or just their trust in the old 'mainline' churches?" *Beliefnet News*; accessed 7 July 2014. http://www.beliefnet.com/columnists/ news/2012/07/have-christians-lost-confidence-in-church-officials.php

148 Ibid.

149 Hugh Kramer, "Why Christianity is on the decline in America," *Examiner*, 3 November 2010; accessed 7 July 2014.

150 Mark 2:1–12 NIV.

151 Luke 5:1–3 NIV.

152 Matthew 5:1–2 NIV.

153 1 Corinthians 7:20 NIV.

154 Judges 7:1–8 NIV.

155 Mark 6:13 NIV.

156 Christina Fox, "Rejected by Men, Even Our Friends," *Desiring God*, 8 July 2015; accessed 30 September 2015. http://www.desiringgod.org/articles/rejected-by-men-even-our-friends

157 1 Corinthians 7:20–24 NIV.

158 Ibid.

159 Dianne Bergant, "Fourteenth Sunday in Ordinary Time (B)," Catholic Theological Union, 8 July 2012; accessed 30 September 2015, http://www.ctu.edu/scripture-reflections/article/fourteenth-sunday-ordinary-time-b (internal citations omitted).

160 Ibid.

161 Ibid.

162 J. L. Calahan, "Second Rejection in Nazareth," *Life and Heart of Jesus* Stu. 78 (2009); Like the Master Ministries (internal citations omitted).

163 "Jesus the Builder," *Theology of Work Project*; accessed 14 September 2015. https://www.theologyofwork.org/new-testament/mark/rhythms-of-work-rest-and-worship/jesus-the-builder-mark-61-6/(internal citations omitted).

164 Bergant, "Fourteenth Sunday."

165 Carey Dillinger, "When Jesus Marveled," *The Expository Files*, February 2001; accessed 6 March 2015 http://www.bible.ca/ef/expository-mark-6-1-6.htm (internal citations omitted).

166 Ibid.

167 "Sacred Space," *Mark 6:1–6*; accessed 14 September 2015. http://www.sacredspace.ie/scripture/mark-61-6-0

168 Luke 4:14–24 NIV.

169 Luke 4:23 NIV.

170 Luke 4:28–30 NIV.

171 Calahan, "Second Rejection."

172 Dillinger, "When Jesus Marveled."

173 Matthew 8:7–8 NIV.

174 Matthew 8:10 NIV.

175 Mark 6:1–6 NIV.

176 Michael I. Norton, Jenna H. Frost, and Dan Ariely, "Less Is More: The Lure of Ambiguity, or Why Familiarity Breeds Contempt," *Journal of Personality and Social Psychology* 2 no. 1 (2007): 97–105.

177 Ibid.

178 2 Timothy 4:14 NIV.

179 Ron Rhodes, "Why Couldn't Jesus Do Miracles in His Hometown," *Reasoning From the Scriptures/Ministries*, The Complete Book of Bible Answers; accessed 30 September 2015. http://home.earthlink.net/~ronrhodes/qjesusmiracles.html

180 Ibid.

181 1 Peter 4:12–14 NIV.

Chapter 6—I Am Barabbas

182 Clark Tanner, *Barabbas and the Gospel*, Sermon Central.com, accessed 18 December 2015. http://www.sermoncentral.com/print_friendly.asp?SermonID=43334

183 Ibid.

184 Excerpts from Gino Cascieri, "Barabbas, The Prisoner Set Free," *Sermon Central*, n.p., accessed 18 December 2015. http://www.sermoncentral.com/print_friendly.asp? SermonID=34827 (internal citations omitted).

185 C. S. Lewis, "Quote" *Goodreads*, 15 March 2013; accessed 5 November 2015, http://www.goodreads.com/quotes/755193-there-is-no-neutral-ground-in-the-universe-every-square

186 "Barabbas," *Gospel Mysteries*, Gospel-Mysteries.Net; accessed 18 December 2015, http://www.gospel-mysteries.net/barabbas.html.

187 Ibid.

188 Ibid.

189 Matthew 23:24 NIV.

190 Patrick Cook, "Barabbas: That's You!" *Sermon Central*. Outreach, April 2006; accessed 18 December 2015. https://www.sermoncentral.com/sermons/barabbas-thats-you-pat-cook-sermon-on-jesus-christ-89885

191 Matthew Henry, *Matthew Henry's Commentary*, verses 28–30, Bible Gateway; https://www.biblegateway.com/resources/matthew-henry/Matthew

192 Romans 6:23 NIV.

193 Galatians 5:19–21 NIV.

194 Jeremiah 17:9 NIV.

195 Romans 5:6–8 NIV.

196 Cook, "Barabbas."

Chapter 7—What the American Church Is Not Building—Disciples

197 Greg Jaffe, "Obama's New Patriotism," *Washington Post*, 3 June 2015; accessed 27 September 2015. http://www.washingtonpost.com/sf/national/2015/06/03/obama-and-american-exceptionalism/?tid=sm_fb

198 Eric Russ, "What Defines a Christian Disciple?" *Discipleship Defined*, 2013; http://www.discipleshipdefined.com/resources/what-defines-christian-disciple

199 Ibid.

200 "Disciple (Christianity)," Wikipedia. https://en.wikipedia.org/wiki/Disciple_(Christianity)

201 "The Conditions of Discipleship," *My Utmost For His Highest*, 2 July 2016; https://utmost.org/the-conditions-of-discipleship/

202 "America's Changing Religious Landscape," Pew Research Centers Religion Public Life Project, 11 May 2015; accessed, 5 November 2015. http://www.pewforum.org/2015/05/12/americas-changing-religious-landscape/

203 Ibid.

204 "Discipleship Works—What a Lot of People Miss About Our Role in Our Discipleship," *The Exchange*, Christianity Today, 27 January 2015; http://www.christianitytoday.com/ edstetzer/2015/january/god-involves-us-in-our-own-discipleship-why-how.html

205 Russ, "What Defines a Christian Disciple?"

206 Billy Graham, "A Choice, a Challenge, a Change," *Decision Magazine*, October 2010; accessed 5 November 2015, http://billygraham.org/decision-magazine/october-2010/a-choice-a-challenge-a-change/.

207 "Introduction," *What Is Discipleship?* Harvest Ministries with Greg Laurie; http://www.harvest.org/knowgod/new-believer/foundations-for-living/what-is-discipleship.html#introduction

208 Dietrich Bonhoeffer, "Daring Thoughts." *Christian History* 1991, Christian History Institute; https://www.christianhistoryinstitute.org/magazine/article/daring-thoughts/

209 John D. Godsey, "Bonhoeffer's Costly Theology," *Christian History* 199, http://www.christianitytoday.com/history/issues/issue-32/bonhoeffers-costly-theology.html.

210 Matthew 8:18–22 NIV.

211 Matthew 5:11 NIV.

212 Mark 8:34–38 NIV.

213 "America's Changing Religious Landscape," Pew Research Centers Religion Public Life,

214 Matthew 6:19 NIV.

215 Adam Clarke, "Genesis 1 Clarke's Commentary," *Clarke's Commentary*, Biblehub; http://biblehub.com/commentaries/clarke/genesis/1.htm

216 John 15:18–19 NIV.

217 Luke 23:34 NIV.

218 2 Corinthians 12:7–9a NIV.

219 "Requirement #2," *What Is Discipleship?* Harvest Ministries with Greg Laurie; http://www.harvest.org/knowgod/new-believer/foundations-for-living/what-is-discipleship.html#requirement-2

220 Ibid.

221 "God and Suffering Are Not a Contradiction," *Sermondigger*, 15 June 2015; accessed 27 April 2016. https://sermondigger.wordpress.com/2015/06/15/god-and-suffering-are-not-a-contradiction/

222 "An Exegesis," *Holy Name of Jesus Parish*, 13 September 2015; accessed 15 February 2016, http://www.hnjchurch.org/app/uploads/2014/10/EB43-Exegesis-24th-Ord-Sun-Sept-13-2015.pdf.

223 Ibid.

224 Matthew 9:9 NIV.

225 Dietrich Bonhoeffer, *The Cost of Discipleship* (New York: Macmillan, 1959).

Chapter 8—The Dirty Little Secret of the American Church

226 Audrey Hector, "Sexual Abuse of Children," *ChristianAnswers.net.* n.d.; accessed 6 May 2016. http://christiananswers.net/q-eden/childsexualabuse.html

227 Valerie Tarico, "The Protestant Clergy Sex Abuse Pattern," TheHuffingtonPost.com, 25 May 2011. http://www.huffingtonpost.com/valerie-tarico/the-protestant-clergy-sex_b_740853.html

228 Ibid.

229 Thornton McEnery, "The World's 15 Biggest Landowners," *Business Insider*, 18 March 2011; accessed 27 July 2016. http://www.businessinsider.com/worlds-biggest-landowners-2011-3

230 Ellen Bass and Laura Davis, "Gizelle," *The Courage to Heal: A Guide for Women Survivors of Child Sexual Abuse* (New York: Perennial Library, 1988), 446.

231 Han Van Den Blink, "Trauma and Spirituality," *Reflective Practice: Formation and Supervision in Ministry* 28 (2008), 41.

232 Ibid., 31 (internal citations omitted).

233 Roland Summit, C.M.D., "The Child Sexual Abuse Accommodation Syndrome," *Child Abuse & Neglect* 7, 1.

234 Jon G. Allen, "Memory," *Coping with Trauma: Hope through Understanding* (Washington, DC: American Psychiatric Pub., 2005), 87.

235 Ibid., 92 (internal citations omitted).

236 Ibid., 79.

237 Ibid., 83–84.

238 Ibid., 88 (internal citations omitted).

239 Allen, "Attachment."

240 Irene Loewen, "Child Sexual Abuse in the Church," *Direction: Justice and Sexuality* 15 no. 1 (1986): 60–72; 6 May 2016 (quoting C. Brandon, unpublished doctoral dissertation, California School of Professional Psychology–Fresno, 1985).

241 Ibid.

242 Ibid.

243 Ibid.

244 Ibid.

245 Josh McDowell and Bob Hostetler, *Handbook on Counseling Youth* (Dallas: Word, 1996).

246 "Matthew 18:6." *Matthew 18*. Biblehub, n.d.; accessed 6 May 2016. http://biblehub.com/matthew/18-6.htm

247 Matthew 18:6 KJV.

248 Matthew 18:6 HCB.

249 "Matthew 18 Pulpit Commentary," *Matthew 18*. Biblehub, n.d.; accessed 6 May 2016. http://biblehub.com/commentaries/pulpit/matthew/18.htm

250 Joy Allmond, "Moving Forward from the Duggar Scandal: Sexual Abuse in the Church and the Epidemic of Silence," *ChristianHeadlines.com*; Salem Web Network, 28 May 2015; accessed 6 May 2016. http://www.christianheadlines.com/columnists/guest-commentary/the-church-sexual-abuse-and-the-epidemic-of-silence.html

251 Ibid.

252 Ibid.

253 Ibid.

254 Ibid.

255 Agostino Bono, "John Jay Study Reveals Extent of Abuse Problem," *Clergy Sexual Abuse and the Catholic Church*, AmericanCatholic.org, n.d.; accessed 6 May 2016. http://www.americancatholic.org/news/clergysexabuse/johnjaycns.asp

256 "Vatican Says 848 Priests Defrocked for Sexual Abuse since 2004," *NY Daily News*, 6 May 2014; accessed 6 May 2016. http://www.nydailynews.com/news/world/time-vatican-releases-wide-raning-statistics-priests-defrocked-rape-child-abuse-article-1.1781825

257 Ibid.

258 Ibid.

259 Ibid.

260 Cathy Lynn Grossman, "Clergy Sex Abuse Settlements Top $2.5 Billion Nationwide," *USA Today*, 13 March 2013; accessed 6 May 2016. http://www.usatoday.com/story/news/nation/2013/03/13/sex-abuse-settlement-cardinal-roger-mahony/1984217/

261 Ibid.

262 Ibid.

263 Ibid.

264 Sarah P. Bailey, "Billy Graham's Grandson: Evangelicals 'worse' than Catholics on Sex Abuse," *OnFaith*, Faithstreet, 30 September 2013; accessed 6 May 2016. https://www.onfaith.co/onfaith/2013/09/30/billy-grahams-grandson-evangelicals-worse-than-catholics-on-sex-abuse/20305

265 Ibid.

266 Ibid.

267 Michael Hanegan, "#SilentCOFC: Child Sexual Abuse and Churches of Christ," blog post, Michaelhanegan.com, 15 July 2014; accessed 6 May 2016. http://www.michaelhanegan.com/blog/silentcofc

268 Ibid.

269 Ibid.

270 Ibid.

271 Ibid.

272 Ibid. (internal citations omitted).

273 Ibid.

274 Ibid.

275 Ibid.

276 Ibid.

277 Ibid.

278 "There Is More Sexual Abuse in The Protestant Churches Than Catholic," *Shoebat: Awareness and Action*, Shoebat Foundation, 6 May 2014; accessed 6 May 2016. http://shoebat.com/2014/05/06/sexual-abuse-protestant-churches-catholic/

279 Ibid.

280 Ibid.

281 Ibid.

282 Ibid.

283 Ibid.

284 Ibid.

285 Ibid.

286 Victor I. Vieth, "What Would Walther Do? Applying Law and Gospel to Victims and Perpetrators of Child Sexual Abuse," *Journal of Psychology and Theology* 40, no. 4 (2012): 257–73 at 258.

287 Ibid., 259.

288 Ibid., 262.

289 Ibid.

290 Ibid.

291 John O. Barres, letter, 30 March 2016.

292 Ibid.

293 Ibid.

294 Romans 15:1 NIV.

CHAPTER 9—WHAT CHRISTIANS (THE CHRISTIAN CHURCH) OWE THE JEWS

295 Sr. Rose Pacatte, "A decade later, 'The Passion' still raises questions of anti-Semitism," *National Catholic Reporter*, 24 February 2014; accessed 18 June 2015. https://www.ncronline.org/news/art-media/decade-later-passion-still-raises-questions-anti-semitism

296 Matthew 27:51–52 NIV.

297 Matthew 27:11 NIV.

298 Matthew 27:25 NIV.

299 Pacatte, "A decade later."

300 Ibid.

301 Ibid.

302 Bishops' Committee for Ecumenical and Interreligious Affairs United States Conference of Catholic Bishops, *Criteria for the Evaluation of Dramatizations of the Passion* (Washington, DC: United States Conference of Catholic Bishops, 1988), 74.

303 Ibid.

304 Pacatte, "A decade later."

305 Acts 1:4–5 NIV.

306 Genesis 1:2 NIV.

307 Kim Fabricius, "Faith and Theology: Ten Propositions on the Holy Spirit," *Faith and Theology: Ten Propositions on the Holy Spirit*, March 6, 2007; accessed 12 February 2015, http://www.faith-theology.com/2007/03/ten-propositions-on-holy-spirit.html?m=1.

308 Karl Barth, *Church Dogmatics*, 2.2 §33 (London: T & T Clark, 2010), 101.

309 George Hunsinger, *What Christians Owe Jews. A Case for Soft-Supersessionism*, February 9, 2015; accessed 11 February 2015, https://www.commonwealmagazine.org/print/36870.

310 Ekkehard W. Stegemann, *Romans 9–11 in Karl Barth's Doctrine of Election*, n.d.; 4, http://www.vanderbilt.edu/AnS/religious_studies/SBL2007/Stegemann.pdf.

311 Ibid. 2.

312 R. R., *"Salvation Is from the Jews": An Assessment and Critique of Karl Barth on Judaism and the Jewish People*, n.d.; accessed 6 March 2015 http://www.kesherjournal.com/index.php?option=com_content&view=article&id=144&Itemid=

313 Michael Vlach, "Karl Barth and Supersessionism," *Theological Studies* 2012; accessed 6 March 2015, http://theologicalstudies.org/resource-library/supersessionism/335-karl-barth-and-supersessionism.

314 Ibid.

315 Ibid.

316 Ibid.

317 Hunsinger, *"What Christians Owe Jews."*

318 Ibid.

319 Ibid.

320 Ibid.

321 "The German Churches and the Nazi State," United States Holocaust Memorial Council, 20 June 2014; accessed 23 April 2015, http://www.ushmm.org/wlc/en/article.php?ModuleId=10005206.

322 Eberhard Busch, "The Covenant of Grace Fulfilled in Christ as the Foundation of the Indissoluble Solidarity of the Church with Israel: Barth's Position on the Jews During the Hitler Era," *Scottish Journal of Theology* 52, no. 4 (1999), 476; accessed 9 February 2015.

323 Ibid.

324 Hunsinger, *"What Christians Owe Jews."*

325 Ibid.

326 Acts 15:7 NIV.

327 Acts 15:8–10 NIV.

328 Acts 15:19 NIV.

329 Amos 9:11 NIV.

330 Hunsinger, *"What Christians Owe Jews."*

331 Ibid.

332 Luke 2:25–32 NIV.

333 Luke 2:38 NIV.

334 John Piper, *"Preparing to Receive Christ: Looking for the Consolation of Israel,"* accessed 15 April 2015, http://www.desiringgod.org/sermons/preparing-to-receive-christ-looking-for-the-consolation-of-israel.

335 Matthew 21:9 NIV.

336 Thomas F. Torrance, *The Mediation of Christ* (Colorado Springs: Helmers & Howard, 1992), 77.

337 The Study Catechism: Full Version, approved by the 210th General Assembly of the Presbyterian Church (USA), 1998; accessed 9 February 2015, Question 52. http://www.presbyterianmission.org/resource/study-catechism-full-version/

338 Hunsinger, *"What Christians Owe Jews."*

339 Karl Barth, *Church Dogmatics*, vol. 2.2, 32–33 (London: T & T Clark, 2010), 198.

Chapter 10—Between a Rock and a Hard Place: The Mediation of Moses (Old) and Christ (New)

340 Mark Tribble, "Moses," Christ as Mediator, HeraldMag, n.d.; accessed 5 March 2015, http://www.heraldmag.org/2007/07ma_5.htm.

341 Jakob Jocz, "Do We Need a Mediator?" Jews for Jesus, n.d.; accessed 4 March 2015, https://jewsforjesus.org/issues-v06-n04/do-we-need-a-mediator (internal citations omitted).

342 Milton Steinberg, *Basic Judaism* (New York: Harcourt, Brace, Jovanovich, 1975), 57–58.

343 Jakob Jocz, *The Jewish People and Jesus Christ: The Relationship between Church and Synagogue* (Grand Rapids, MI: Baker Book House, 1979), 280.

344 Deuteronomy 30:19 NIV.

345 Jocz, "Do We Need a Mediator?"

346 Ibid.

347 Ibid.

348 Exodus 19:6 NIV.

349 Ibid.

350 Ibid.

351 Walter A. Elwell, entry for "Mediator, Mediation," *Baker's Evangelical Dictionary of Biblical Theology*, n.d., http:classic.studylight.org/dic/bed/view.cgi?number-T467.

352 Ibid.

353 Ibid.

354 C. H. Spurgeon, "The Mediation of Moses No. 2398," n.d., https://bible.org/seriespage/mediation-moses-no-2398.

355 John MacArthur, "Jesus Christ, Greater than Moses." n.d., http://www.gty.org/resources/study-guide-chapter/1607.

356 Deuteronomy 34:6 NIV.

357 MacArthur, "Jesus Christ, Greater than Moses."

358 Ibid.

359 John J. Parsons, "Moses' Prophecy of Messiah," *Yeshua—the Prophet Like Moses*, Hebrew4Christians, n.d., http://www.hebrew4christians.com/Articles/Like_Moses/like_moses.html.

360 Elwell, "Mediator, Mediation."

361 Ibid.

362 Ibid.

363 Ibid.

364 Ibid.

365 Tribble, "Moses."

366 MacArthur, "Jesus Christ, Greater than Moses."

367 Ibid.

368 Hebrews 3:4 NIV.

369 MacArthur, "Jesus Christ, Greater than Moses."

370 Parsons, "Moses' Prophecy of Messiah."

371 Elwell, "Mediator, Mediation."

372 Don Schwager, "The Letter to the Hebrews: a commentary & mediation," R.C. Net, n.d., http:www.rc.net/wcc/ readings/heb3.htm.

373 Ibid.

374 Matthew Henry, "Matthew Henry's Commentary Galatians 3:19," *Matthew Henry's Commentary,* Biblehub, n.d., http://biblehub.com/commentaries/mhc/galatians/3.htm.

375 Gerald O'Collins and Michael Keenan Jones, *Jesus Our Priest: A Christian Approach to the Priesthood of Christ* (Oxford: Oxford UP, 2012), 1.

376 Brett R. Scott, "Jesus' Superiority Over Moses in Hebrews 3:1–6," *Bibliotheca Sacra* 155 (1998): 201–10; Gordon.Edu, 5 May 2015, https://faculty.gordon.edu/hu/bi/ted_hildebrandt/ntesources/ntarticles/BSac-NT/Scott-Heb3Moses-BS.htm (internal citations omitted).

377 Ibid.

378 Ibid.

379 Ibid.

380 Tribble, "Moses."

381 Esther Bhasme, "Exodus Exegesis," *BIBL* 2553, 13 November 2009, 7.

382 Jeremiah 31:1 NIV.

383 Jeremiah 31:33 NIV.

384 Jeremiah 31:34 NIV.

Chapter 11—If Christ Had Not Come

385 Browning, "If Christ Had Not Been Born," Sermonoutlines.org, n.d., http://webcache.googleusercontent.com/search?q=cache%3ANY_rYqYNzBUJ%3Awww.sermonoutlines.org%2FBrowning%2520Sermons%2FIf%2520Christ%2520Had%2520Not%2520Been%2520Born%21.doc%2B&cd=1&hl=en&ct=clnk&gl=us.

386 John 15:22 NIV.

387 Browning, "If Christ Had Not Been Born."

388 Ibid.

389 John 1:1–3, 14 NIV.

390 Luke 2:14 NIV.

391 "Silent Night, Holy Night," *The United Methodist Hymnal* number 239, translated by John F. Young (stanzas 1–3) and anon. (stanza 4), hymnsite.com.

392 "What If Christ Had Not Come Into the World," *Sermons.* TEXsource, n.d., http://www.texsource.com/bible/sermons/117.pdf.

393 Ivor Powell, "The World Without Christ." *Johnny the Baptist,* n.d., http://www.johnnythebaptist.org/ivorpowell/The%20World%20Without%20Christ.pdf.

394 Ibid.

395 Ibid.

396 Hebrews 7:18–21 NIV.

397 Torrance, *The Mediation of Christ.*

398 George Hunsinger, classroom lecture, Princeton Theological Seminary.

399 Torrance, *The Mediation of Christ.*

400 Powell, "The World Without Christ."

401 Ibid.

402 Jarrett Aycock, *If Christ Had Not Come and Other Sermons.* (Kansas City, MO: Beacon Hill Press, 1998), n.p. http://wesley.nnu.edu/wesleyctr/books/0501-0600/HDM0577.pdf

Chapter 12—Missional Objectives of the Authentic Church: The Poor, Homeless, Displaced and Aliens

403 Dr. Darrell Guder's contribution to the church has been the development and application of missional theology. Though he did not coin the phrase, he did much to explain and develop its application to the church. The church is reflective of the incarnational Jesus Christ who called the church, the special agency elected by Christ, "to be his witnesses in the world."

The most important objective or mission of the church is to be a witness in the propagation or proclamation of Christ's teachings of the word and in deed. One cannot separate the verbal witness of the person representing Christ from his or her life and conduct. This is why the church and its elected representatives are called out to be His witnesses.

Dr. Guder believes that the incarnational witness of the church happens when the elect proclaim and emulate the wonders and goodness of God. This is called *martyria*, when the person is what the gospel proclaims. That is where many times we, the elect, fall short. Though we are not perfect, we must be obedient. When this occurs, we are able to complete the task of what Christ accomplished on the cross for all humanity. Dr. Guder relies on many themes from the gospel of Mark where he demonstrates that evangelization is a process that develops over time for a convert to become a disciple of Christ (process evangelization). He also uses much from the book of Peter to explain how the church is called out of this world as a "royal priesthood" and "strangers and aliens" to this world as examples of the incarnational witness of Jesus Christ in the world. This is the overriding mission of the church.

Dr. Guder challenges conventional thought on evangelization and its obsession with "getting people saved". He believes this undermines the true, authentic work of Christ by diminishing Christ's mission to a pattern and practice of counting so-called salvations. He cautions against parachurch organizations doing the work of the church, which is not to be done independently or outside the church and is in fact the mission of the church. This certainly would be problematic to many organizations such as the Billy Graham Organization and others.

Dr. Guder believes that this is only for the work of the church, *kiononia*, that the community of the elect are called to finish the work done on the cross by Christ for all humanity. Dr. Guder describes regular theology as what is done in the seminaries, and irregular theology as what is done outside of seminaries. This is an important distinction for Dr. Guder's theory of missional theology. He believes much of our theology and witnessing needs to be done outside the church in everyday language so others outside the church can understand the gospel and come to follow and be disciples of Christ. He believes so strongly in the practical application that his seminal publication, *Be My Witnesses*, is written with no footnotes or quotes so people outside the church can understand they too are called for mission. Dr. Guder believes everyone in the church is called for mission, not just pastors or priests, and in turn, all are obligated in that mission so more will join in the elect.

A fellow colleague at Princeton Seminary, Dr. George Hunsinger told us about a discussion he had with Dr. Guder at his dinner table. They wanted to coin a term that would embrace and explain the purpose and mission of the church, so they came up with the new subject name entitled missional hermeneutics, the study of the purpose and mission of the church. I believe these concepts are important to understand and apply. Dr. Guder used a very interesting example in his book *Be My Witnesses* to demonstrate this point. When God freed the Israelites from bondage and slavery, their purpose was to be witnesses to the wonderful acts of the only true God in a pagan world as well as live in joy. It is the same for the church (elect) now, whom as Dr. Guder says "manages the grace of God for humanity." In Christ, we have been forgiven of our sins to be of service in the world for now until eternity.

How do we accomplish this with what Dr. Guder calls the end of Christendom? Students of missional theology and hermeneutics try to answer this question and apply it to ministry and mission. Mission and evangelization cannot be done in the old way alone; we must continually understand and evaluate what we do, make changes, and commit to those changes as society changes. That is the continual challenge and evolution of evangelism and mission. As do others, I believe evangelism is about relationships, about developing relationships over time, and about having conversations that help those on their individual pilgrimages to know Christ. This will never change!

The challenges the church faces in the modern era are far different from those it faced and had to overcome centuries or even decades ago. Dr. Guder suggests that in the Middle Ages, the church was concerned with "getting the heathens saved"; this attitude was very common also in early America. Dr. Guder suggests this type of conversion undermines true conversion and discipleship. Overzealousness can undermine the authentic experience of the conversion.

Dr. Guder believes conversion is a process that takes time to develop someone into a disciple of Jesus Christ. We have read of the Pauline conversion; what happened was specific to the apostle, but even after his conversion, Paul was sent on a journey by the Holy Spirit to develop into a disciple. He did not fully realize himself as a disciple instantly, but it began the process. This ought to be the same for the elected in the church and those who come to Christ through their encounters with process evangelism.

I am not sure that missional theology is consistent with my upbringing as a young Catholic and in my later years in Christian, nondenominational churches. The church's missional work includes the CYO (Catholic Youth Organizations) basketball and youth leagues and CCD classes; these are effective in engaging many with the mission of the church. But how far has the church gone to build disciples?

The challenge of what former president of Princeton Seminary John Mackay said, "Let the church be the church," is far more difficult than one may believe.

In my early tradition, I think the Catholic Church was more concerned with being institutionalized than being an institution. The difference is dramatic. One is a successful organization, the latter successful in the mission of the church. Many nondenominational churches are so consumed with getting everyone saved that that is all that matters, and they neglect follow-up or discipleship programs. The number of conversions is the most important objective, not building long-lasting relationships and disciples. This is where my old and new denominations are lacking and could benefit from a study in missional hermeneutics.

Dr. Guder's contributions to the church actually go further than the church; they extend to all humanity. He has developed a practical theology that will allow the church to properly and effectively continue the work Christ did on the cross and in turn bless all.

404 Jurgen Moltmann, *Passion of Life: A Messianic Lifestyle* S.l. (Philadelphia: Fortress, 1978).

405 Matthew 25:40 NIV.

406 Ligonier Ministries, the teaching fellowship of R. C. Sproul, "Strangers and Aliens No Longer," 11 November 2014, www.ligonier.org/learn/devotionals/strangers-and-aliens-no-longer.

407 Psalm 69:8 NIV.

408 Luke 4:24 NIV.

409 Chawkat G. Moucarry, "Aliens, Strangers, and the Gospel," Ri Weal Intervarsity, 20 March 2002; accessed 7 July 2014. https://ism.intervarsity.org/resource/aliens-strangers-and-gospel

410 Ibid.

411 Ibid.

412 Ibid.

413 Charles Van Engen, "Biblical Perspectives on the Role of Immigrants in God's Mission." *Journal of Latin American Theology* 3 (2008): 22–32.

414 Ibid., 23.

415 Ibid., 22.

416 Ibid., 27.

417 Ibid.

418 Ibid., 29.

419 Ibid., 31.

420 Ibid., 32.

421 Miguel H. Diaz, "On Loving Strangers: Encountering the Mystery of God in the Face of Migrants," *Word & World* 29 (2009), 236.

422 Carol Meyers, *Exodus*, New Cambridge Bible Commentary (New York: Cambridge UP, 2005), 201.

423 R. K. Harrison, *An Introduction and Commentary* (Downers Grove, IL: Intervarsity, 1980), 202.

424 Elliott Wright, *Go Free* (New York: Friendship, 1973), 55.

425 Dr. Eugene Boe, Rev. Dale Hanson, Rev. Paul Larson, et al., "Statement on Missional Theology," CLBA Study Committee on Missional Theology, May-June 2010, http://www.clba.org/wp-content/uploads/2015/07/Statement_on_Missional_Theology.pdf, 3.

426 Darrel Guder, "Missional Church: From Sending to Being Sent," *Missional Church: A Vision for the Sending of the Church in North America*, ed. Darrell L. Guder (Grand Rapids, MI: Eerdmans, 1998), 6.

427 Boe et al., "Statement on Missional Theology," 3.

428 Ibid., 4.

429 Mark Glanville, "An Extraordinary Conference (at Which I Get to Speak): A Missional Reading of Scripture," *For He Has Made You Beautiful*, WordPress, 7 November 2013; accessed 1 November 2015. https://markrglanville.wordpress.com/2013/11/07/an-extraordinary-conference-at-which-i-am-speaking-a-missional-reading-of-scripture/

430 Ibid.

431 Boe et al., 4.

432 Ibid., 13.

433 Moucarry, "Aliens, Strangers, and the Gospel."

434 Ibid.

435 Ibid.

436 John T. Carroll and James R. Carroll, *Preaching the Hard Sayings of Jesus* (Peabody, MA: Hendrickson, 1996), 7.

437 1 Peter 2:11–12 commentary, http://www.preceptaustin.org/1_peter_211-12.html.

438 James Zondervan, "Strangers in the World," Christian Reformed Church, 6 August 2012, http://crcna.org/resources/church-resources/reading-sermons/strangers-world.

439 Ibid.

440 David Klinghoffer, "What the Scriptures Say About Immigration," *Faiths and Prayers*, Beliefnet, May 2005, http://www.beliefnet.com/Faiths/Judaism/2006/05/What-The-Scriptures-Say-About-Immigration.

CHAPTER 13—THE MUSTARD-SEED PRINCIPLE OF BUILDING A MINISTRY

441 "Mustard Seed," Wikipedia, 6 March 2015.

442 Ibid.

443 Ibid.

444 "Parable of the Mustard Seed," Wikipedia, 6 March 2015.

445 Matthew 13:31–32 NIV.

446 Mark 4:30–32 NIV.

447 Luke 13:18–19 NIV.

448 "Parable of the Mustard Seed" Wikipedia, 6 March 2015.

449 Ibid.

450 Ibid.

451 Ibid.

452 Charles R. Erdman, *The Gospel of Matthew: Pocket Commentaries on the New Testament.* (Philadelphia: Westminster, 1919).

CHAPTER 14—HOW TO START YOUR MINISTRY AND OBTAIN TAX-EXEMPT STATUS

453 IRS Exempt Organizations 501(c)(3) Tax Guide for Churches & Religious Organizations, Publication 1828 (Rev. 8-2015) Catalog Number 21096G Department of the Treasury Internal Revenue Service. https://www.irs.gov/pub/irs-pdf/p1828.pdf